T0380199

TEACHING TENNIS
IN FRANCE:

TEACHING TENNIS
IN FRANCE:
ORIGINS, HISTORY,
DEVELOPMENTS & OUTLOOK

NICOLAS STANAJIC PETROVIC

TEACHING TENNIS IN FRANCE:
ORIGINS, HISTORY, DEVELOPMENTS & OUTLOOK

iUniverse books may be ordered through booksellers or by contacting:

iUniverse
1663 Liberty Drive
Bloomington, IN 47403
www.iuniverse.com
844-349-9409

Because of the dynamic nature of the Internet, any web addresses or links contained in this book may have changed since publication and may no longer be valid. The views expressed in this work are solely those of the author and do not necessarily reflect the views of the publisher, and the publisher hereby disclaims any responsibility for them.

Any people depicted in stock imagery provided by Getty Images are models, and such images are being used for illustrative purposes only.
Certain stock imagery © Getty Images.

ISBN: 978-1-6632-6480-0 (sc)
ISBN: 978-1-6632-6481-7 (e)

Library of Congress Control Number: 2024914523

Print information available on the last page.

iUniverse rev. date: 02/04/2025

Cover illustration: *Painting by my friend Dimitri Lorin in 2011.*

Dimitri was ranked in the French first series (number 36 in 2000), and reached 302ⁿᵈ place in the ATP rankings in 2002, when he had the honour of playing Rafael Nadal on clay at his home in Mallorca in a satellite tournament (the old name for future tournaments). Passionate about painting and art, he naturally turned to this sector. He first opened a gallery in Hong Kong in 2013 - Avenue des Arts Paris-HK - before moving to California in 2017 where he is director of "Lorin Gallery".

CONTENTS

ACKNOWLEDGEMENTS

I would like to thank two people in particular, without whom this project would never have seen the light of day: Mr Paul Jalabert and Mr Didier Masson.

Paul Jalabert is the living memory of French amateur tennis. Born in 1927, he was French Junior Champion in 1946 and played in the French Open at Roland Garros 17 times between 1947 and 1966. He rubbed shoulders with all the great names in French and international tennis, and above all he has one of the largest collections of tennis archives (images and videos). He has written an _Album de souvenirs filmés du tennis français_ which was published in 2010.

Didier Masson is a well-informed teacher and former regional technical adviser to the Picardie league (1973-1988). He is the guardian of the legacy of master teacher Alfred Estrabeau (1906-1999). He is the author of several books, including _Le rôle du bras libre_, published in 1984 and selling over 6,000 copies.

He recently published _Un tennis fin dans un corps sain_ (2020).

Sadly, he passed away on 1 December 2022 after a very long illness, and I would like to dedicate my book to him in particular.

The upstream work was particularly rewarding and it was with a great deal of passion and self-sacrifice, but also thanks to the help and support of Paul and Didier, that I was able to obtain the testimonies of key players in French tennis, ranging from former amateur and professional players, sports historians in general and tennis in particular, technical managers from the French Tennis Federation and the National Technical Directorate, colleagues/brothers who teach at clubs in France and/or abroad, to internationally renowned French coaches.

After Paul and Didier, I'd also like to thank the people with whom I've had numerous discussions, people without whom it would have been difficult for me to put together this book, which is the fruit of three years of reading, research, reports and summaries in parallel with my professional activity as a full-time club coach.

I've chosen to list these resource people in alphabetical order, as I don't want to give more importance to any one of them.

Once again, all these men and women have been kind enough to answer my questions and queries, and I'd like to thank them warmly!

Allan Trevor, a former Australian professional tennis player (ATP number 54 in 1984), moved to Marseille where he became sporting director of CSM in 1991. He coached Arnaud Clément when the latter was a teenager.

Beust Patrice, former professional player and director of France's first tennis academy. He has coached many French players (including Yannick Noah). He was head of the continuing education department for professional teachers at the FFT.

Borfiga Louis was director of the INSEP Pôle France (1990-2006), during which time he trained ten future ATP top 100 players, including four future top 10s. A former sparring partner of Bjorn Borg, he was National Technical Director of the Canadian Tennis Federation between 2006 and 2021.

Bory Eric, sports director of TC St Germain les Corbeil (Essonne Committee, Ile de France League), also a PE teacher, was trained very early on by Bernard Pinon in situation-based teaching. He was also my guide for many years.

Brossard Philippe, director of the Fédération Nationale des Enseignant de Tennis (the only union in the sector for many years), is the author of the book _Prof ou champion de tennis_ published in 1991.

Cassaigne Alain attended the Cochet courses at the RCF at theageof eleven. He obtained his monitorat in 1972, later becoming national coach and then assistant DTN, in charge of the INSEP, where he was the first coach to bring in a sophrologist (1984-85).

Cherret Pierre, currently director of the Tennis Training Institute (LIFT), was previously technical director of the French Tennis Federation (2018-2021). He was Cédric Pioline's coach when Pioline reached the Wimbledon final (1997).

Clastres Patrick, professor of sports history at the University of Lausanne, has published numerous works, notably on the history of tennis (he himself was classified in the second series). He was commissioned by President Giudicelli's team to supervise the writing of the book on the federation's centenary.

Couvercelle Jean was a sports journalist specialising in rugby, golf and tennis for the daily newspaper France Soir from 1967. He was the founder and editor-in-chief of the famous monthly Tennis Magazine, the first issue of which came out on 1 April 1976.

Crognier Lionel, Director of the Sports Science Faculty at the University of Burgundy, organiser of the two conferences held in Dijon in 2008 and again in 2021 on the theme of "Tennis in tomorrow's society".

Darmon Pierre, French number one from 1959 to 1968, finalist at Roland Garros in 1963. He was coached by the illustrious master teachers Alfred Estrabeau and Jacques Iemetti. He also trained with Henri Cochet and René Lacoste.

De Camaret Régis, took up tennis at the age of 17. He was a self-made man who observed and interviewed many of the champions of the time (Nastase, Pietrangeli, Rosewall). Even though he never obtained his monitorat, he was one of the most successful coaches in the 1980s on the fringes of the FFT.

De Roubin Odile, former professional tennis player (1/4 finalist at the French Open in 1973). CTR for Yvelines in 1982, then head of training for the under-12s at the FFT, author of the book *Le guide du tennis naturel*, published in 1983.

Delpierre Isabelle, granddaughter of Marguerite Broquedis, the first French athlete to win an Olympic gold medal in any discipline (women's singles at the Stockholm Olympics in 1912).

Deniau Georges, who became a coach in 1961, set up the first tennis clinics in France in early 1970. Successive coach of the French and Swiss Davis Cup teams, he is the author of several books on technique. He was also a technical consultant for *Tennis magazine for* almost forty years.

Di Maggio Eric, coach at Elite Tennis Center in Cannes, has worked with Patrice Hagelauer at Sophia Country Club and was also a member of Team Daniel Contet. Eric has also worked for the Qatar Tennis Federation, in China and Singapore.

Dron Sever, a graduate of the Bucharest Institute of Sports (Romania), was granted political asylum in France in 1972 and then qualified as a monitor under Jean Paul Loth and Georges Deniau. His coaching credits include Henri Leconte (Roland Garros finalist in 1988) and Julie Halard-Decugis (world number one in doubles in September 2000).

Durr Françoise, winner of Roland Garros in 1967, lived through the beginnings of the Open era. Appointed captain of the French Fed Cup team, she played an active role in the creation of the WTA to promote women's tennis.

Fizaine Roland, Technical and Sports Advisor for the Alsace League from 1981 to 2016, BE1 then DE trainer in Strasbourg, is passionate about the history of tennis. He was also a member of the jury for the BE and DE exams for many years.

Garnier Pierre, a former coach with the Pays de Loire league, is currently self-employed and organises training courses on the theme of motor preferences. He is an avid collector of tennis rackets and magazines.

Glaszmann Caroline, currently a development advisor for the Alsace league, her father and grandfather were the first to set up a tennis school for youngsters in Alsace. Ranked in the first series in 1973, she had the particularity of playing her backhand with both hands.

Gouzenes Alban began teaching in 1980 alongside Romanian coaches Ion Tiriac and Sever Dron. He was lucky enough to assist master teacher Estrabeau. A coach with the Paris league, he also taught at Racing Club de Paris before becoming CTR (Guyane then Lorraine).

Kronenberger Alain, current President of CA Montrouge (Ile de France League), was CTR of Hauts de Seine before joining the DTN. He played an active role in thedevelopment of the black book (federal training reference system) in the 1990s.

Lacaze François, after obtaining his monitorat in 1968, taught for twenty-four years in various clubs in the Paris region. He is the author of the book *Le coup droit*, published in 2020 and the fruit of thirty years of research.

Lamarre Thierry, who started out as a very high-level aviator, discovered tennis by chance while doing his military service in the Joinville battalion with a certain Gilles Moretton. He soon decided to make teaching tennis his profession. He set up the PTR France agency in 1997. To date, he has trained over eight hundred coaches in the American method.

Letort Olivier, holder of the BE3 since 1998 following his work on evolutionary tennis, actively participated in the creation of mini-tennis in France from 1986, alongside Jean Claude Marchon (1933-2020). He is the man behind the different formats of the game. He created Tennis Cooleur and trains many teachers in his teaching methods.

Lovera (born Sherriff) Gail, born and trained in Australia by her father Ross Sherriff, considered one of Australia's greatest coaches. She rubbed shoulders with and played with all the great Australian champions before becoming French in 1969.

Massias Jean-Claude became the very first CTR for the Ile de France region in 1970-71 after obtaining his tennis instructor's diploma in 1969, followed by a teaching diploma in sport. He went on to become director of the INSEP and then national technical director of the FFT for 12 years (1996-2005).

Michelin Nelly is a clinical psychologist who specialised in top-level sport for ten years, helping athletes to manage their emotions. She worked with Yannick Noah in 1983.

Mourey Alain is a PE teacher and the author of several books on tennis education. He was CTR in Burgundy and was involved in the creation of the black book in the 1990s. He has been recognised as an expert by the ITF.

Peltre Marie-Christine, retired from the Education Nationale (Professor of History and Geography), ex - 15, she was President of the Brittany League before becoming vice-president of the FFT under the presidency of B. Giudicelli (in charge of tennis culture in particular).

Pestre Bernard, former national coach (1984-96), in charge of BE2 training at Roland Garros from 1996 and member of the exam jury. Founder of the Training and Education Department at the DTN in 1997, he will also be its director.

Pestre Gérard, former director and founder of Trans-Faire, with whom I completed the BE2 Executive Training and Sports Management option in 2005/06. An expert in training engineering. He pioneered the organisation of tennis camps for young people in France in the 1970s.

Pestre Jean-Paul, ex-director of ACTJ, my trainer for the BE1 diploma promotion 2000/2001. Jean Paul and his teaching team trained over 300 teachers between 1992 and 2006. ACTJ was also a pioneer in the organisation of sports courses for all, particularly tennis courses from the late 1970s onwards.

Peyre Guillaume is a high-performance coach (he took Marcos Baghdatis to the Australian Open final in 2007) and a former member of Team Lagardère (coach to Nicolas Mahut and Richard Gasquet). He worked for the Chinese Tennis Federation for eight years (in charge of the best male and female players).

Piffaut Jean-Christophe, former director of the Tenniseum at Roland Garros, was involved in every stage of the museum's creation. A member of the first team at TC Chavril (a suburb of Lyon), he was ranked negative.

Poey Dominique, originally from the Basque country, naturally started out playing rugby before becoming one of France's top juniors in 1970. He joined the DTN in 1978 as head of the second national tennis-study programme, inaugurated that same year in Poitiers.

Rebuffé Christian, a trainer with Trans-faire since it was founded in 1993, has experienced the transition from the BE to the DE from the inside. He was a member of the technical team of the Val d'Oise league. I was lucky enough to have him as a colleague at Trans-faire between 2008 and 2011, after having had him as a trainer in 2006!

Renoult Marc, head of education at the DTN, was CTR for Seine Saint Denis and also head of the federal club of professional tennis teachers for many years.

Rouchon Anne-Marie, French number eight in 1964, joined the DTN where she was co-responsible for the regional future programme.

Sautet Aurélie, daughter of the late Philippe Sautet (designer of the first soft ball ever with Jean Claude Marchon in 1986), was used as a 'guinea pig' in her father's trials (CEO of Nassau

France at the time and later creator, with his brother Christophe Lesage, of the first birth year tournaments).

Segur Catherine, former director of the Essonne league (1979), took the 1st degree federal initiator course supervised by JC Marchon (1933-2020) in 1976, then obtained her monitorat at the age of over forty in 1982. For many years, she ran a club in Brunoy: Renaud TC (Essonne committee, Ile de France league).

Simon Brigitte, a former professional player (semi-finalist at Roland Garros in 1978), taught for twenty years after her playing career before turning to mental coaching and nutrition.

Sumyk Sam was born in Brittany and moved to the United States in 1990, shortly after obtaining his BE. He worked at an academy in Florida, where he immediately turned his attention to coaching female players. He has coached Belarusian Victoria Azarenka, Russian Vera Zvonareva and Spanish Garbine Muguruza to great success.

Thamin Jacques, France's fifteenth-ranked player in the 1970s, travelled the world playing in a series of tournaments on the international circuit at the very start of the Open era, notably in Asia. He became a professional teacher in 1973. He is the author of the book *Mes belles rencontres de Borotra à Federer*, published in April 2022.

Thorel Eric, federal initiator at TC Revel (Occitanie league) for two seasons, moved to the United States at the end of the 1980s where he trained in American teaching methods (USPTA and Bollettieri training) before joining PBI in 1990. He remains with the American-Canadian company to this day.

Torre Paul started out in Rouen with master teacher Jacques Langanay. He is one of the few French players (along with F. Jauffret, E. Deblicker, P. Portes & G. Moretton) to have had the privilege of facing Sweden's B. Borg during the French Open at Roland Garros.

Toumieu André, born in 1961, was one of the very first French players to play his backhand with both hands (following in the footsteps of Jean Claude Barclay, François Pierson and then Hervé Gauvain). Never had the support of the FFT despite being ranked -30.

Valentin Gérard was one of the very first people to be awarded the monitorat (class of 1966), and for many years taught at club level (Charleville Mézières, Champagne League), before joining the DTN in 1984. He was director of the Pôle France in Reims before being co-responsible for the Programme Avenir National (PAN) with Alain Solvès.

But also:
Blanco Jean François, Cabale Yves, Chiambretto Laurent, Collombel Frédéric, Davies Chris, Griffon Clément, Guillon-Schutzle Monique, Hagelauer Patrice, Jenkins Keith, Lepelletier Patrick, Loliée Éric, Marty Jean-Claude, Peter Jean-Michel, Rome Philippe, Simonet Christian, Solvès Alain, Tauziat Nathalie.

17 July 2019: Meeting with Didier Masson, for an afternoon of exchange around technique. Here on the only tennis court available to his FFT-affiliated club in the commune of Bueil (Comité de l'Eure, Ligue de Normandie).

24 July 2019: Reunion with Paul Jalabert, illustrious champion of the amateur era (1946-1966) and living memory of French tennis. A moment of sharing at his home in the Var. An exceptional man with incredible energy and enthusiasm when it comes to talking about tennis.

ACRONYMS USED

AAA	Amateur Athletic Association (1880)
ACTJ	Association Centres de Tennis pour Jeunes (1978-2006)
AFPT	Association Française des Professeurs de Tennis (1929-1968)
ANET	Association Nationale des Éducateurs de Tennis (1994-2012)
(BE)ES	Brevet d'Etat d'Educateur Sportif (1963)
BSP	Brevet Sportif Populaire (1937)
CCNS	National Collective Agreement on Sport (2005)
CNES	National Confederation of Sports Educators (1991)
CQP AMT	Certificat Qualification Professionnel Assistant Moniteur de Tennis (2008)
CREPS	Centre de Ressources d'Expertise et de Performance Sportive (1945)
CSIT	Centre Scolaire d'Initiation au Tennis (1938)
CTR	Regional Technical Advisor (1960)
(DE)JEPS	State Coaching Diploma in Youth, Popular Education & Sports (2008)
DTN:	Direction Technique Nationale (1963)
ENEP:	Ecole Normale d'Education Physique (1933-1975)
EPS	Physical and Sports Education (1945)
ESG	Education Sportive et Générale (1941-1944)
FFLT	Fédération Française de Lawn Tennis (1920-1976)
FFT	Fédération Française de Tennis (1976)
FNDS	National Sports Development Fund (1978-2005)
FNEPT	National Federation of Tennis Teachers and Professors (1974)
ILTF	International Lawn Tennis Federation (1913-1976)
INS	National Sports Institute (1945-1975)
INSEP	Institut National du Sport et de l'Education Physique (1975)
ITF	International Tennis Federation (1977)
LIFT	Institut de Formation du Tennis (2018)
OPCA	Organisme Paritaire Collecteur Agréé (1994)
PAN	Programme Avenir National (1996)
PTR	Professional Tennis Registry (1976 in the United States and 1997 in France)
RCF	Racing Club de France (1882)
SNBET	Syndicat National des Brevetés d'Etat de Tennis (Paris, 1971)
TCSG	Tennis Club Saint Germain Les Corbeil (1976)
UNPT	Union Nationale des Professeurs de Tennis (Côte d'Azur, 1970)
USFSA	Uniondes Sociétés Françaises des Sports Athlétiques (1891-1920)
WCT	World Championship Tennis (1982-1989)
WTT	World Team Tennis (1973)

ACRONYMS USED

AAA	Amateur Athletic Ass. Union (1950)
ACTI	Association Cannes de Tennis pour l'enfance (1990 à 2000)
AEPT	Association Française ... Professeurs de Tennis 1929-1968
ANET	Association Nationale des Educateurs de Tennis (1993-2012)
BREPS	Brevet d'Etat d'Educateur Sportif (1960s)
BSP	Brevet Sportif Populaire (1937)
CCNS	National Collective Agreement on Sport (2005)
CNES	National Conference of Sports Education (1960)
COPAMT	Comité ...
CREPS	Centre de Ressources, d'Expertise de Performance Sportive ...
CST	Centre ...
DTR	Regional Technical Advisor (1960)
DRJPS	State Coaching Diploma in Youth, Popular Education & Sports (2008)
DTN	Direction Technique Nationale (1993)
ENEP	Ecole Normale d'Education Physique 1933-1975
EPS	Physical and Sport Education (1945)
ESG	Education Sportive et Générale 1941-1944
FFLT	Fédération Française de Lawn Tennis (1920-1976)
FFT	Fédération Française de Tennis (1976)
FNDS	National Sports Development Fund 1976-2000
FFEPT	National Federation of Tennis Teachers and Professors (1968)
ILTF	International Lawn Tennis Federation (1913-1975)
INS	National Sports Institute (1945-1975)
INSEP	Institut National du Sport et de l'Education Physique (1975)
ITF	International Tennis Federation (1977)
IFT	Institut de Formation du Tennis (2018)
OPCA	Organisme Paritaire Collecteur Agréé (1990)
PAN	Programme Avenir National (1990)
PTR	Professional Tennis Registry (1976 in the United States and 1992 in France)
RCF	Racing Club de France (1882)
SNBET	Syndicat National des Brevetés d'Etat de Tennis, Paris, 1970
TCSG	Tennis Club Saint Germain Lès Corbeil (1970)
UNPT	Union Nationale de Professeurs de Tennis-Côte d'Azur, 1970
USFSA	Union des Sociétés Françaises de Sports Athlétiques (1887-1920)
WCT	World Championship Tennis (1968-1989)
WTT	World Team Tennis (1973)

FOREWORD

I was born on 5 June 1971 in Clichy la Garenne in Hauts de Seine (92), but I grew up in Essonne (91), south of Paris, in one of the very first Kaufman & Broad villages, where my parents, both Parisians, decided to settle in 1973: Saint Germain-Les-Corbeil.

Naturally, I started out playing football, first in the family garden and then against garage doors, before my parents finally signed me up for the local club at the ripe old age of six, in 1977!

Like most boys of my age and generation, I dreamt of being a professional footballer, lulled by the exploits of the Saint Etienne 'Greens' led by Michel Platini and Johnny Rep (my very first nickname - I was blond and curly as a child) but also by the Liverpool 'Reds' who held a real fascination for me.

In those days, youngsters my age followed the matches more on the radio - the European Champion Clubs' Cup was only played on a few Wednesdays a year, and you had to fight hard with Mum to get permission to watch, as school was the next day... But I have to admit that the oratorical talents of the late Eugène Saccomano (1936-2019) gave me goose bumps and, above all, the desire to go to the stadium to see my heroes in 'real life'.

Fortunately, my father, a child of the baby boom, born of the union of two Yugoslav immigrants and better known as Petrovic (pronounced 'itch') than Stanajic - a nickname in old Serbo-Croatian attributed to his paternal grandfather when the latter arrived in France - was himself a keen sportsman, football of course like any self-respecting 'Yugoslav' but also and above all rowing.

He won the hundredth Championnats de la Seine, the oldest sporting competition ever held in France (the first was in 1853), the day after I was born!

As much as his passion for football helped me later on, his background as a former top-level rower (as we say in the jargon...) weighed me down because he turned out to be a poor 'coach': I understood a little too late that the two sports, rowing and tennis, were the opposite of each other!

Rowing is a closed-skills sport where the aim is to get from point A to point B without having time to think, whereas tennis is more of a 'cerebral' open-skills sport where numerous parameters have to be taken into consideration with every ball hit, every point played, every match... So his remarks and other advice during matches, and/or worse, after a big defeat, were far from having the desired effect... A few examples..:

"How could you lose to a guy who weighs a hundred and ten kilos? You're not hitting the ball hard enough. Why are you sending all the balls back into your opponent's racket?

It's not difficult to put the ball on the right when the player is on the left"...And stop playing in the service boxes, extend your arm for God's sake!

My father was never politically correct, but deep down he was a true competitor and above all a sportsman at heart, very attached to club spirit and respect for the rules, even if for him it was less important to take part than to win - not just anyone can be a baron!

Thanks to my father, I was lucky enough to be able to go to the Parc des Princes in Paris at a very early age. - in 1975 - for the visit of the green team from St Etienne and then regularly thereafter to cheer on Paris Saint Germain and in particular its successive Yugoslav stars: Pantelic, Šurjak, Susic, Halilhodžić, Vujovic and yes there were already "itch" who delighted the Park long before the arrival of Zlatan (a Swede of Yugoslav origin as you can guess from his surname!).

And what about tennis?

I discovered it at the end of the seventies and beginning of the eighties on television when I was fascinated by the Wimbledon finals between Borg and McEnroe, finals symbolised by a blatant clash of styles, even for the laymen that my father and I were.

As for me, I was immediately fascinated by the Swede with the long hair and the three-day beard... Even though colour television was already widely available in homes at the time, it was hard to know where that bloody white ball was (it turned yellow at Wimbledon in 1986 -a British tradition).

It also took a huge effort of concentration to follow the ball as it sailed up and down the screen, a bit like in the very first video game, the famous 'pong', inspired by table tennis! And it wasn't easy to follow a white ball over light grey grass, especially on the central path that led from the baseline to the net.

And yes, at that time, exchanges of more than two shots from the back of the court on London grass were at least as rare as snow in spring in the Paris region...

And not just because of the equipment available at the time: wooden rackets, very small heads, giving no margin for error (hence the famous "look at your ball" advice) and making passing shots very risky, except for the Swede...

The grass of the 1980s did not have the same properties as the grass we know today: the bounce was much lower...

Our British friends have always claimed loud and clear that they have never touched their rubber, but the 2001 final between a certain Goran Ivanisevic - who was born in Yugoslavia in 1971 and became Croatian twenty years later - and Australia's Patrick Rafter sealed the end of the serve-and-volley rule at Wimbledon, ushering in a new era for tennis in the 21st century: the back-court brawl!

It was only very recently, in the latest edition of the book entitled _Wimbledon The Official History,_ published in 2020, that the author, one John Barrett, a former British player, member of the All England Lawn Tennis and Croquet Club since 1955 and now vice-chairman of the tournament's organising committee, admitted that the grass at Wimbledon had indeed undergone modifications coupled with a change of balls in order to alter its bounce, as can be seen on page 397 of his book:

"Another factor at Wimbledon that contributed to the disappearance of volleyers was the change in playing properties of the courts. From 2000 the seed that was used became 100% perennial ryegrass, which gave better wear than the mixture of 70% and 30% creeping red

fescue that had been used before. The courts, dressed now with the same loam used to prepare cricket wickets, were also firmer: balls which on the greener, lusher courts used to shoot through on a low trajectory now bounced higher".

So it was after following the exploits of the Swede Bjorn Borg, who held a real fascination for me, that I finally decided to leave the Saint Germain Les Corbeil football club to join the village Tennis Club in June 1982, at the age of eleven. A crime of lèse-majesté just before the opening of the football World Cup in Spain...

But in those days, and with the education I had received, you didn't spread yourself too thinly over several activities at once - and there weren't many of them - but you did have to give your all to the one you had chosen to invest in.

This didn't stop me from continuing to take an interest in football, playing with friends (the most fun way to improve your physical condition and coordination at the time), following the exploits of Michel Platini's Les Bleus and making regular trips to the Parc des Princes. But I have to say that TCSG very quickly became my 'main residence', even though the club had no reception area (more commonly known as a 'club-house') and the six courts were mainly reserved for adults, I spent my days on the wall with the other kids my age - the best training, you might say!

And then I was lucky enough to grow up in the 1980s, at the very time when the little yellow ball was sweeping France and Yannick Noah's victory at Roland Garros on 5 June 1983 (the very day I turned twelve and when I had only been a member of the FFT for a year) led to a tidal wave in the clubs!

I spent some of the most extraordinary years a kid, then a teenager and finally an adult with a passion for the yellow ball could have at TC St Germain Les Corbeil, having been a member of the club from 1982 to 2007, a quarter of a century without interruption.

Not only did I train there as a player, first in the hands of the late Jacqueline Leneuf - whom everyone from Essonne in the 1980s knew - then under the guidance of those who became dear friends, first Frédéric Collombel from 1987 and then Éric Bory from 1990, two passionate and experienced coaches who are still at TCSG - what loyalty!

But it was also there, and with the encouragement of Éric and Fred, that I did all my teacher training: from 1st degree federal initiator in 1991 (when I was a history student at the University of Paris IV Sorbonne) to BE2 teacher in 2006!

Of course, I'm very proud of what I've achieved with the club where I grew up and every time I go back to France, TC St Germain Les Corbeil is a must for me and it's always a great pleasure to meet up with friends, their children and former pupils - in short, my second family!

So, almost forty years after I took my first steps on a tennis court, my passion for the sport, its history, reading, teaching and the evolution of techniques made me want to put it all down in this book, which I hope you'll enjoy reading and, above all, which will enable you to find out more about a whole host of subjects, as I myself have learned a great deal during these three years of research!

The aim of this book is first and foremost to describe the development of the federation and all the players who have contributed to the development of tennis teaching in France.

I felt it was very important to try and put all the events and decisions taken into context so that we could understand the whys and wherefores.

So I wanted to retrace the history of tennis teaching in France without bias or judgement, because I wanted this book to be as neutral as possible.

Of course, you will see that at times I wanted to give my opinion on certain decisions taken, but always taking into account the context and keeping a certain distance: "it's better to try to understand than to condemn without knowing".

Thank you very much in advance for your attention. The history of teaching our sport is so rich!

July 2018 at TC Saint Germain les Corbeil (Essonne Committee, Ile de France League). On the right in the photo, my friend Fred Collombel, on the left Éric Bory, also a loyal friend. Always a pleasure to see them again! In the background, on the left, court number six where I took my entrance test for the TCSG tennis school in June 1982 with the late Jacqueline Leneuf (1927-2005).

Opposite, a photo taken in June 1984 exactly two years after my entrance tests for the TCSG tennis school.
Old-timers will recognise the "mateco" cement courts, which were later replaced by porous concrete.

INTRODUCTION

Although codified by the English in 1874 and quickly introduced to France on the beaches of Normandy, the Atlantic and the Côte d'Azur by our British friends, tennis in its current form is no less derived from a monastic activity that appeared in France in the 11th century and was played assiduously first in the Middle Ages and then throughout the modern era by the clergy, the nobility and the monarchy until the French Revolution in 1789:
jeu de paume.

The first female paume player in the Western world to have a written record was the Frenchwoman Margot la Hennuyère, better known as Margot de Hainaut.

The latter beat the best paumiers in 1427 in Paris, as recounted in the _Journal d'un bourgeois de Paris (Diary of a Paris burgher)_ kept between 1405 and 1449:

"In the year 1427, there came to Paris a woman named Margot, quite young, like 28 to 30 years old, who was from the country of Hainaut, and who played the best paume that any man had ever seen, and with this played in front hand after hand very powerfully, very maliciously, very skilfully, as a man could do, and few men came to whom she did not win, except the most powerful players".

So I like to say that tennis is first and foremost a French game, invented by the English!

Major Wingfield (1833-1912), the father of lawn tennis, had the ingenious idea of packing his kit into a portable case containing four rackets, rubber balls, a net, pegs and lines to mark out the court.

And that was long before the arrival of the big sports chains!

The first lawn tennis balls were made of rubber, using a process developed by the American chemist Charles Goodyear (1800-1860) himself, so as not to damage the grass so dear to our friends across the Channel (_source: Jean-Christophe Piffaut, L'invention du tennis, 2007_). This portable kit could be set up just about anywhere (like the croquet game, which was very popular in Great Britain), and when the British arrived in France on holiday, they didn't hesitate to set up their courts on the beaches along the coast.

This very friendly game, which can be played by both men and women, is going to win over our fellow citizens very quickly!

The year 1877 is a milestone in the history of tennis in France, because it was then that ten Englishmen living in Paris founded the very first tennis club in France, in Neuilly sur Seine, on the Ile de la Jatte to be precise:

Decimal Boating & Lawn Tennis Club.
And it was not far from the Ile de la Jatte that the English, once again, built the first regular asphalt tennis court in 1885 for the Société Sportive de l'Ile de Puteaux, on the very spot where the tennis events of the 1900 Olympic Games were to be played in Paris (*see La Vie au Grand Air magazine, 6 May 1900*).

These same Englishmen were even behind the creation of the first clay courts in France at the end of the 19th century!

History has it that the Renshaw twins (William, seven-times singles champion at Wimbledon and five-times doubles champion with his brother Ernest between 1881 and 1889), who were giving lessons on the grass courts at Cannes, came up with the idea of covering them with a red powder to make it easier to see the lines in summer, when the grass was yellowed by the sun.

The powder came from broken clay pots from the neighbouring town of Vallauris: clay was born!

Many other clubs, or societies we should say, were soon created (Tennis Club de Dinard in 1879 - rightly considered to be the first French tennis club, since it was created by French people only, unlike the Decimal - then followed the Racing Club de France in 1882, the Tennis Club de Paris in 1895...).

1891 is a second date worth remembering, with the creation of the first French Amateur Tennis Championship and the founding of the Union des Sociétés Françaises des Sports Athlétiques (USFSA), which promoted the spread of sporting activities in France, including tennis, by organising numerous inter-club tournaments well before the founding of the Fédération Française de Lawn Tennis (FFLT) in 1920, which would only abandon the word "lawn" much later, in 1976...

In this book, we take a step back in time to retrace thehistory oftennis teaching in France, from the first master teachers, the true artisans of the "white ball", The most famous of these were Martin Plaa (1901-1978) and his disciple Alfred Estrabeau (1906-1999), via the Suzanne Lenglen Tennis Schools set up throughout France just before the Second World War, to the Federal programmes devised and distributed in France from 1992 via the National Technical Directorate (DTN) and its Training and Teaching Department set up in 1997.

We will also see that a number of important events had an impact on the way tennis was taught in France, including the creation of *Tennis de France* magazine in 1953, and the events of 1968, which helped to popularise tennis and ensure the survival of the Roland Garros tournament, which had been under threat for some time.

This was followed by the development of the French teaching method, which from 1972 onwards helped to introduce more and more young people to tennis, and finally, later in 1978, the creation of _Tennis Info_ magazine by the federal authorities (the FFT was the only sports federation to have its own magazine at the time) helped to better disseminate the federation's messages to its clubs and therefore to its members.

As the only federal newspaper to be sent free of charge to all affiliated clubs, _Tennis Info_ aims to be the magazine that directly serves the clubs, the living fabric that makes up the leagues, but also all players, whatever their level.

Unless it was created with a view to thwarting the expansion of the new all-tennis monthly that had appeared two years earlier: Jean Couvercelle's famous _Tennis Magazine_?

In any case, all these publications have enabled our sport to penetrate homes and convert a greater number of players, regardless of the type of tennis they play: recreational and/or competitive!

We will also look at the role played by national education teachers of physical education and sport (PE) in improving teaching techniques after the Second World War.

These men and women have played a very important role in the spread and democratisation of tennis in France, particularly among young people.

We will also see that the training of tennis instructors and teachers has been considerably professionalised and developed since the beginnings of the federal diplomas in the 1950s (educator and teacher) to the current DEJEPS, thanks in particular to the emergence of a training engineering trend in the 1980s, leading to the creation of state-approved training organisations.

Finally, it should also be noted that individual initiatives outside the FFT have helped to advance and progress the way tennis is taught, or rather coached in France, as a distinction must be made between competitive tennis - coaching - and introductory tennis for the general public, aimed primarily at leisure and relaxation - teaching - as the former cannot exist without the latter.

Here we look at the training camps and academies set up on the French Riviera in particular by former professional and/or amateur players with a passion for tennis, not forgetting the contribution made by "foreigners": Thomas Burke (United Kingdom), Joseph Stolpa (Hungary), Gail Sherriff (Australia), Francis Rawstorne (South Africa), Sever Dron and Ion Tiriac (Romania), Bob Brett (Australia), etc.

Finally, on the eve of the Paris 2024 Olympic Games, we'll be going back a hundred years to when French tennis first entered its golden age on the international stage, dominating virtually every major competition, first with the great Suzanne Lenglen, followed by René Lacoste, Jean Borotra, Henri Cochet and Jacques Brugnon, better known as the 'Musketeers'.

We'll see that these great names in French tennis, each with their own nickname: 'la Divine', 'le Crocodile', 'le Basque Bondissant', 'le Magicien' and 'Toto', have left an indelible mark not only on the history of tennis but also on the history of teaching. These characters are also an integral part of France's cultural, sporting and industrial heritage!

Suzanne Lenglen was the first to think about developing a teaching method and came up with the idea of group lessons, leading to the creation of the first tennis schools.

René Lacoste is the man who invented the ball-throwing machine for self-initiated training, as well as the leather grip for a better grip on the racket (before that, the hand was in direct contact with the wood of the racket, something difficult to imagine today, when you change grips like you change your shirt!)

He was also the father of the anti-vibrator, designed to overcome the severe vibration problems he encountered when developing the metal racket he designed in 1963, which was used for the first time that same year at the Wimbledon tournament by French champion Pierre Darmon.

The racket became very popular a few years later, when Lacoste sold the patent to the American company Wilson Sporting Goods, which marketed it under the name Wilson T2000.

Used since 1967 by the American Billie Jean King, she won Wimbledon that year, becoming the first player in history to win a Grand Slam with a metal racket 'made in France'.

The model was popularised by his compatriot Jimmy Connors in the early seventies, and he played with it for eighteen years, winning all eight of his Grand Slam titles.
!
Frenchman Patrick Proisy reached the final of Roland Garros 1972, wearing the original model designed by René Lacoste.

A revolutionary racket at the time, as it was a little lighter than wooden frames and a little easier to handle. Above all, it offered an excess of power, provided the ball was perfectly centred.

Henri Cochet, for his part, was immediately interested in spreading the sport, becoming a propagandist for the federation before turning his attention to training, not hesitating to observe the country's best players and to offer advice, thereby becoming the very first national instructor. And we shall see that of the four musketeers, it is undoubtedly he who has left the greatest legacy in terms of thinking about teaching and coaching.

As for Jean Borotra and Jacques Brugnon, they did not hesitate to travel the world, along with Henri Cochet, to meet the best players from every continent and observe their training methods.

So perhaps our next Olympic Games, organised for the third time in the City of Light after 1900 and 1924, will be followed by a new golden age for French tennis, currently in the doldrums?

We have every right to believe that, as we will see, we have excellent coaches in all areas (technical and physical), good trainers, a very dense network of young players and a sport that is as popular as ever among the French population, but which is also being challenged by new practices (padel tennis in particular, but also beach tennis and, to a lesser extent, pickleball).

According to recent statements by Arnaud Di Pasquale, head of the Padel mission at the FFT since March 2021, padel tennis currently boasts 300,000 regular players in France and could lead to a decline in interest in our good old tennis.

? Or is it just a complementary activity to revitalise life in all the clubs affiliated to the FFT?

Time will tell!

PART ONE

THE ORIGINS OF TENNIS TEACHING IN FRANCE

"The first concern of the English, when they emigrate and go to plant their flag on new land, is to first build a church, then a school, and thirdly, a "lawn-tennis" court"
"E. de Nanteuil, La Paume et le Lawn-Tennis, 1898.

The first traces of educational thinking, Burke/Broquedis (1910-1913)

At the beginning of the 20th century, tennis was mainly played at low tide on the beaches of the Opal Coast by middle-class Parisians, whose main aim was to get some fresh air, get their bodies moving and, in short, have a good time among people from good families.

At a time when paid holidays did not yet exist (it was not until 1936 and the arrival of the Front Populaire in government), tennis was only played by a tiny minority of privileged people whose aim was to indulge in the habits and customs of the English nobility.

It's worth remembering that back in the Middle Ages, the ancestor of tennis, jeu de paume, was described as "the game of kings, the king of games". The game of tennis, now codified and regulated, was soon to experience the same craze, and the law of 1 July 1901, which authorised the free formation of associations, was to accelerate the phenomenon: Whereas in 1900 tennis was played in just nineteen civil societies (not yet called clubs), in 1912 the USFSA already counted 1,226 civil societies throughout France, 133 of which declared tennis to be part of their activities (*cf. Jean Michel Peter, Tennis, "Leisure class" et nouvelles représentations du corps à la Belle Époque, STAPS review 2010/1, n° 87*).

Played primarily as a leisure activity for men and women of equal status, tennis began as a distinctive form of entertainment, a simple pastime for people from good families.

Research by historian Patrick Clastres shows that most of the tennis clubs that sprang up in France before the Second World War were set up as commercial companies rather than associations.

As these structures have required substantial investment (land, construction, maintenance, etc.), the first users are also the first promoters and shareholders of the clubs, which are for the most part very closed circles.

Little by little, tournaments were organised during the summer period, initially by the various hotels located near the French coast (Channel, Normandy, Brittany, Basque Country, Côte d'Azur) and then very quickly by the clubs themselves.

So, gradually and quite naturally, players will seek to develop their game in order to be competitive: sometimes it will be a question of winning friendly games, sometimes of shining in tournaments.

And the first teachers were British exiles, the most famous of whom at the beginning of the 20th century was a certain Thomas Burke.

This Irish-born man began his career as a teacher at the Lansdowne Club in Dublin, where he coached his compatriot Joshua Pim (1869-1942), a doctor who won the men's singles at Wimbledon twice (1893-1894).

Burke moved to France in 1897 at the request of a certain German player, Victor Voss (1868-1936), who made him his personal 'coach' on the Côte d'Azur.

We can deliberately use the term "coach" here, as Burke spent a whole year looking after just one player, the German who became his employer. Voss was a finalist at the Nice Lawn Tennis Club and then at the Monte Carlo tournament during the period when he benefited from Burke's teaching and coaching.

After this coaching episode, Burke became a teacher at the Tennis Club de Paris (1898), before going on to teach at the Nice LTC (1900), then at the Carlton Lawn Tennis Club in Cannes, before ending his career as a tennis teacher not far from the capital on the island of Puteaux.

He died in 1920, but his three sons (Tommy, Albert and Edmund), all born in France, took up the family torch.

Even back then, tennis was often a family affair!

One of the very first issues of _Tennis_ magazine, founded in January 1910 by two French professors, Etienne Micard (1889-1910) and Max Decugis (1882-1978), contains information about Thomas Burke.

This magazine, written exclusively by players and teachers, was created above all to communicate the latest tennis news in France and to compensate for a lack of general information, as can be read in the introduction to the first issue:

"While England, the United States and Germany have their own Lawn Tennis & Badminton, American Lawn Tennis, Lawn Tennis und Golf, the 20,000 or 30,000 tennis players in France are still ignoring each other.

Tennis now fills the gap. Written exclusively by players, it is aimed solely at those who know how to breathe life into the ball, who know the delicious anguish of waiting for the unexpected leap of the serve, or who, two steps away from the net, keep their cool in the face of the drive launched at full speed".

So, as you can see, this is a magazine created by specialists for specialists only!

And the founders were quick to justify the title they had chosen as soon as the first issue appeared:

"Why Tennis tout court and not Lawn Tennis? The reason is simple. While English players, favoured (?) by the humidity of their climate, can bounce their lobs on magnificent lawns, French players have only ever played lawn tennis on the fine sand of a beach or on the crushed brick of a regulation court".

In my opinion, and in the midst of the 'entente cordiale' between our two nations, this remark is more of a desire to set ourselves apart from our British neighbours than an actual reality!

But let's get back to Thomas Burke, because in an article in the same _Tennis magazine_ entitled '_The Teachers' Match_', the editors give a very interesting account of the match between the experienced Irishman and the young French teacher Eugène Broquedis (1890-1913), who was just twenty years old.

Young Eugène's father, Émile Broquedis, was a master paume player (i.e. a paume teacher and racket maker) and his sister Marguerite was to become France's best pre-war player, but more on that later.

We learn from this report that this was only the third game organised in Paris between two teachers, who had much better things to do:

"Was it that professionalism in lawn tennis wasn't catching on in France, or were French players so perfect that they didn't need lessons any more? Not at all, but Tom Burke, who was almost the only teacher in France at the time, had other things to do than show off. He had no shortage of customers, taking up his days, and it's very hard work sending balls back for eight hours a day... Since then, things have changed, players have multiplied; teachers have been trained in France and have educated the young neophytes while training the old ones."

These statements show that tennis had become a very popular activity in Parisian clubs by 1910. The instructors were very busy and teaching was based solely on individual lessons. Even then, a distinction was already being made between initiation and training. But what may have been true in the capital was certainly not the case across the country.

In December 1936, the monthly bulletin of what was then called the AFPPT (Association Française des Professeurs et Professionnels de Tennis) listed just 79 teachers in the whole of France (56 French and 23 foreign teachers, including British, of course, but also Italians, Germans and Russians). We can therefore safely assume that there were still very few teachers in 1910, as the report on the match between Burke and Broquedis makes clear.

But let's go back to this report, which seems to indicate that the game between the two men was indeed an exhibition, the main aim of which was to attract new followers:

"Why should two teachers, competing in a friendly exhibition, show the spectators anything other than lesson shots, classic shots? This match should serve as an advertisement for them; if they show the customer gestures that seem acrobatic, or extraordinary efforts, the customer will be afraid, he will say: tennis is a fearsome and difficult and tiring game, and he will not take a lesson."

The aim was to make people believe that tennis was an easy and enjoyable sport; in short, this exhibition served as propaganda for the teachers, at a time when they were the only masters on board (the Lawn Tennis Federation was not founded until ten years later, in 1920).

We learn that Broquedis will emerge victorious from this match (we can quite rightly assume that Burke, close to retirement, has decided to pass the torch to his young apprentice - the two men are teachers at the same club). And after this victory over the Irishman, Broquedis intends to challenge the teacher from the Tennis Club de Paris, a certain Ware, the author of the report added:

"If this match is concluded with Ware, I for one will give it all the publicity I can; such encounters are better, for sporting propaganda, than a match between two young lunatics, who in front of an anguished harem of oxygenated suaves, shoot each other with balls 'out' for an hour...with no result other than winning a nickel-plated ebonite bowl or a pushed-back mahogany calendar."

The author seems to be making fun of amateur players, who are nevertheless the clients of these teachers, unless he wants to imply that professionals are much better than amateurs?

To conclude this article, we note that on the eve of the First World War, tennis, which was still in its infancy in France, was intended to be a noble sport, as the players wanted to emphasise technical precision, fluidity and consistency more than physical strength and speed.

But very early on, the tactical and strategic dimension of the game was highlighted as a key area to work on, well before technique!

In 1912, Etienne Micard wrote in the magazine *Tennis:*

"In tennis, the head includes intuition, resolution and attention. Through intuition and deduction, you'll be able to understand the reasons for things that are, or should be [...] Then you have to analyse your opponent's game and try to guess his intentions".

As well as being a sport and an athletic discipline, tennis is presented very early on as a strategic game in which reflection, patience and intelligence are at least as important as the stroke.

A year later, in an article entitled *Le style en tennis (Tennis style)* published on 1 November 1913 in the magazine *La Vie au grand air,* Marguerite Broquedis (1893-1983), Olympic tennis champion in Stockholm in 1912 in the women's singles (the first ever Olympic title won by a French sportswoman in any discipline), wrote the following:

"The accuracy of the eye, the sense of distance, the ability to manage quickly in difficult situations, the subtlety to penetrate the tactics of the opponent and to conceal one's own, constitute a wealth of technical knowledge, a general intelligence of the game, a quality of personal initiative which, combined with the elegance of the gesture, make it possible to achieve a style which can be described as truly pure, because it is made up at the same time of a happy harmony of movements and of a very practised science".

In these words, which show just how open-skilled the game of tennis is, with so many parameters to take into account, we find the four areas that every competitor needs to master in order to perform as well as possible: tactics, mindset, technique and physique.

And when the editors of the same newspaper ask her to explain the style of a player, Marguerite Broquedis explains:

"Style reflects the temperament of the subject, his taste and his personality. A beautiful style is always interesting to the technician who knows all the difficulties and surprises that tennis has to offer; it seduces the lay spectator, who is rarely insensitive to the simple, precise and skilfully calculated grace of the movements. It can also be said that style, if it claims to be truly beautiful, must suffice with great sobriety of movement through the application of only strictly useful efforts, and that anything that is a fancy gesture is both an error of taste and often the testimony of an imperfect knowledge of the technique of the game".

This presentation, made in 1913 by the player Marguerite Broquedis, sets out the ambiguities surrounding technique: it's true that everyone has their own style, but on the other hand, there are 'codes' that must be respected. The gesture mustbe beautiful and fluid, whichmeans thatin addition to his or her style, the player must strive for efficiency. This equation is still relevant today!

Marguerite Broquedis is a very special figure in French tennis.

Born in Pau in 1893 to a father who was a master peacock player, she naturally began playing paume with her two older brothers (Eugène and Louis). Later, the family moved to Paris, and they all started playing tennis. Emile, the father, made a made-to-measure racket for his daughter, and the two boys quickly became so adept at tennis that they became tennis teachers in Puteaux.

Marguerite was not to be outdone, and she soon had to find male training partners. She hits like them, attacks, goes to the net:

"She had all the strokes, but above all a dazzling forehand drive, a splendid volley and a serve that few other women could match" said the Parisian player Pierre Albarran (1893-1960), who knew Marguerite well and was one of Suzanne Lenglen's lovers (*sources: P. Albarran and H. Cochet, Histoire du Tennis, 1960*).

Above all, as sports historian Jean-Michel Peter (Université Paris Descartes) points out, she attracted the best players from Racing Club de France, as much for the quality of her game as for her natural beauty, and they did not hesitate to bring her to the Croix Catelan to train with her.

The magazine *Fémina* of 1 August 1910, for example, stated:

"In the past, women tennis players were not very feared partners and it was certainly not very gallant, but certainly successful, to hit them with difficult shots [...] Today, they have acquired the suppleness, vigour and certainty of vision and judgement that protect them from petty male treachery".

But also in 1911 in the all-male *Tennis* magazine:

"Watching Mlle Broquedis perform is pure pleasure. Flexibility, elegance, harmony: nothing is missing. The forehand is powerful, sufficiently long and strong; the backhand, though the weaker part, is broad and graceful; the serve has a lovely arch. Seeing Diana's beautiful, sculptural stance at the racket, one is reminded that tennis is a game revived from the Greeks.

Marguerite's list of achievements was not as extensive as it should have been (due to the first world conflict), but it is worthy of respect: in addition to her Olympic title in women's singles in Stockholm in 1912, she won the first edition of what was then called the World Championship on clay at the Parc de St Cloud on the Stade Français courts (1912) and was the only player in history to beat Suzanne Lenglen in a tournament final, and on clay at that (French Women's Singles Championship in 1914 on the RCF courts at Croix Catelan).

In my opinion, she deserves to be honoured in the very heart of the Roland Garros stadium: wasn't she supported by Baron Pierre de Coubertin himself, who, after seeing her play, personally approved her participation in the tennis event at the Stockholm Olympic Games, enabling her to win the first Olympic gold medal in the history of French women's sport?

Ted Tinling (1910-1990), a former British tennis player who became a stylist (he designed dresses for all the players of the fifties, sixties and seventies) and who worked alongside both Broquedis and Lenglen, even confirmed her aura across the Channel:

"Broquedis was the subject of the first fashion column devoted to tennis ever published in a newspaper [...] she was the first to suggest that tennis could be beautiful. It all comes from her. And above all, she was more elegant than Lenglen.
(Source, Libération 30 May 2020, article by Gil Dhers, Marguerite Broquedis, la grande oubliée du tennis).

In my opinion, this French player deserves to be in the International Tennis Hall of Fame!

In fact, she wrote an article in the special Tennis issue of the magazine *La Vie au grand air,* published on 30 May 1914 and entitled *"Tennis, the favourite sport of young girls"*, in which we read:

"Of all the sports available, tennis is the physical exercise best suited to young girls. The effort she has to put into a severely played game forces her to make movements that are wide, broad, very often complete, supple and energetic. She does this without sacrificing any of the grace and elegance that should characterise a woman's gestures; but these gestures, when executed in this way, lose their natural effeminate languour and take on a character of decision and authority, indicative of a certain self-control.

Because of the rapid movements it requires, tennis demands of the young girl a sporting quality that nature has always given her sparingly: speed [...] tennis therefore appears to be the most complete sport for women".

I therefore think that Amélie Castera Oudéa, the current Minister for Youth and Sport in the Macron government, Amélie Mauresmo, director of the Roland Garros tournament, and Caroline Flaissier, very recently appointed director general of the FFT, should look into the case of Marguerite Broquedis, an unjustly forgotten player in French and international tennis and a great icon of women's sport...Ladies, it's up to you!

Max Decugis, landmark writings

After the article about Marguerite Broquedis published in the magazine *La Vie au grand air,* Max Decugis (1882-1978) wrote one of the very first collections on tennis that same year, published by Slatkine and very soberly entitled *Tennis.*

The preface to this book, written by a certain Henri Wallet (1850-1926), who was to become the first president of the French federation (1920-1925), having previously been elected president of the international federation in 1914 (under the anglicised name of Henry Walley), tells us something about the French mentality of the time with regard to sport in general and tennis in particular:

"My dear Decugis, you must know our compatriots well to have thought it would be useful, indispensable, to give them some advice.

The proverbial lightness of the French is found in sports more than anywhere else. Whereas for many years sports had been taken very seriously in foreign countries, in France they existed only as amusements, only as pastimes; their organisation was non-existent and the practice of the game followed the will of each individual. As far as tennis in particular is concerned, whereas in England, Germany, America and Austria, players who devote themselves to methodical and regular work improve their form considerably, in France, our players are still tramping around without making any progress. As for trying to remedy their imperfections, by the special study of a move, by the desire to acquire a faculty which they lack, or which they have incomplete, it is too much to ask of them."

This preface, very serious and at the same time full of self-deprecation - worthy of the posts on the FFL (Fédération Française de la Lose) Facebook page, which was created a century later - suggests that France has fallen slightly behind in the desire to improve and train its practitioners!

But this has to be qualified by the fact that the preface is written by a man who sees tennis primarily in terms of performance, whereas the majority of players at the time took to the courts to relax, get moving - in short, to have a good time without any ulterior motive!

Let's go back to Max Decugis' book, which can be considered the very first French compendium of technical, tactical and physical advice.

The author is France's greatest champion of the era, so his book is sure to be a big hit!

After meticulously detailing all the shots used in tennis (with the exception of the return of serve?) and reviewing all the different effects that the player can impart to the ball, Max Decugis gives his advice on how to improve your game in a section entitled 'Training'.

Very avant-garde - let's not forget that this book was published just before the First World War - Max Decugis does not ignore the mental aspect, dietetics or even healthy living in his training method, of which the following are some general principles:

1. *"Repeat all the shots one by one many times.*

2. *If you don't have anyone to play with, use a wall: the ball will be faster, more regular and you'll get a great eye speed.*

3. *You learn a lot by watching good players play.*

4. *Work on the different game situations but focus mainly on your opponent's weak point.*

5. *Find a fast, accurate pick-up because you can't make progress and pick up your balls at the same time. To be good, you have to hit a lot and often.*

6. *You don't have to play against the strongest to progress, because if you do, you're forcing your talent and you're not doing any good.*

7. *Don't give up, keep going even if you've had enough.*

8. *However, to train properly, it's not enough to just play tennis. Other exercises are essential for acquiring breath, speed of movement and stamina. These include jumping rope and short sprints from 10 to 25 metres.*

9. *Going to bed early, getting a good night's sleep, eating sensibly and staying well hydrated will save you a lot of discomfort".*

More than just playing points, the author stresses the need to repeat all your shots over and over again, and not to hesitate to do what would later be called 'scales'.

And he doesn't forget to warn:

"I wouldn't advise a beginner to try and slavishly copy the style of one player or another... shots can't be reproduced like photographs.

In the descriptions of the different strokes, I have tried to give the movement; but each will produce it according to his personal conformation".

This last remark is of course very interesting and above all very clear-sighted and we shall see later that other teachers and trainers will also insist on this point, but the federation will take another direction, that of model teaching, which is much more convenient, especially with a view to disseminating the practice, because there is no room for questioning, for questioning...!

It's worth highlighting the important role played in the spread of tennis in France byone of the very first illustrated French sports magazines, the famous *La Vie au grand air,* which was launched in 1898 and closed for good in the spring of 1922.

Based on the model of the British magazine *The Field,* founded in 1853 and considered to be the world's oldest publication devoted to outdoor sports and leisure activities, and which was responsibleforthefoundation of the All England Croquet Club at Wimbledon in 1868, *La Vie au grand air was* to make the game of tennis known to as many people as possible on an almost daily basis.

This weekly magazine even went so far as to devote a special thirty-page issue to tennis, which was published on 30 May 1914 with a dense and substantial table of contents and articles written by specialists:

1. a survey in the form of interviews with players and female players on the most formidable opponents they have encountered during their careers.

2. an article *on Courage and reflection in tennis* by Max Decugis

3. *The evolution of tennis* as seen by the first president of the fledgling international federation, Frenchman Henry Wallet

4. a paper by New Zealand champion A-F Wilding (1883-1915) on *the influence of athleticism in tennis*

5. an article *on Patience and regularity* by German champion Otto Froitzheim (1884-1962)

6. an article entitled *Une balle ou deux?* by Jacques Quellennec (1887-1977) in which the author questioned both the abuse of the volley service and the foot faults that this sequence provokes.

7. *Tennis finesse* as seen by Maurice Germot (1882-1958)

8. the paper signed by Marguerite Broquedis and entitled *Tennis, the young girl's favourite sport*

9. *The intuition of the tennis player* by the French player William Laurentz (1895-1922)

10. *Ground games and volley games* by French player André Gobert (1890-1951)

11. an article entitled "*Installation of courts and formation of clubs*" written by Miss Adine Masson, daughter of Armand Masson, founder of the Tennis Club de Paris, in which we learn that since the creation of the French Tennis Championship (1891), not a single provincial has managed to enter his name in the competition!

12. a piece on *The weapons of our champions,* which tells us how tennis rackets and balls were made on the eve of the First World War!

So there's a lot of talk about tennis in the press, and foreign players also have their say.

The English champion Miss Lambert Chambers (1878-1960), seven-time singles winner at Wimbledon and Olympic champion in London in 1908, revealed her training tips in an article entitled *How to improve your game,* published in the magazine on 21 June 1913, in which she explained:

"Some players find it very difficult to improve their game [...] in my opinion, it's because they're not using the right methods [...] don't play a practice game like a match game, where you avoid your weak shots, your only aim being to win [...]. Work on your weak shots until they become your strong shots. Get a devoted friend to send you the ball where you want it again and again: your patience will be rewarded by continuous progress.

Another system: work against the wall, which has the advantage of always being there, and means you don't have to disturb anyone... Only work with a specific object, with a weak point in sight [...] keep an eye on the best players and try to penetrate their methods.

The match game is a different matter: here, you have to avoid weak moves, the sole aim being to win. One of the secrets of success is the gift of anticipation. There's a natural genius in anticipating shots, but it has to be cultivated. Watch your opponents first, and you'll often find that they always hit back with the same shot...".

For Miss Chambers, it is more important to strengthen his weaknesses than to work on his strengths, a dilemma on which not all coaches have the same point of view.

She also stressed the fact that you shouldn't try to work on everything at once: the player should concentrate on one shot and one shot only, and we'll see that this principle will later become one of the pillars of federal teaching.

The English champion also needs to work on consistency and anticipation.

The French player William Laurentz also gave his recommendations in an article entitled *"L'entraînement pour le tennis"* (*"Training for tennis"*) published in the magazine on 20 May 1919:

"Before the war we neglected physical preparation too much. Apart from Gobert and, above all, Miss Lenglen, everyone arrived on the court with training done somewhat haphazardly.

In my opinion, playing the game isn't enough [...] you also need to develop your breathing and leg work. Skipping and breathing movements seem to me to be particularly appropriate [...]. Miss Lenglen, our best French player [...] is an example of methodical training. Fieldwork, physical training and swimming, carried out rationally and continuously in a beautiful climate where life in the open air is possible in both winter and summer, have produced the splendid results we are familiar with [...].

In short, tennis is an excessively hard game, for which a player, even a very gifted one, needs great physical qualities, because nothing is more discouraging than to see victory slip from your grasp through fatigue or lack of breath".

Full of common sense, these remarks by William Laurentz are still relevant more than a century later!

What's more, Lenglen chose to move to the Côte d'Azur very early on to take advantage of a climate that was more conducive to training and, above all, more beneficial: what could be better than being able to train outdoors for most of the year to adapt to all conditions (wind, heat, sun, etc.)? And Laurentz was quick to point out that poor physical condition undermines a player's confidence and therefore his mental state! The year was 1919!

Little by little, thanks to the articles published in the magazine *La Vie au grand air*, tennis became more familiar to a larger number of French people and from 1920, the date of its creation, the federation took over from the daily press in an effort to propagate the sport.

The time of the first master teachers

In the inter-war period, there were not many tennis teachers, but they were already hierarchically organised according to a model that was to last for many decades: first you were a teacher, then you could become a master teacher for the most skilful rackets in hand, or perhaps for the most experienced?

Diplomas were first awarded under the supervision of the ministerial department responsible for sports, then from 1920 (when the FFLT was founded) jointly with the federation. Finally, in December 1929, the newly-created Association Française des Professeurs et Professionnels de Tennis (AFPPT) came on board.

This organisation, founded by the great champion Martin Plaa (1901-1978), is an association of professional tennis teachers and players (at the time, tennis teachers had the status of professionals because they earned income from their tennis-related activities).

In the context of the times, it is very important to stress that those considered to be professionals, i.e. all those teachers and other master teachers who were paid to teach, had absolutely no right to take part in the most prestigious events, which were, in the order in which they were created and with their original names, Wimbledon, The Championships (1877), the United States Championship (1881), the French International Championship (1891) and the Australasian Championship (1905): Wimbledon, The Championships (1877), the United States Championship (1881), the French International Championship (1891) and the Australasian Championship (1905), to which must of course be added the Davis Cup (1900).

It should be noted that when they were created, these four championships (not yet known as Grand Slams) were all played on natural grass (ours opted for clay in 1912 and never changed surface again - a French speciality!).

At that time, only amateurs were allowed to take part - tennis teachers were excluded!

As sports historian Patrick Clastres pointed out during his speech at the Dijon symposium in June 2021:

"From the very beginnings of tennis in France, two worlds coexisted and battled [...] that of amateurs with a taste for the game and that of professionals who made a living from their art. The famous musketeers erased the master teachers from history, even though they were much better than them with racquets in hand!

In fact, Jacques Brugnon himself (1895-1978), alias Toto, one of the famous Musketeers, was the one who first hinted at this fact in a special issue of _Tennis de France_ magazine, published in 1977 to mark the fiftieth anniversary of France's first Davis Cup victory and entitled _L'épopée des Mousquetaires._

On page 106 it states:

"At the time, we were lucky enough to have at our disposal a wonderful coach whose dedication was matched only by his talent. Martin Plaa was capable of playing every day four or five sets with Borotra, as many with Cochet and Lacoste (when the latter was in the team) and he retained enough enthusiasm to play with me the few games I needed... It always seemed to me that in these long games that Martin Plaa played at full speed against our singles representatives, he was above all concerned with making them work without worrying about who would win or who would lose.

At the time, then, competitive tennis was an activity for moneyed amateurs (at least for all those taking part in the events that came to be known as Grand Slam tournaments in the 1930s), and it remained so until 1968, when our sport became 'open'!

Throughout this period, access to the most prestigious tournaments was reserved solely for a minority of players, in accordance with a code of amateurism that was promulgated in London in 1880 by the founding meeting of the Amateur Athletic Association of England (AAA), which stipulated that
:

"An amateur is any gentleman who has never taken part in a public contest open to all comers or for money derived from admissions to the field or otherwise, or who has never at any period of his life been a teacher or instructor of exercises of this kind as a means of livelihood."

And these two worlds, amateurs and professionals, are grouped together in two different organisations:

➤ The UFSA tennis committee for amateurs. This committee became independent in 1920 within the FFLT, which advocated amateurism.

➤ The professionals grouped around the master teachers, who were theiheirs of the last master clam-makers and who created their own organisation in 1929 (Assoc ation French Association of Tennis Teachers and Professionals)

It's important to remember that two of the four musketeers (Jean Borotra and René Lacoste) picked up their first tennis racket late in life, during language stays in Great Britain in 1912 for Borotra, who was just fourteen, and in 1919 for Lacoste, who was fifteen!

And when you consider that René Lacoste took part in the Wimbledon tournament for the first time just two years after discovering tennis, losing 6/0-6/0 to Australian player Pat O'Hara Wood (1891-19691), it's worth putting things into context.

! In fact, it was his first experience on grass, something unthinkable today!

When the young Jean Borotra, who had already played Basque pelota, received a tennis racket for the first time, he was naturally very comfortable:

"When I hit the ball, with the racket as if it were a pala, it took the lady of the house a long time to believe that I'd never touched a tennis racket!

As a result, during my stay in England, I was invited almost every day to go and play with all the friends of the lady of the house, because the news had spread and everyone wanted to see this 'Basque phenomenon' who jumped, leapt and soon was playing better than them! (cf. Daniel Amson, Borotra de Wimbledon à Vichy, 1999)

More than the skill of the novice Borotra, racket in hand, we can highlight in this example the importance of learning transfers and moreover many players from the country Basque and trained in pelota during their early childhood became excellent tennis players. Dominique Poey, who spent almost forty years with the FFT (1978-2015), told me in an interview in July 2021 that he became one of France's best juniors in the early 1970s, thanks to his initial training as a pelota player:

"Because the pala handle is flat rather than round, when I first started playing tennis I naturally put lift into all my forehands and because I was left-handed, I quickly got up to -15!"

But let's get back to Borotra, considered by all his peers to be one of the greatest players of the first half of the 20th century, and without wishing to offend him, it is inconceivable in this day and age to think that it was possible to play the leading roles having started out so late in the game!

All the more so as he had to stop very quickly after starting out - due to the First World War -only playing his first tournament at the age of 21!

But two years later, in 1921, he managed to beat the best French player of the time, a certain André Gobert (1890-1951).

Martin Plaa, who hails from the Basque country, started out as a champion paume player, but soon turned to tennis to become a great player: he has a complete, consistent and, above all, very precise game. At a very young age, he decided to take up a career as a tennis teacher and soon became the coach of the Musketeers!

His lessons are given on a one-to-one basis only, with Martin Plaa as the teacher.

He is regarded as an excellent teacher, but also as a force of nature, as he can train one of the Musketeers for several hours and then do the same with the others, as Jacques Brugnon confirms!

It's hard to imagine a coach/sparring today doing a session with Federer, then another with Nadal and finally with Djokovic...

At the time, group lessons did not exist, and no attempt was even made to consider them, as master-teachers felt that they did not allow them to focus on the pupil.

These masters are in fact true craftsmen, in the noblest sense of the term, Martin Plaa being of course the best known.

Later, his disciple, the famous Alfred Estrabeau, as well as Jacques Iemetti (1922-1969) and a few others passed on the legacy.

In the *official bulletin* number 114 of May 1947 (the forerunner of Tennis Info) of what was still called the French Lawn Tennis Federation, which I managed to obtain, we can learn that at that time only 98 teachers were practising in the whole country (which included not only metropolitan France but also French Algeria as well as Morocco and Tunisia) for a total of just under 60,000 members of the Federation (59,359 to be exact).

This gave a ratio of one teacher for every six hundred and five licence-holders in 1947.

It also states that to become an instructor (i.e. the first level), the required ranking is 30 (which was the first level of the French ranking at the time). To become a teacher, you need to have worked as an instructor for at least a year and obtained a ranking of 4/6.

Lastly, a master teacher must have worked as a teacher for at least ten years, and can only hope to earn this title if he or she has been ranked in the top French series...

In 1947, among the 98 professional teachers listed, there were 33 monitors, 47 teachers and 18 master teachers...

All these teachers are members of the Association Française des Professeurs de Tennis, a kind of teachers' union (created in 1929 by Martin Plaa himself) and each year they negotiate with the Federation the maximum rate to which they are entitled according to their grade.

In May 1947, for example, we learned that an instructor could not receive more than 200 francs net in fees for an hour of individual tuition (300 francs net for a teacher and 350 francs net for a master teacher).

And it is specified in this *official bulletin* of May 1947:

"In spa towns, seaside resorts, health resorts, etc., and during the periods referred to as "seasons", the prices indicated may be increased by 100 francs to compensate for accommodation, hotel and travel expenses, etc., incurred by members of the AFPT. In the same places and during the same periods, civil servants, physical education teachers in secondary schools, etc., who hold a diploma, may only teach tennis professionally with the authorisation of AFPT.

These net fees do not apply to group courses organised by the federation and which are the subject of special agreements between the federation and AFPT members.

So we can see that very early on, professional tennis teachers united within a corporation - the AFPT - to protect their interests and assert their rights against those who might do them harm, but we'll come back to that later!

As we can see, there were not many master teachers, and one man more than any other was soon to be considered one of the greatest pedagogues and one of the finest teachers: Alfred Estrabeau (1906-1999).

Also from the Basque country, and trained in paume like his illustrious teacher Martin Plaa, young Alfred was ranked in the first series at the age of 16 in 1922.

He very quickly obtained the title of master teacher and first became coach of the Belgian Davis Cup team, then those of India, Poland and Spain, before becoming Martin Plaa's assistant to coach the French team at Roland Garros.

The team was made up of René de Buzelet (1907-1995), Christian Boussus (1908-2003), Marcel Bernard (1914-1994), Jacques Brugnon (1895-1978), Jean Borotra (1898-1994) and Henri Cochet (1901-1987).

Alfred then became head coach of the French team between the 1930s and the 1950s, assisted by the man who can be considered the federation's first national coach.

Henri Cochet himself!

Alfred Estrabeau was quickly portrayed as the "educational gentleman" of tennis, in that he always found a trick to correct a fault or reinforce a weakness.

It's great for both training the very best and introducing novices.

The trainer of many French champions, including Bernard Destremau (1917-2002) and Henri Bolelli (1912-1984), he also advised the former French number 1, Pierre Darmon (finalist at Roland Garros in 1963), who considered Alfred to be the best technician of his time. He was also the private teacher of Jacques Chaban-Delmas (1915-2000), ranked -4/6, who was mayor of Bordeaux for almost half a century (1947-1995) and prime minister in the Pompidou government (1969-1972).

These are the words of Alban Gouzenes, which I collected in May 2020, about Alfred Estrabeau, whom he had the good fortune to meet regularly in the 1980s when he was a coach with the Paris league:

"The image I have of him is very personal.... I was his assistant every Sunday afternoon, giving lessons to young league players, including Géraldine Caes, whom I coached at the time (1981). She became French champion on the Roland Garros courts, in an individual draw of 64. At the time, the FFT was headed by Jean Paul Loth and its president Philippe Chatrier.

in his estate in the north of the Seine et Marne, at "Tijeaux", (Brie cheese country) manor-style in the middle of a park planted with trees over a hundred years old (it seems to me that he lived there with his wife). He had a covered clay court with, if memory serves, a small covered area, an observation room attached to the court. He was a small man, with the title of 'master teacher', so 3rd degree, and I worked during the week with Sever Dron (himself a BE2 teacher). Sever told me to make the most of the opportunity to be Estrabeau's assistant. France, I also worked with Jacques Malosse and another 'MP' in Essonne whose name I can't remember - in fact it was Pol Guillemin (1919-1997).
the chance to work with 3 'masters'... aware of the prestigious nature of these titles.
that this qualification was given to them on an honorary basis (there must have been only 5 of them in France, perhaps) for the fact that they had been at the forefront of tennis teaching in France, they were people of great experience... their words were marked by those who had lived through the evolution of racket grips and the rackets themselves and other equipment. Alfred gave his 'lessons' in white trousers, he was in his late sixties, (I even remember someone older, maybe 70) he needed a sparring partner during the sessions with his best pupils (which is what I did). Taking a lesson was a privilege and the pupil was aware of it, the words were poised and fair. Sometimes the demonstrations were astonishing because their efficiency in balance or precision was worthy of a martial arts master. Looking back, I admit that I understood the art of tennis and was influenced by it to the same extent as Brechbuhl

(the Swiss master). There was a certain academicism in his teaching of technique, but he was also very open-minded. Estrabeau had a whole arsenal of self-made gadgets to convey technical messages. Tools that made it easier to discover new sensations. To this day, another teacher, Philippe Boyadjian (Luxembourg), also demonstrates the same originality and creativity in his teaching tools. Estrabeau was captivating in his sessions I was perhaps even too young to appreciate the substance. No matter, as a young coach, I have moulded myself in this atmosphere of excellence. Estrabeau was like other great composers whose music accompanies a career. I don't know whether he was taken seriously or not by the younger generations, but the next generation I could identify as a 'money' generation like Pierre Barthès or the other great centres that sprang up in the 1980s. Estrabeau, on the other hand, favoured the individual lesson with a capital 'L'.

He needed a sparring partner because observation was the basis of his method.

had a solid base of knowledge in biomechanics and that his interventions were highly personalised: he manipulated the joints, placed holds, the pelvis, applied pressure, played with balance, corrected a head carriage, an osteopath of the sporting gesture...

The lesson wasn't predominantly physical, but I do remember some subtle physical engagement on the part of the students. So there you have it Nicolas ... my remaining memories ... after an introspection of my memory! It was yesterday and it was 40 years ago... it only has the value of my memories as a young coach ....

And I would add ... Estrabeau conveyed a man of small stature and natural elegance, an aristocrat of sport and teaching... He practised off the beaten track, and when he retired to his home I didn't feel that he was being sidelined, but rather that his passion for teaching tennis was indivisible.

Far ahead of his time, he was a pioneer whose teaching focused above all on the technical fundamentals (the basis of the champion's movements), which he specified as follows for right-handed players:

- ➔ Anticipation (glance to be ahead of the ball)
- ➔ Catch the ball early to be able to play fast
- ➔ Strike the ball in front of the body, using the left leg to support the forehand.
- ➔ Balance (he points out that any movement tends to destroy the balance of its author)
- ➔ Control and precision (with the hand, sense of touch)

For Alfred Estrabeau, more than a role model, a master tennis teacher is above all a guide, an adviser who must ensure that each individual's style and natural disposition are respected, and this is where he would later make his mark!

For him, it is very important to define each player's style beforehand, as the work and training should enable the development of personal qualities.

In his book *Apprendre le tennis,* published in 1952 and co-written with his colleague Jacques Feuillet (1898-1988), also a master teacher and head of training at the FFLT, Mr Estrabeau defined three essential qualities to be developed in order to become a good tennis player:

➜   Moral (later called mental)
➜   Physics
➜   Execution (i.e. technique)

Alfred Estrabeau goes further, saying that *"wanting to play in a way for which you were not made is the worst mistake of all: even with practice a little cat will never become a tiger!*

And he takes the example of the Musketeers, explaining first of all that René Lacoste defeated the strongest with his moral qualities rather than his physical ones.

These are the words of the famous American player Bill Tilden (1893-1953) in 1927:

"The implacable regularity with which this boy with the impassive face responds to all my attacks has a disastrous influence on my nervous system. I'm filled with a wild desire to throw my racket at his face. There's something merciless about such an opponent. His nickname, 'The Alligator', suits him perfectly... Every time, I know I'm in for a physically and morally exhausting fight.

Henri Cochet, for his part, had an extraordinary eye for detail that enabled him to be ahead of the ball and therefore to hit it much earlier than any other champion at the time.

This could perhaps be explained by the fact that he was introduced to tennis at a very early age, unlike his compatriots Borotra and Lacoste?

Henri Cochet's father was the groundskeeper at the Tennis Club de Lyon, so he was lucky enough to be able to watch the players from an early age and knew everything there was to know about the game of tennis from the age of seven!

Tilden, once again, said of him: *"He plays tennis that I don't know"*.

Later, in his autobiographical book *My Story* published in 1948, the American champion spoke of Henri Cochet in the following terms:

"Cochet, the genius of French tennis, revolutionised the game for us, rejecting the old theories and inventing a new style. His ball attack at the top of the bounce and the perfect coordination of his movements enabled him to achieve maximum efficiency with minimum effort. I don't know any other player with such a sense of anticipation and of exactly where to place a tennis ball. And his ease is such that it gives the impression of laziness, but I know from experience that no player is more of a fighter, more determined to win, although always with exemplary correctness and loyalty."

Finally, Jean Borotra made the most of his exceptional natural physical qualities to develop a highly offensive game, which has led to him being described as the first server-volley player in the history of the game.

The physical dimension of his game outweighed his lack of technical mastery. Henri Cochet, his Davis Cup partner, said of him in 1980:

"His volleys were the most sparkling, served up by extraordinary physical strength. Every shot he played had just one aim: to win the point as quickly as possible with a decisive blow at the net. No other player put so much physical effort into catching balls that seemed out of reach, showing that what seems impossible is sometimes achievable.

And in his many post-war "propaganda tours" on behalf of the federation, Henri Cochet would say of his colleague Borotra's setback:

"He was the last great champion to fully extend his thumb behind the handle of his racket to hit his backhands. But it should be noted that he applied this principle to a very specific technique. While theory demanded that the head of the racket be raised at least to the level of the hand during the stroke, Borotra, without worrying about this obligation and because he felt perfectly at ease that way, hit his backhand balls by holding his racket with the head lower than the hand and the handle higher with his thumb firmly arched behind it... Notwithstanding these fantasies, Borotra's backhand was sensational. He was so sure of it that he made it his favourite attacking stroke to prepare, when he could, for his climbs to the net. But it was an exclusively personal stroke that no one tried in vain to imitate. A few daring players tried it. It didn't work.

In fact, it was after the First World War, when he served in the French army of occupation in Germany, that he was given this advice by the teacher at the Wiesbaden club.

The latter advised him not to change the basis of his movements, even though they were unorthodox because the young Borotra had never taken a lesson!

But our Musketeers were above all inspired by Suzanne Lenglen (1899-1938), who taught the theory of angles to the young Henri Cochet and inspired his friends with her fierce determination never to give up on the court.

The creation of the federation: to spread the practice more widely

Our federation was founded in 1920 under the name FFLT (Fédération Française de Lawn Tennis).
Tennis was played mainly on grass at the beginning of the 20th century.
The word "lawn" was used until 1976, when the name was changed to FFT (Federation Francaise de Tennis).

When it was founded in 1920, our federation set itself the following main objectives:

1. Register and affiliate all clubs and courts

2. List teachers working in France in affiliated clubs

3. Rank competitors from affiliated clubs according to the federal ranking

4. Attempting to develop the practice throughout the country

5. Ensuring respect for amateurism

In one of the earliest FFLT directories in my possession, dating from 1928, we learn that from 1925 the young federation kept a register of French and foreign teachers working in France in affiliated clubs.

In 1928, it had just four hundred and ninety-five affiliated clubs (also known as associations and/ or societies). These clubs are, of course, spread throughout mainland France, but they are not the only ones.

The federation has 53 affiliated clubs in the French protectorates abroad:

→ Algeria: 20 clubs in the regions of Algiers (7), Constantine (9) and Oran (4)
→ Madagascar: 1 club
→ Morocco: 16 clubs
→ Tonkin (part of present-day Vietnam): 7 clubs
→ Tunisia: 9 clubs

The same directory provides valuable information on the ranking of French players in 1927: there were 1,348 ranked players and 547 female players. And at the time, the federal ranking only had three series and a much smaller number of levels (14) than today (24):

→ 1st series: 21 male and 17 female players (the best French players)
→ 2nd series: 7 steps from 0 to 15
→ 3rd series: 6 steps from 15/1 to 30

Sociologist Stéphane Mery explains in an article published in issue 52 of the _Lettre fédérale des enseignants professionnels_ in April 2008:

"In 1909, tennis was much less widespread than in the 1920s. There were few competitors and few opportunities to play (5,360 members of sports clubs in 1912 and 17,000 members of the federation in 1924)... This was not necessarily due to the fact that the sport had become more popular.

In 1900, tennis was a leisure activity reserved for adults, some of whom played competitively. The game was a pretext for a "salon discussion" between people from "good families".

At a time when tennis is being 'federalised', its image is somewhat at odds with the aspirations of everyone: some see it as a sport for the rich, while others see it as a mindless distraction! During this period, there was a noticeable divergence of interest between the clubs - which catered for a high standard of play with great social potential - and the young federation, which tended to promote more sporting, less elitist and more democratic objectives (cf. Aurélien Zieleskiewicz, _La transmission du tennis en France : sociographie d'une relation de service_).

In fact, for a very long time, at least until the early 1960s, the federation struggled to get its message across to clubs, most of which were still privately owned. And these clubs were unwilling to allow the fledgling federation tointerfere in their internal affairs...

These structures are very closed, modelled on the British country club model, and they want to organise the sport as they see fit, sometimes applying their own rules to tournaments they organise themselves, which is not without its problems for the federation, whose aim is to bring all the clubs together...

At that time, the clubs decided on their own policy without the federation having any say (cf. Anne-Marie Waser, _La genèse d'une politique sportive : l'exemple du tennis_). So from the outset, there was a clash between recreational tennis and performance tennis, and both the federation and the clubs had to juggle constantly between the two - it wasn't easy to find the right balance, even today!

Quite naturally, the FFLT chose to rely on its champions, who improvised themselves as teachers through general publications. Most of them were self-taught, but that didn't matter! And two of these champions would go on to produce educational documents that the federation would use over several decades to try and spread the sport, particularly among the younger generation.

They were Suzanne Lenglen and Henri Cochet, who set up their own teaching methods, initially in the Paris region - in keeping with the Jacobin tradition - and then slowly in the provinces with the proliferation of Suzanne Lenglen schools and Cochet courses.

SECOND PART

THE ROLE PLAYED BY SUZANNE LENGLEN AND THE MUSKETEERS

"The champion is an accident of nature whose exceptional qualities enable
him to perform certain tasks better than any of his adversaries.
Suzanne Lenglen, 1937, <u>Introduction to tennis, essential principles and physical preparation</u>

Suzanne Lenglen's teaching legacy

French tennis obviously owes a great deal to the woman who was nicknamed the Divine on the courts, the famous Suzanne Lenglen, whose court A at Roland Garros, inaugurated in 1994, was named after her in 1997.

Suzanne was the first major world star in sport, and in tennis in particular: the first non-Anglo-Saxon player to win the Wimbledon tournament (1919), it is probably thanks to her that the word champion was given a feminine form.

The Centre Court was built and inaugurated in 1922, over a hundred years ago, so that more British people could enjoy it at Wimbledon!

In fact, contrary to popular belief, women were almost never denied the opportunity to take part in sports in the 1920s, as Pierre-Marie Bartoli recalls in her thesis, defended in 2020 and entitled _Les dieux du kiosque_ :

"The _only thing is that it doesn't go against the dress that their femininity imposes on them. Tennis, a sport in which the best players are compared to dancers, is obviously part of this. As is figure skating, whose icon is also a woman in the person of the Norwegian Sonja Henie, triple Olympic champion (1928, 1932 and 1936) and who later became a film star_".

Suzanne is considered to be the first player in the history of tennis (men's and women's) to turn professional after signing a $50,000 contract on 2 August 1926 with an American promoter and sports agent named Charles C. Pyle (1882-1939).

The signing of this contract with the man who, at the time,was nicknamed 'cash and carry' led to her being banned not only from Wimbledon's All England Club, but also from the FFLT... Indeed, the president at the time, Albert Canet (1878-1930), who was very attached to the principles of Baron Pierre de Coubertin (1863-1937), reaffirmed on this occasion the FFLT's vocation to be "_essentially a federation of amateurs_".

And he took a very dim view of the development of sports exhibitions across the Atlantic from 1920 onwards.

He did not fear the loss of Lenglen, because those who would later become the Musketeers were already at the forefront of the major tournaments and so the Divine's successor seemed assured!

But the debates about amateurism at the time, particularly in France, were very lively, and our federation stuck to its position for a very long time: the best players should remain amateurs. All this is very well recounted by my colleague Chris Davies, in the first part of his book _Balles neuves,_ published in April 2019 and which I can only recommend reading.

Long before 1926, Suzanne Lenglen was accused of undermining amateur status through her links with the Patou fashion house.

The collaboration between the fashion designer and the champion is in some ways akin to a relationship with a sponsor. The fashion world took an interest in tennis and very early on saw it as a potential advertising medium.

But the federation was tolerant of Suzanne, who was helping to popularise our sport in France. Tennis was beginning to recruit a following among the working classes, and that suited the young federation just fine!

Lenglen officially announced his decision to make a profit from his fame in 1926 by saying:

"Since tennis is a lifetime's work, if we have to spend our lives learning to play for nothing, why isn't there a gallery of amateurs watching for nothing?

With this statement, she raises a problem in an environment where, for several decades, the defenders of amateurism (traditionalists) and those who would like to allow everyone to benefit from the democratisation of tennis, which is becoming a spectator sport, will be at loggerheads.

A certain Jean Schopfer (1868-1931), a former tennis player and the first French winner of the French International Tennis Championship in 1892 (an event played on grass and at the Racing Club de France), and a novelist known under the pseudonym Claude Anet, defended Lenglen in the biography of the champion that he published in 1927, presenting professional tennis as the future.

We'll see later that positions will eventually evolve somewhat to adapt to different situations.

But it was above all thanks to Suzanne Lenglen that the Musketeers became unstoppable, with French tennis becoming the number one in the world between the wars.

More generally, the sporting France of the Roaring Twenties (1920-1936) was presented as invincible, a period when French sportsmen and women excelled in all the leading disciplines of the era: Our jockeys swept all the races at the Longchamps racecourse, the racing driver Robert Benoist (1895-1944) was unstoppable at Montlhéry and on every racetrack in Europe, and our cyclists, led by a certain André Leducq (1904-1980), were the bosses in the Tour de France.

And then, it's not a good idea to cross swords in the ring with our boxer Georges Carpentier (1894-1975), the first French professional boxer to become world champion in English boxing by defeating the American Battling Levinsky at his home in the United States in front of 20,000 people (1920)!

As for our tennis players, they shone on every continent and in every major tournament, whether in singles or doubles, on clay or natural grass: Brugnon, Borotra, Cochet and Lacoste won no fewer than six Davis Cups and almost eighteen Grand Slam tournaments in singles and twenty-three in doubles between 1924 and 1932!

Lenglen is said to have groomed the future Musketeers at least as much for her contempt for American champion Bill Tilden as for her fierce desire to see her comrades bring the Davis Cup home.

Lenglen had not forgotten the affront she suffered one summer day in 1920, when she bumped into Bill Tilden on one of the pheasantry courts in the Parc de Saint-Cloud.

Nearly half a century before the battle of the sexes between the American Billie-Jean King and her compatriot Bobby Riggs in Houston, this confrontation turned into a humiliation for Suzanne, as reported in Fabrice Abgrall and François Thomazeau's excellent book *La Saga des Mousquetaires,* published in 2008:

"Bill Tilden, who describes Lenglen as a mixture of peripatetic and prima donna takes this game very seriously, all too happy to put the woman who tarnishes her aura in her place. There's no chivalry with Big Bill. He hits with incredible violence, alternating between drop shots and deep balls. Tilden played with such energy and aggression that he inflicted a severe and degrading 6-0 defeat on his opponent.

Suzanne Lenglen returned to the dressing room in tears. Overwhelmed and offended, the Divine was brought back to her human condition. In the dressing room, she swore to herself that she would avenge the affront.

And if she, the Divine, can't beat this woman-hating superman, she'll leave it to others. And these others are the ones who will later take on the nickname of the Musketeers..."

But even more than that, we can consider and affirm that Suzanne Lenglen was a forerunner in the teaching of tennis and all that revolves around it, for the following reasons, which we will develop:

1. She herself was coached by her father, Charles Lenglen, who can be considered the first "daddy coach" (there were many more to follow...).

2. It opened its own tennis school in 1936 (by popularising group lessons), a school that would be officially recognised as a federal training centre by the federation, taking the name Ecole Française de Tennis (fifty years before the creation of the Centre National d'Entraînement-CNE).

3. In 1937, in collaboration with a British professional dancer, she wrote an introductory book on tennis, in which she described her method of introducing the player to technique, physical preparation and the mind (the last two concepts being new at the time).

It inspired the French Tennis Federation, which in collaboration with René Lacoste and Jean Tissier, among others, developed the first teaching method for tennis in 1942: _the Lenglen method_, which can be considered the first federal teaching document.

This document served as the basis for the development of the Centres Scolaires d'Initiation au Tennis (CSIT) throughout France, the first tennis schools for young people, also known as Suzanne-Lenglen centres or schools.

Born with asthma, Suzanne's health was very fragile (she died of leukaemia in 1938, before her 40th birthday).

Her father Charles introduced her to sport at a very young age, convinced, quite rightly, that it would enable his daughter to combat her health problems effectively.

After practising a number of sports from an early age, including running, cycling, swimming and dancing (disciplines that help develop coordination, endurance, speed and balance), Suzanne took her first steps on a tennis court at the age of 10.

Her parents have a country house on the Côte d'Azur, with a terrace overlooking the tennis courts at Nice's Parc Impérial!

It should be noted that the information on Suzanne's first steps in tennis is more laudatory and precise in Anglo-American historiography than in French archives.

Indeed, even before she turned professional, relations between the Lenglens and the federation were already conflictual: a bourgeois family involved in the development of tennis on the Côte d'Azur - Charles Lenglen ran the Nice LTC - the Lenglens opposed the federation's Parisian centralisation (a conflict that continues to this day with the families of budding champions).

So you have to look in the _New World Encyclopedia_ (American encyclopaedia) to find very precise information.

This is hardly surprising, given that Lenglen spent two full years touring the United States when she turned professional in 1926.

In the _New World Encyclopedia,_ we learn that Charles Lenglen decided to introduce his daughter to tennis in order to develop her athletic talents and strengthen her frail body.

He immediately saw tennis as a sport, a very complete game for Suzanne.

At that time, in 1909, tennis teachers were in very short supply, so Charles improvised himself as a coach for his daughter: first he observed the ladies playing and realised that their game was too slow and too patient for his daughter's overflowing character.

So he took inspiration from the men's game (which is more aggressive) to build a real training programme for his daughter:

1. Rehearsals at the wall and then at the basket for consistency: he doesn't hesitate to place targets (hats, handkerchiefs and pouches) in different places on the pitch.

2. Physical preparation to develop footwork: skipping, sprinting, running, etc.

3. Exchanges with men to get more rhythm

Very quickly, the young Suzanne developed a very attacking game of serves, volleys and smashes that were very hard-hitting and destabilising for all her opponents.

Above all, she follows a very methodical training programme, working on her footwork (skippingrope), vision and striking.

This intensive preparation, rare in those days, soon gave her a clear advantage over the other players!

Her parents set up a system of psychological intimidation very early on, to "influence the tenacity" of their daughter, they say: praise and monetary rewards after each good training session ("extrinsic motivation"), but also bullying and insults when Suzanne's investment is not deemed sufficient...

It's a questionable method of intimidation, even if it has always been used, hasn't it, Mr Dokic, Mr Pierce and Mr Tomic, to name but a few?

But this method would develop in Suzanne a fierce hatred of defeat and give her two qualities that are essential in tennis: fighting spirit and tenacity!

So it was only natural that, having become an icon, first in England, then in the United States and finally everywhere else, Suzanne returned to Paris to work with the French federation from the spring of 1933, giving demonstrations and lessons in the newly-built Roland Garros stadium.

Although Lenglen was banned after his stint with the professionals, the federation was aware of his reputation, not only internationally, but also in France, and used this reputation as propaganda, in other words to try and convert young people to tennis.

A book by English biographer Peter Kettle, published in June 2020 and entitled _The Suzanne Lenglen phenomenon: myths & reality_, even tells us that Suzanne Lenglen was initially the director of a French Federation tennis school located in the Roland Garros stadium before becoming a teacher and opening her own school at Tennis Mirabeau in February 1936, with the financial support of the Federation and her lover at the time, a certain Jean Tillier. Lenglen's speech at the inauguration of her school in the presence of sports personalities (including boxer Georges

Carpentier and Jean Borotra) and politicians was broadcast on British television, with the champion saying the following in the language of Shakespeare:

"Group lessons are better than individual lessons, especially for children".

This statement obviously met with a particularly favourable response from the young lawn tennis federation, and this first "Suzanne Lenglen" school will be branded FFLT. In a win-win agreement, the federation would rely on Lenglen to open the Ecole Française de Tennis in the second arrondissement of Paris, a training school for tennis teachers, with Lenglen as technical director.

The Suzanne Lenglen school welcomed only children and young teenagers in its first year, before opening its doors to adults in 1937.

In an interview published in the newspaper *Le Figaro* on 20 August 1936 and entitled "*L'enfant ses sports: le tennis*", Lenglen said:

"Tennis is extremely important in a child's physical education, because it develops the most essential of athletic qualities: the coordination of movements of the whole body [...] contrary to what the vast majority of people believe, tennis is played very little with the arm [...] as at no time does it require brute force, it is a sport that is particularly suitable for children, for whom purely forceful exercises can have regrettable consequences [...] I have found that children who play tennis do not use their arms [...]....] As at no time does it require brute force, it is a sport particularly suited to children, for whom exercises of pure strength can have regrettable consequences [...] I have found that most pupils find it easier to correct their faults by seeing the teacher rectify the mistakes of their classmates. It is only through comparison and instinctive imitation that children are able to correct their faults. That's why I insist on group lessons. All the more so as it creates an extremely healthy sense of competition between pupils.

Lenglen's words in 1936 were very avant-garde and are still valid today. And above all, what a marvellous platform to serve the interests of the federation in its desire to develop the sport among the younger generations.

It was also Lenglen who is said to have inaugurated the first Centre Scolaire d'Initiation au Tennis in May 1938 (shortly before his death) at the Stade Pierre de Coubertin, Porte de Saint Cloud, in Paris, but this claim is not confirmed by the sources.

Suzanne recorded her vision of tennis and how she went about teaching it in a document that she co-wrote and published in 1937 with her English friend, Margaret Morris (1891-1980), a professional dancer.

This document, which covers all the subjects she herself had set out in a first work written in English and published in New York in 1920 under the title _Lawn Tennis for girls, covered techniques and advices on tactics for beginner players,_ can certainly be considered to be the 1ˢᵗ teaching document never to have been published in France.

Entitled _Introduction to Tennis. Principes essentiels,_ consists of two parts:

The first deals with technique and the importance of choosing the right equipment, and is written by Suzanne herself!

The second part was written by Margaret Morris, a member of the British National Council for Physical Education, and aims to _"put the tennis player in a physical condition to execute the various movements that will be imposed on him by the practice of the game"._

As you may have guessed, this development deals with physical preparation as well as breathing (mental) and seems very avant-garde, especially as the author draws his inspiration from dance and music!

It should be noted that this book was prefaced by Jean Borotra and René Lacoste, two of the greatest French champions of the time, and they were full of praise when presenting their compatriot:

"Suzanne was the first of us... almost as a child, she managed to conquer Wimbledon, a veritable citadel of Anglo-Saxon sporting superiority...

For the general public, all these victories and successes were simply the expression of extraordinary athletic superiority...

Those of us who knew her well knew that Suzanne was much more than a simple phenomenon of muscular coordination and balance.

We all knew what ardour, will and enthusiasm his magnificent personality contained".

It is interesting to note that Jean Borotra and René Lacoste put more emphasis on Suzanne's physical and mental qualities in their presentation, but made no mention of her technical mastery.

Jean Borotra himself based his game on physical strength and athleticism, while René Lacoste's patience and psychological qualities made more than one opponent cringe... And the two men were more keen to highlight the champion's perseverance than her natural qualities.

What is most striking about the first part of this book is Suzanne's belief that "the game is the highest and most complete expression of sport".

It identifies two essential characteristics of tennis before going on to describe the technique of the main shots:

1. Its role in the physical and intellectual training of young people

2. A means of distraction and a source of health for practitioners

These two characteristics mentioned by Suzanne in 1937 are still relevant at the time of writing, so I think it's very important to continue to emphasise them in our tennis schools: tennis is first and foremost a game and should remain so.

Play against yourself and play against your opponent or with your partner!

Before giving a technical description of the main strokes, a description that would be invaluable to future instructors of the Brevet d'Etat, particularly in the context of the demonstration test, which would be the flagship event in the 1970s, Suzanne Lenglen first outlined four fundamental principles:

"First of all, it is essential that the player never loses sight of a certain number of points which are common to all strokes and which are absolutely essential to their correct execution. There may be different styles, depending on the shape of the skeleton or the muscular qualities of each individual.

But the following four points are absolutely universal and enter into the composition of all shots. Neglecting them will inevitably lead to inferior execution; they really are the essentials of tennis".

1. "Watch the ball" (attitude of attention/concentration/reaction/anticipation)

2. "Bend your knees" (lower centre of gravity)

3. "Bodyweight forward" (advanced strike plan / accompaniment / transfer)

4. "Profile position (remote control)

<u>*Watch the ball.*</u>

"Nothing is more difficult for beginners than to position themselves correctly in relation to the ball, neither too far nor too close. To achieve this, it is essential to judge not only the direction of the ball but also its speed as soon as it leaves the opponent's racket. Only when the trajectory of the ball and its landing point have been accurately calculated can the player get to the right spot to hit it in the right conditions. It is infinitely difficult for anyone to judge the speed of an object coming directly at them.

This is the case for the player; he can only achieve this appreciation of the speed of the ball if he doesn't lose sight of it, even for a fraction of a second, during its entire course. Strange as it may seem, this absolute concentration of the gaze on a moving object is infinitely difficult to achieve.

31

Very often, the player thinks he is looking at his ball because he sees it as part of the whole spectacle placed before his eyes, and he is quite astonished when it comes close to him to realise that he has made an enormous error of judgement about its real position. He had either not been looking at the ball, which he could see very well, to the exclusion of everything else, or his attention had been diverted from it for a brief moment, and however brief it was, that moment had been enough to distort his judgement.

Even among the greatest players, this concentration on the ball is sometimes difficult to achieve. For beginners and average players, it requires a constant effort; it cannot be repeated often enough that you have to look at the ball, not only when it is coming towards you, but also when it has just left your racket, and while your opponent is hitting it; it is by never losing sight of it, by identifying yourself with it so to speak, and only in this way, that you will manage to be close to it when the moment comes to hit it".

The focus here is on one of the greatest challenges in tennis, whatever the era: the ability to control the trajectory of the ball, to read its path so as to anticipate the rebound and position yourself as well as possible before the shot.

So not only do you have to look at the ball, you also have to remember to act: move, position yourself, hit and replace yourself.

Bend your knees.

"At first sight this may seem of secondary importance. In reality, knee flexibility is almost as important as concentration on the ball. As we have seen, tennis is a game of quick starts in different directions and sudden stops followed by new starts. Only perfectly elastic knees can cope with this need.

What's more, perfect balance is absolutely essential when executing your shots. This balance cannot be achieved with stiff legs. Perfect knee flexibility is as essential for tennis as it is for skiing."

Suzanne Lenglen emphasises the role of the lower body as a motor. Tennis is a sport of reaction and action, and the player must take care to lower his centre of gravity slightly so that he can act as quickly as possible and, above all, as precisely as possible.

The parallel with skiing is interesting, but also surprising because it was not widely practised in France at the time and was much less popular than boxing, which I think could have been highlighted here?

Body weight forward.

"I cannot stress enough the extremely important role played by the distribution of body weight. This essential point is unfortunately lost sight of, not only by most players, but also by many professionals.

However, it is obvious that to give the ball maximum speed and power, the body's weight must be used to the maximum. This weight must therefore be directed forward. In the same way that a boxer cannot hit with power when moving away from his opponent, a tennis player cannot give speed or weight to his ball if he hits it when the weight of his body is exactly vertical or behind the vertical.

It is therefore essential that the ball is struck at a moment when the weight of the body is moving forward. This does not mean that the ball should be struck while the player is walking forward. On the contrary, the conditions of perfect balance necessary for the execution of shots are more completely achieved when the player's feet are immobile.

But it is possible to be immobile with the weight of the body forward, vertical or backwards. And the critical moment of the stroke, i.e. the moment when the racket hits the ball, must take place when the body's weight is really moving forward.

This comment highlights four essential elements of the strike: rhythm, the strike plane, the transfer of body weight forward (support) and balance.

Profile position in relation to the net.

No tennis shot should face the net. During the preparation of all shots, the player must position himself clearly in profile. The need for this position, unfortunately neglected by most players, is easily understood for the following reasons.

As we shall see later, the drive, backhand and serve movements cause the torso to rotate about half a circle around the hips; if this rotation is started facing the net, it will naturally end parallel to it, and the ball will be thrown in the direction of the width of the court rather than the length.

Finally, and this applies not only to the drive and serve, but also to the volley, it is infinitely easier to carry the weight of the body in a given direction by placing the body in profile to that direction rather than facing it.

All you have to do is try to push a heavy object such as a car or a piece of furniture; instinctively, the body will move in the direction it is facing so that it can use its weight to the maximum.

The profile position is therefore also the essential corollary of the "weight forward" rule.

". These four essential points are to be found in the detailed structure of every move in the game. That's why it's essential never to lose sight of them and to try to follow them in all circumstances.

As you will have gathered, this last statement refers to support, and for Suzanne in this area, open support (facing the net) is out of the question!

The practitioner, the player, must always look for support in line, i.e. he must always be in profile to be able to play the ball in the best conditions.

In fact, this was to remain the case with the spread of the French teaching method in the seventies and eighties, before finally being overturned in the early nineties!

We shall see that the principles set out by Suzanne Lenglen in her book were also to be found in the works of the eminent master teachers Alfred Estrabeau and Jacques Feuillet in particular.

After listing the fundamental principles, Suzanne goes on to describe the main moves in detail:

Forehand, backhand, follow through, forehand volley, backhand volley, serve, smash and footwork!

In her description of each of the shots, she first warns the reader about the "common mistakes to avoid".

In her first book for young girls, written in 1920 and published only in English, she had already warned against the temptation to use a single grip for the forehand and backhand:

"Even *though the great British champion of the early 20ᵗʰ century, Reggie Frank Doherty (1872-1910), used the same grip to hit his forehands and backhands, I think we should abandon this idea.*

Very few players can play with a single grip and the fact that most players, especially young girls, who have a very weak backhand owe it to the fact that they don't change grips."

And he goes on to say, in a sentence that refers very precisely to both the eastern forehandand backhand grip:

"The common mistake that is often the cause of a weak backhand is having the wrist in front of the racket and pulling it (eastern forehand grip, piston backhand) *instead of behind it to propel it* (eastern backhand grip)".

At the time, changing grips was very difficult because racquet handles were very large and did not make it easy to move the hand and fingers. To make it easier to change grips between forehand and backhand, Lenglen suggested supporting the racket at its heart with the free hand (left for a right-hander and the opposite for a left-hander) when in the waiting position:

"Beginners are often troubled as to how they shall change the grip from forehand to backhand, and vice versa.

If you rest the neck of the racket in your left hand you will find the change very easy".

Among the common mistakes to avoid for what she calls the "drive", i.e. shots from the baseline, apart from not changing your grip between the forehand and the backhand, she lists the following:

1. Body weight not carried sufficiently forward: *"under no circumstances should the torso lean backwards".*

2. Too close to the net: *"If the balls of the feet face the net, it is practically impossible to turn the body sufficiently".*

3. Faulty wrist action: *"The wrist action, of which some mediocre players are so proud, is in reality a lamentable habit whose only result is toadd another element of difficulty to the precision of the shot.*

At his school, pupils spend long hours practising their movements before they can finally kick a ball!

This is confirmed by the words of Borotra and Lacoste in the preface:

"By setting up her school, Suzanne wanted to make tennis, the "real" tennis, accessible to as many people as possible. Through this little book, in which she has brought together the essential principles of our beautiful sport, she has made tennis accessible to everyone.

The ideas it expresses on the need for an intimate link between the concepts of physical culture and sport could serve as the basis for an entire system of physical education. The French Tennis Federation immediately saw the value of this effort and gave it its support... This work of sports propaganda, of which this little book is an expression of daily and practical utility, gives him a new title for our recognition".

From then on, Suzanne Lenglen was to earn her living not by playing but by teaching, in the interests of the federation, which quickly understood its interest in rehabilitating her image after having banned her from the organisation between 1926 and 1928.

A popular figure, she also appeared in adverts extolling the virtues of an exercise bike and the comfort of unisex shorts, products that she didn't hesitate to recommend to her students!

Many future champions got their start at the Suzanne Lenglen schools, which subsequently proliferated, including a certain Patrice Beust (a member of the French Davis Cup team from 1963 to 1969 and a doubles specialist), who began playing tennis in 1955 at the age of 11, as he told me in an interview in April 2020:

"The lessons, which were given at the "petit Coubertin", near Porte de Saint-Cloud, took place on Thursdays (the school holiday at the time) and were played on one half of the court for 15 minutes. One Thursday in four was reserved for service, with eight players on each side. I'd like to take this opportunity to point out that, having never played before, I got my first taste of the game at that school,

35

and of the volley in particular, as it was the first shot I learnt, and it has steered my entire career towards the volley. Later, after reading a lot of books on tennis, I concluded that it was more effective to teach tennis by starting with the simplest things. It's then easier to add more preparations for shots from the back of the court, than doing away with preparations when you come to the net."

Patrice's comment confirms that a beginner's first concern is to tame the ball's bounce and master how to read its trajectory.

The challenge was made all the more difficult at the time by the fact that surfaces, particularly covered surfaces, were extremely fast (parquet), that balls were as hard as stone (felt was much finer) and that wooden rackets, which were very heavy (around 400 grams) and had a very, very small sieve (around 420 cm2), were the same for everyone (it was not until the 1960s that the first 'junior' rackets arrived on the market), leaving no room for approximation...

Sending the damn ball back before it bounces and escapes us is still the best response: "take the ball by the scruff of the neck" as the old-timers used to say!

Obviously, when the champion died and following pressure from the parents of the pupils at the eponymous school, the federation decided to support the reopening of the Lenglen School, as reported in the sports section of the *Echo de Paris* newspaper on 9 October 1938:

"At the request of the parents of the pupils of the Suzanne Lenglen School, the staff of our great champion have decided to continue her work and reopen the school as usual. The school will operate under exactly the same conditions (lessons entirely free of charge, balls and racket provided by the federation) and Suzanne Lenglen's staff, to whom she instilled all the elements of her remarkable method, will continue to apply all its principles.

The French Tennis Federation, appreciating the considerable importance of this work for the development of French tennis, has decided to lend its support to the continuation of the Suzanne Lenglen School by appointing a technical committee [...] The admirable work of sports education conceived and carried out by Suzanne Lenglen will thus become permanent".

The federation also quickly decided to capitalise on the champion's popularity to set up the first real federal teaching method, with the aim of spreading tennis throughout the country. And it was a certain René Lacoste, then president of the federation, who wrote this collection with the help of Jean Tillier (who was Lenglen's lover for a time), Henri Darsonval (1891-1972), Henri Cochet (1901-1987) and Bernard Destremau (1917-2002).

This group of five experts created the first teaching method to be disseminated by the federation when it was published in 1942: *La Méthode Suzanne Lenglen*.

For thirty years, this method would remain the benchmark for introductory tennis, even though more pragmatic approaches would emerge in the meantime, but more on that later. Henri Cochet also played an important role from 1933, when he decided to embark on a career as a professional player and trainer/expert.

This is how the Lenglen and Cochet schools came to exist side by side in the major Parisian clubs after the war.

Henri Cochet "talks to young people

Like Mademoiselle Lenglen, Henri Cochet left his mark on the history of tennis education in France, but in a slightly different way.

While Lenglen concentrated his efforts more on mass initiation, with young people in general and girls in particular, Cochet was more interested in perfecting and training promising young pupils.

He wrote two books in the 1930s and, above all, spent several decades backstage at Roland Garros, watching the players train, offering advice and trying to give them the benefit of his experience as a former world number one.

Later, after three world tours on behalf of the federation and to promote tennis, during which he was able to see all the national champions, he would be a great help not only to young players but also to trainers.

Unlike Lenglen, he published his first book in French in 1932 (*Tennis, sa technique et sa psychologie*), which was translated into English the following year under the title *The Art of tennis: more useful to the novice than a season's play*.

This book is very interesting because from the very first pages, Cochet warns:

"It is important for everyone to choose, either instinctively or intelligently, the method of play and the kind of style that suits them best... The way you will play exists within you, in power, before you touch a racket for the first time. There is a 'natural' way for you to play, only one.

I think that's an essential point, and it's still relevant as I write these lines, but it's not always easy for practitioners to find their own way, their own styles.

Also, even teachers and coaches always tend to reflect and advise on the basis of their own experience, their personal experience, without taking into account the specific characteristics of the people they are working with.

And Cochet added:

"In sports, style refers to a personal way of performing certain sporting gestures. And in the case of the tennis player, it's a physiological product... For each player, there is a normal way of playing, and that's what should constitute his style. Anyone who deviates from this to follow the 'classic' average is making a mistake.

So each player will have to find his own style and develop a tactic based on his physical characteristics. And therein lies the subtlety of the game of tennis, a duel sport in which there is no direct contact with the opponent during the match (well, normally... sic).

An article published in *Le Figaro* on 6 December 1938 tells us more about Cochet's vision:

"I'm giving up professional tournaments or exhibitions almost completely to devote myself to teaching: I don't think you can do both things well at the same time. But I'm going to try to apply in my lessons a method other than that which consists first of indicating the regulation positions for executing the various shots and then of tirelessly returning balls to the pupil.

My intention is above all to take into account the personal style of the players and thus give each of them their best performance. I think it's a mistake to advocate one technique over another.uniform [...] The fact that there are fewer champions has two main causes: too much emphasis on uniform technique and an almost absolute lack of fighting spirit".

In the same article, we learn how Henri Cochet became a teacher, as the journalist who interviewed him, a certain Maurice Capelle, explains:

"Cochet left us because at 2pm he had to "undergo" the wrath of the examiners from the Association Française des Professionnelles de Tennis. He was at the Pierre de Coubertin stadium at the appointed time in front of Messrs Gallay, Darsonval and Tissot (the examiners). He played a few balls, gave a few tips to a player and... received his official teacher's and coach's licence, which in this case is the ultimate."

It's unlikely that Cochet has received any training whatsoever to become a professional teacher - his experience as a player and his aura are enough to earn him a place among his peers!

In his second collection, written in collaboration with Eugène Broquedis (the older brother of the champion we mentioned earlier) and published in 1938 under the title *Tennis, Henri parle aux jeunes,* the champion went even further:

"For those of you who have never played tennis before, I'm not saying do what I tell you, I'm just telling you what I do... To play tennis well, the first thing you have to do is not play it at all".

A very strange piece of advice, you might ask?

Not so much, in fact, because he invites neophytes to observe first, to watch the best players play, how they position themselves on the court, what their tactics are, why do they miss, how do they win the point? In fact, Cochet himself, whose father was a groundskeeper at the Lyon tennis club, spent his early years watching all the members strolling around the club's courts, hitting balls as best they could?

The ability to observe that is so dear to federal teaching methods and that will be found in all the assessment criteria for future BE and then DE candidates has its roots in the words of our musketeer to young people before the Second World War!

Finally, he advises that you should first practise controlling the ball against the wall, playing a little every day to get used to reading trajectories and improving your placement.

It is interesting to note that his approach does not deviate too much from Lenglen's, in that he will first list what he calls the fundamentals before turning his attention to the technical description of the various tennis strokes.

For Cochet, racket grip, low knees, stance, support, distance, shot pattern and balance are the elements that every player must focus on first and foremost.

In his description of the different strokes, he distinguishes :

1. **Groundstrokes**: serve, forehand, backhand and return of serve

2. **Playing at the net**: high volley, low volley, half-volley, smash and passing shot

3. **Special shots**: shop, drop shop and lift. Cochet explains: "These three shots are not part of my current repertoire, although I do use them from time to time, but I recognise that they are not particularly suited to my style of play.

4. **Acrobatic shots**: all those that are an adaptation to an embarrassing situation and do not allow the fundamental principles set out above to be respected. He goes on to say: "*After all, you have to get the ball over the net... Doing them well makes it easy to forget the fatigue of a five-set match*".

Finally, Henri Cochet does not forget to mention physical fitness and concentration, without however offering any specific advice on how to develop these two areas:

"*Physical fitness is the most important thing. If you're in good shape, you'll be in excellent spirits and your nerves will be in perfect balance*".

So it was two champions of the inter-war period, Suzanne Lenglen and Henri Cochet, who were the first to take an interest in the sport and pass on their experience to younger players. Suzanne focused more on young beginners and women, while Henri Cochet tried to teach the basics of coaching.

It is very important to emphasise that, although they both set out empirical principles, they avoided proposing rigid teaching methods, preferring to stress that each learner had to adapt his or her approach according to his or her physical and psychological dispositions.

So Cochet, who was short (1.68m), was aware that he could not play the same tennis as his friend Borotra, to whom he gave back twenty centimetres!

The presidency of René Lacoste (1940-1942): a turning point but also a troubled period

Although René Lacoste's term of office was very short, it was crucial, not only for the future financial health of the federation, but also for the development of tennis teaching and practice, which have always been priorities since the federation was founded.

But this mandate was exercised in very special circumstances, as Paris and a large part of the country were occupied by the German army.

It is therefore important to remember that the federation did not really have a free hand in choosing its president, a choice that fell exclusively to the General Sports Commissioner, a Vichy minister and therefore close to Marshal Pétain, who between August 1940 and April 1942 was none other than Jean Borotra.

As "Minister for Sport" in the Vichy government, Jean Borotra took some very radical decisions:

→ It bans professionalism in two sports federations: tennis and wrestling
→ It immediately bans the following four sports: XIII rugby / table tennis / jeu de paume and badminton

So Jean Borotra is showing his commitment to ensuring that tennis remains an amateur sport, while at the same time showing his contempt for other racket sports by banning them altogether!

Perhaps he wanted to use this decision to promote tennis, thinking that it would serve the interests of the federation?

This is very likely because his collaborator at the time, a certain Joseph Pascot (1897-1974), then Director of Sport at the Ministry, was a former rugby union international, and therefore also had ideas to put forward by banning the practice of XIII...

The press of the time, in particular the dailies L'_Echo de Paris_ (1884-1944), _Aujourd'hui_ (1940-1944) and _Paris-Soir_ (1923-1944), all of which were banned after the Liberation on suspicion of collaboration, provide us with information about the tennis propaganda activities that took place during Lacoste's presidency.

An article published on 15 November 1941 in the "Sports" section of the daily _Paris-Soir_ relayed the initiative of _Smash_ magazine, in agreement with the federation, to distribute propaganda films aimed at young people and entitled "Mousquetaires".

Three films were shown for the young players:

1. A slow-motion shot of Suzanne Lenglen, unreleased in France
2. A slow-motion film by René Lacoste
3. A film retracing the 1932 Davis Cup victory

"The commentary will be provided by our juniors' mentor, Antoine Gentien, alias "Coco". reads the article.

In another article dated 26 September 1942 and published in the daily newspaper _Aujourd'hui_, we learn that the federation organised a quality gala at Roland Garros for the benefit of prisoners, with the following programme:

1. A match between Yvon Petra and Bernard Destremau
2. A meeting between the 'semi-old' Boussus and the young Abdesselam
3. A demonstration by René Lacoste himself of the "Suzanne-Lenglen" introductory tennis method

"René Lacoste will play a set against some of the best students trained at the Lenglen school, in aid of prisoners," it reads.

State control over the organisation of sport therefore began under the Vichy government, which set up a General and Sports Education (EGS) programme focused on the development of mass sport and the rejection of professionalism.

This idea was first mooted under the Front Populaire government with the creation of the BSP (Brevet Sportif Populaire) in 1937 by a certain Léo Lagrange (1900-1940), a socialist.
!
He, too, was fiercely opposed to spectator sport (professional sport), and saw sport more as a way of maintaining his health.

Under the Vichy government, a new subject was introduced at school: General and Sports Education (EGS), which was renamed Physical and Sports Education (Éducation Physique et Sportive) in 1945.

Sports (EPS). In addition to gymnastics, which has long been part of the school system, there are team sports, individual sports and sports games!

So we're opening the door to tennis!

But let's get back to our dear Lacoste, because it was under his mandate that the federation took over the concession of the Roland Garros stadium (February 1942).

The stadium was specially built to host the 1928 Davis Cup final, which pitted the Musketeers' France (winners of the event for the very first time the year before in the United States, and therefore directly qualified for the 1928 final under the 'Challenge Round' principle in force at the time, which was not abolished until 1972) against Bill Tilden's United States.

At the time, there was no sports stadium capable of hosting such an event, for which there was a great deal of popular interest, so an agreement between the management of the Stade Français, represented by its president Emile Lesueur (1885-1965), and the Racing Club de France, whose president was none other than Pierre Gilou, captain of the Davis Cup team, agreed to finance the construction of the stadium after the City of Paris had granted them a plot of land on the site of the former Jean Bouin stadium.

The Roland Garros stadium was built in eight months, a feat in those days, and it was Emile Lesieur himself, a former rugby international, who demanded that the new stadium bear the name of his fellow HEC graduate, a stadium player like himself and a hero of the First World War: Roland Garros (1888-1918), an aviator who died in combat.

The Roland Garros stadium concession will be awarded to the joint Stade Francais / Racing Club de France agreement for a period of twenty years, with the land remaining the property of the City of Paris.

It is therefore reasonable to believe that Lacoste and Borotra used their connections and support from the Vichy government to obtain the resumption of the stadium concession from the founders and on behalf of the federation as early as 1942, six years before the end of the original lease?

In a report by Robert Gallay (1878-1954, secretary general of the federation who refereed the 1928 Davis Cup final) published in the official bulletin of May 1947, we read:

"The takeover of the Roland Garros stadium required more than a year of negotiations and steps; these were in fact undertaken in September 1941 and ended with the agreement of the City of Paris, which signified its acceptance of the transfer of the lease in November 1942; fortunately, the agreement between the two parties (FFLT and Stade-Racing committee) had only required six months of conversations, and the federation could take possession of the Roland Garros stadium from February 1942."

In any case, it is undeniable that this operation was a stroke of genius, as it would become very profitable for the federation several decades later, when the revenue from the French internationals (ticket sales and TV rights), in the best years, provided up to 75% of the FFT's annual budget!

It was also under René Lacoste's presidency, with a view to democratising access to the sport, that the number of Centres Scolaires d'Initiation au Tennis (CSIT) was increased. These had been created a few years earlier by a certain Camille Grégoire (General Secretary of the Federation), a creation made possible thanks to the collaboration of Suzanne Lenglen:

"It's not a question of producing champions every fifteen minutes, but of bringing tennis to the masses and recruiting more and more new fans," he says.

Finally, it was René Lacoste himself, after obtaining the agreement of the Lenglen family (let's not forget that Suzanne died in 1938) who, as we pointed out earlier, decided to work with a group of experts (Tillier, Darsonval, Destremau and Cochet) to develop the first teaching method, based on Lenglen's work.

The Suzanne Lenglen Method was therefore born in 1942, it was labelled FFLT and was of course used to operate all the new centres:

"There is no point in showing you the importance of the Lenglen method, without it, the tennis initiation centres would lose all their effectiveness; it was in fact necessary to create for them a guide, a method on which the best teachers were in agreement, and this was the case, since in numerous meetings they took part in its elaboration;

The Suzanne Lenglen method was in a way the crowning achievement of the federation's teaching work".

says Camille Grégoire at theOrdinary General Meeting of the French Lawn Tennis Federation on 15 March 1947.

The CSITs are in a way the ancestor of our tennis schools. They were set up in 1938, initially in Paris, on the Alsacienne courts, before spreading to the provinces, encouraged by the federation, with financial support from the secretariat and then the Ministry of Sport, and the participation of physical education teachers.

By using the term "schools", the federation wishes to emphasise that these centres are intended solely for young people. The federation, which has little or no control over the internal organisation of clubs, hopes to encourage youngsters to take up the sport by working with schools (collèges and lycées)!

These "school centres", which may be called tennis schools, are generally set up on the initiative of either local councils or school headmasters who apply to the Secretary of State for Youth and Sport. It is the regional leagues and this same secretariat that give their agreement to the opening of school centres.

The aim is first and foremost one of "propaganda" (there is in fact a "press and propaganda" committee within the federation which, as well as having its own official magazine - the forerunner of Tennis Info, with which younger players are all familiar - organises, on request, what it calls "propaganda tours" with screenings of films from the federation's film library -slow-motion replays, Davis Cup matches, etc.) and to spread the word about tennis among young people.

But it's also a question of training new players at an accelerated rate and improving the skills of players in clubs, and we'll talk more about this later.

Very early on, the federation became interested in developing tennis for young people, at a time when tennis was still played mainly by middle-aged men and women in clubs. And these adults do not wish to be disturbed in their leisure activities…!

René Lacoste's term of office came to an abrupt end in August 1943, a few months after Jean Borotra decided to leave the Vichy government to join the Free French Forces in North Africa (Joseph Pascot became General Sports Commissioner).

For example, the newspaper _Tous Les Sports_ (the official weekly of the French national sports committee and sports federations) of 28 August 1943 stated:

"Mr René Lacoste having found it necessary, due to his professional commitments, to relinquish the presidency of the FFLT, the General Commissioner for Sport, after thanking and congratulating him on the impetus he has given to the sport, has appointed Mr Raymond Rodel to take over the presidency on 1 September.

And while René Lacoste had decided to requalify his friend Henri Cochet as an amateur so that he could take part in the French tournament during the war, his successor, Raymond Rodel, created a special commission within the federation to promote tennis:

"I want to develop people's interest in tennis, I want to make it better known and better loved," said Rodel when he took up his post.

And he naturally asked the former glories of tennis to join, convinced that these champions would do more than anyone else to raise the profile in France of a sport they had made famous the world over. So Decugis, Germot, Gobert and Cochet, our most illustrious 'rackets', answered President Rodel's call.

In 1943, Henri Cochet was appointed Director of the French Tennis Propaganda Department, with the primary mission of discovering and preparing the young people who would one day have the honour of being part of our national team: detection, training and selection were the responsibility of our former champion, who can be considered the very first national instructor never to have held this position!

Cochet explains his role in more detail in an article published in the newspaper _"L'écho de Paris"_ on 3 December 1941 entitled _"Promoted to the position of great propagandist of French tennis, Henri Cochet goes in search of future champions to teach them the art and obligations of this role":_

44

"It's the role of the champion to evangelise the sporting crowds. I'm not going to be an educator, just a propagandist. I won't be teaching tennis, I'll be publicising its charm and seduction through lectures, talks and screenings. And if I visit the Suzanne Lenglen schools, for example, I won't be presenting myself as a teacher or examiner, but as an adviser at most.

President Rodel and Cochet knew each other well, having toured Asia in 1929 with Jacques Brugnon and Pierre-Henri Landry (playing in Japan and Vietnam in particular). The two men began to think about the most effective way of dealing with young people.

They've decided to build on what the federation has done in this area in previous terms of office, which I think is a very intelligent move on their part:why would they necessarily want to call everything into question?

A great deal of work had gone into setting up the Suzanne-Lenglen schools and developing them throughout France:

"The Suzanne-Lenglen schools have taught orthodox technique to a great many beginners. Thanks to this method, children starting out in tennis no longer have any excuse for not knowing how to hold their racket, or for misplacing their feet".

We read in an article entitled *"Les tournée Cochet"*, published on 15 January 1944 in *Le mémorial de Gaillac,* a provincial weekly newspaper.

And the same article gives us a little more information on the initiatives taken by Cochet as director of the federation's propaganda department:

1. Bringing as many children as possible to the Suzanne-Lenglen schools
2. Focus on the development of the most gifted children coming out of these schools

To develop the first point, Cochet set up propaganda tours visiting secondary schools in Paris and the provinces, convinced that the best means of propaganda is to go and find young people at home.

These tours will focus on three areas:

1. Sports talk on the physical and moral benefits for young people of playing sport in general and tennis in particular
2. Demonstration/exhibition in the company of one of the members of the propaganda committee, during which Cochet and his partner try to explain and demonstrate the various tennis strokes.
3. Doubles sets played with the most talented juniors in the audience

So Cochet and the propaganda committee wanted to rely on young people who were already convinced and who would themselves become the best propagandists for their lay comrades. !

When it comes to developing the most gifted children, Cochet naturally relies on the clubs:

"Clubs need to organise themselves to group together young people who show particular talents and to follow them effectively", he said in the aftermath of the Second World War.

Three "Ecole des Juniors" centres were created in collaboration with the RCF, the TCP and the Tennis Club de France (Neuilly), which can be considered as the first training centres for young players within these three Parisian clubs.

After the war, the aim was to capitalise on the growing interest in tennis both internationally and in France.

By the end of 1946, there were more than five thousand pupils in the various school centres covering more or less the whole of mainland France: Besançon, Brive, Cannes, Clermont-Ferrand, Fontainebleau, Grenoble, Limoges, Lyon, Montluçon, Montpellier, Moulins, Nancy, Nice, Paris, Pau, Reims, Rouen, St Quentin, Toulouse, Versailles and Vichy.

This represents a total of 59,359 members of the French federation, including 4,949 in North Africa (2,621 in French Algeria, 1,610 in Morocco and 718 in Tunisia).

It is therefore interesting to note that almost 8% of licence holders played tennis outside mainland France in 1946!

He also pointed out that many future players in French tennis (players, coaches and technical staff of the federation) discovered tennis in North Africa, including :

Robert Abdesselam (Algeria), Pierre Darmon (Tunisia), Patrice Dominguez (Algeria), Françoise Durr (Algeria), Guy Forget (Morocco), Patrice Hagelauer (Morocco), Paul Jalabert (Algeria), Gérard Valentin (Morocco) to name but a few!

The Lenglen method (1942)

Right from the introduction, René Lacoste warns:

"This book is primarily intended for all those, club managers or teachers, who will respond to the Federation's call to create and run a Suzanne Lenglen centre in the coming years...

Its presentation has been designed to make it a useful guide for any tennis player, teacher or amateur, who wants to give good advice to a youngster... Run, hit, apply yourself. It'sallabout returning the ball at all costs...

Follow the example that Jean Borotra, the finest figure in French sport, has always set for his young emulators on the courts and in life... In the most desperate situations, he never said to himself: "all is lost".

So even though it focuses mainly on initiation, the method has a threefold aim:

1. Introducing tennis to a large number of young people aged between 11 and 15 (propaganda)
2. Identifying future talent
3. Training managers

Using the Lenglen method, the federation aims to introduce as many children as possible to tennis.

But also to inculcate the best principles in many more pupils than she could have trained through individual lessons.

By encouraging French clubs to set up Lenglen centres (tennis schools), the federation hopes to enable teachers to train the maximum possible number of up-and-coming young players in the minimum amount of time and on the minimum number of courts.

Based above all on the assimilation of racket grips, gestures and the right attitude, it is nevertheless specified in the introduction:

"The advice given - after consultation with all the French specialists - remains general enough not to restrict the development of personal qualities".

This remark is very interesting because it shows that the experts of the time were aware that each player had to develop his game according to his own qualities. An avant-garde theory that was not always respected...

At the Lenglen centres, the sessions (lasting one or two hours) are organised in a very methodical way, with students quickly divided into three different levels:

1. Level A → beginners or inexperienced players (no exchanges possible)
2. Level B → players judged capable of returning balls sent by the teacher
3. Level C → players judged suitable for discussion with the teacher

And there is no room for fantasy: *"A pupil who learns too slowly or badly must be eliminated from the centre. A pupil in class B or C who holds up his classmates must be sent back to the lower class".*

Although the method focuses on initiation and improvement, it also includes advice on training, as well as corrective measures to address the main shortcomings encountered by experts.

But all this is done in directive form:

example: "*The player picks up the ball too far away, too low, at the end of his leap → the teacher forces him to stand one or two metres inside the court to return the serve*".

The Lenglen method was therefore based on model teaching: the teacher (the maître) showed and the pupil executed. It was very off-putting insofar as the students only really hit a few balls. Centred on gesture, discipline and repetition, it is similar to a military method where the learner is more subject than actor.

But it has the merit of existing and will play a significant role in the development of tennis in France.

PART THREE

THE DEVELOPMENT OF THE FIRST TENNIS SCHOOLS

"The way you will play exists within you, in power, before you touch a racket for the first time", Henri Cochet, 1932, *Le tennis, sa technique et sa psychologie.*

The federal initiative to professionalise teaching

Faced with the difficulty of increasing the number of introductory tennis centres for schoolchildren, particularly in the provinces, due to a shortage of teachers and a lack of facilities, the federation decided to organise technical teaching courses at the Paris French Tennis School (the school created by Lenglen in 1936 and which has since been given the status of a federal training centre), by organising 3 training sessions during the year (March, May and November), each of which could accommodate a maximum of 30 participants, although candidates still had to be found!

Wishing its best players to remain amateurs and therefore not wanting them to embark on a teaching career, the federation came up with the ingenious idea of relying on students at the Ecole Normale d'Education Physique, allowing them to learn to play tennis free of charge during their two-year training course, as reported in an article published in *L'Express de Mulhouse* on 9 June 1938, entitled "Un professeur de tennis dans chaque lycée et collège de France" ("A tennis teacher in every lycée and collège in France"):

"What we need to do is teach children what tennis is and get young people to love it. To do that, you need teachers. We don't have enough of them. So we need to train them [...] why shouldn't the students at the Ecole Normale de l'Education Physique, who are preparing for their PE instructor diploma, learn the principles of tennis at the same time? Why shouldn't they give tennis lessons to children in secondary schools after their course?

Where will they be assigned? [...] the federation, in every town where there is an affiliated club, and there are some just about everywhere, will make a court available once a week to the teacher and his pupils.

As for the ancillary costs that the operation will generate - rackets, balls, training for pupils -we have been told that the Ministry will cover these costs:

"This teachers' school will cost money. The government will pay for it. Lessons will take place at the Stade de Coubertin, under the technical direction of Suzanne Lenglen, assisted by a number of professionals [...] arrangements with ball and racket manufacturers are also planned so that these accessories cost as little as possible [...] All in all, young people will be taught a whole range of tennis-related sports. We could do no better than to direct them towards this sport, which has the advantage of being practised by both men and women, and which is a useful and enjoyable complement to the essential physical training.

Clearly, the federation was riding the wave of Lenglen and the musketeers by presenting, quite rightly, the hygienic virtues of playing tennis in order to obtain financial support from the government, at a time when people were just beginning to realise the importance of healthy physical activity. And tennis had the advantage of being a mixed sport that did not contradict the hygienic theories of the time.

As a result, the federation will be able to train tennis teachers at a lower cost, but not all of these students from the Ecole Normale d'Education Physique will pass the exam at the end of the two-year training course:

"On graduating from the French Tennis School, students will sit an examination before a committee made up of two members of the amateur federation and two professionals. If they pass, they will leave with a diploma corresponding to their ability: 3 categories are planned, as for other teachers; MONITOR (strength of a 3rd series player); PROFESSOR (top player of the second series), and COACH (1st series)".

Just after the end of the Second World War, the FFLT tried a pirouette to attract the best players from its affiliated clubs, as stated in an official FFLT bulletin dated May 1947:

"We thought that to remedy the shortage of teachers, we could encourage clubs to set up a tennis school run by one of their good players, who would have spent a fortnight in Paris beforehand. The advice they would be able to give, either at their club or elsewhere, would be on a voluntary basis, otherwise they would lose their amateur status.

This is how the federation announced the beginnings of the special status of federal educator, which was unofficially created in 1958 before being made official in 1975.

A virtuous and rather good idea, but one that will very quickly become unhealthy because men will be rubbing shoulders with men who, for the same activity, will not be treated in the same way...

Although they have been trained as volunteers, it is clearly stated that these "educators" cannot be paid for their advice...

However, in the article published in <u>*L'Express de Mulhouse*</u> in 1938, the journalist clearly states:

"We would remind you that it is in the interest of all professionals to have a diploma because, as we said recently, the federation will advise its clubs to choose qualified instructors..."

It was a double standard that raised questions and, above all, one that was to last for many decades. Later, with the arrival of the Open era, the spread of tennis and the massive influx of players into the clubs, the federation decided to make the compensation of these assistants official by creating the title of federal educator in 1975, which led to unhealthy competition between, on the one hand, state-qualified professional teachers who had received lengthy training and, on the other, federal educators with much more basic initial training.

And this is still the case today, with the DEs on one side and the CQPAMTs (assistant tennis instructors) on the other, qualified as professionals to sow even more confusion among players...

Let's go back to 1947, because having found a way to make up for the shortage of teachers, the federation and the AFPT jointly wanted to propose to the Ministry of Sport that only State diplomasbe awarded, as can be seen in the federation's official bulletin of May 1947:

"Subject to acceptance by the Direction Générale de l'Education Physique et des Sports, it has been decided to award State diplomas to tennis teachers who are members of the Association Française des Professeurs de Tennis, as well as to candidate teachers who will be recognised as worthy in the future".

The federation added that *"these diplomas will be awarded by the ministerial body responsible for sports, with the collaboration of the FFLT and the AFPT".*

By applying to the Ministry as early as 1947 for the creation of a state diploma to teach tennis, the federation and the AFPT have, in my opinion, a common interest:

1. A way for teachers to be recognised by the state as a corporation

2. A way for the federation to interfere more easily in club life

But it is also, and above all, because it intends to rely on PE teachers to run the CSITs at lower cost, that the federation must undertake to protect the teachers in the clubs: even if they are reluctant to embark on collective lessons, they are still the cornerstone of club organisation and the federation cannot fall out with them.

The Ministry did not respond favourably to the request, and it was not until the 1963 law that regulations were introduced for the teaching of sporting activities, which naturally included tennis.

The (federal) diplomas used up until now have been accused of legalising dubious situations, particularly those of top-level athletes, and this is true of allsports, not just tennis.

For my part, I think that this is also partly the responsibility of the students, the learners, who always want to play like this or that champion, isn't that still the case today?

And what could be more tempting for a neophyte who wants to perfect his game than to enlist the services of a former player, even if the latter has no knowledge or even teaching skills?

It was a time when champions and former champions were each publishing books in which they taught 'their tennis', a style of teaching that took absolutely no account of the student and his or her abilities, but was modelled on the tennis of the 'master'. And this state of affairs was to last for many years.

During an interview with former champion Pierre Darmon in May 2020, he told me that he had wanted to pass his tennis monitorat (which he brilliantly obtained in 1973) more for fear of being trapped when asked about the publication of his book *Le tennis en dix leçons,* published the same year and for which he had not written a single line in the paragraph on technique (his name having been used by the publisher to facilitate sales).

Mr Darmon never wanted to teach, he just wanted to be credible in relation to this publication, and that's a credit to him!

As we shall see, this approach was to last for many years, leaving an indelible mark on the structure of tennis teaching in France.

But let's now look at how these CSITs were organised

CSIT, tennis schools open to all, well almost all...

Spreading the practice, particularly among the youngest members of the sport, was a key issue for the federation's management from the outset.

And very opportunistically, they used the Debacle (France's capitulation to the German invasion) and the Vichy government (1940-1944) to convince the Ministry of Sport of the importance, and rightly so, of offering physical education and sport to our young citizens.

In July 1940, Jean Borotra was appointed General Commissioner for Education and Sport with the aim of promoting sport throughout France:

"The new regime (Vichy) wanted to restore morale, but it also wanted to get young people back into shape according to the principle of "Being strong to serve better".

So the federation took advantage of the war and then the occupation to approach the Ministry and position itself to obtain funds to open introductory tennis schools for youngsters (aged 10-13) in a win-win agreement: efforts aimed at the youngest players to train good citizens / development of tennis propaganda.

Borotra and Lacoste naturally took advantage of their respective aura to defend the interests of the federation and obtain the support of the Vichy government in this civic undertaking.

But it was also a rather troubled period for the federation, because let's not forget that from October 1939, the Roland Garros stadium was used as a transit camp for "undesirable foreigners" for several months.

Although Borotra disassociated himself from the regime in April 1942, a few months after his friend Lacoste resigned as president of the federation, it cannot be denied that both men took advantage of the regime to serve the interests of the FFLT.

The Roland Garros tournament, which was quite rightly cancelled in 1940, resumed the following year under the name Tournament de France (1941-1945), with participation restricted to male and female players who were members of an FFLT club.

But let's get back to the introductory tennis activities!
Of course, affiliated clubs offered to introduce young people to the sport, but there were very few of them - less than a thousand clubs spread across the country in 1946 - and above all, access to them was very elitist.
And the federation had very little leverage over the clubs:

"The successive teams of national leaders from 1945 to the end of the 1960s worked to develop tennis at a lower cost, taking advantage of school structures rather than clubs, as their power over associations was very limited at the time. With meagre resources, they set up CSITs with the help of the Secretary of State for Youth and Sport, who paid an annual subsidy for the running of these centres". (Source: Anne Marie Waser, La genèse d'une politique sportive : l'exemple du tennis, 1992)

In fact, between the post-war years and the end of the 1960s, the federal authorities simply followed the path laid out by Lenglen and the Musketeers, concentrating their efforts more on detection and selection than on the development of mass tennis.

But how could it have been otherwise at a time when sports facilities are in short supply and French young people are a long, long way from receiving the same sports education as their Anglo-Saxon counterparts.

In a surprising and unexpected way, individual initiatives are going to change things and I would like to mention here the action of the Glaszmann family in Alsace.

Roland Glaszmann, in an autobiographical novel written in 1989 and entitled *Tennis, quand tu nous tiens!* which was unfortunately never published:

"My father, Louis, was a tennis enthusiast, and back in 1927 he helped build the first indoor tennis court in eastern France, using an old disused factory. The best players in Alsace came to train there. So, after the Liberation in 1945, my father and I decided to set up a tennis section within CS Barembach, the football club of which he was president. My aim was to introduce the young people of our village to tennis. I organised the physical and tennis sessions myself on my grandparents' private court, and I did it all on a voluntary basis. I didn't receive, nor did I ask for, any help from the tennis federation, with which I had no contact at the time. I supplied the balls and rackets myself. My school was the first tennis school to be set up in Alsace. It was entirely free and aimed at young people from Barembach. I set the age limit at twelve, asked parents for a medical certificate and set up a short fitness test for admission. It worked well, so much so that very quickly I was able to talk about this tennis school to the big clubs in the region and encourage them to take part.
(source, Anne-Marie Waser, Actes de la recherche en sciences sociales, 1991-1992)

Caroline, Mr Glaszmann's daughter, a former development advisor to the Alsace league, who was France's number thirteen player in 1973 and a world champion in the over 65s with France in 2021, told me in an interview in March 2022:

"My father received very positive feedback from the start of his initiative and he quickly proposed to the Alsace league authorities the creation of a youth commission, which the league accepted. My father was the first chairman and in 1949, he set up the first Alsace youth championships (cadet categories - 15/16 years old - and juniors 17/18 years old). Naturally, all the major clubs in the region set up tennis schools modelled on my father's school. The following year, young players from twelve of the fifteen or so clubs in Alsace took part in the regional championships.

Roland Glaszmann's initiative is of course remarkable, but it remains isolated, even if it is at the origin of the development of tennis in the Eastern region and has certainly helped to develop competition at the level of the Alsace league.

Although he himself had no teacher training, many of the youngsters trained by Mr Glaszmann went on to become champions of Alsace.

And Caroline, his daughter, was ranked -15 in 1973, despite hitting her backhand with both hands at a time when it was banned by the federation:

"As I won the Alsace championship in my age category, I was selected to take part in training courses organised by the federation. These courses took place twice a year (at Christmas in Monte Carlo and at Easter in Le Touquet) and lasted a week. They were run by two women: Jacqueline Kermina and Florence de la Courtie. There weren't many of us, just a few players from clubs in Paris and a few from the provinces, including myself. It was very well organised, we had physical training in the morning and tennis training every day, interspersed with friendly matches between us. However, I couldn't play my backhand with both hands because my technique wasn't compatible with the federal vision of the time. We often played a tournament in a row. I remember playing mixed doubles at Le Touquet with the Australian Ian Fletcher, who was an excellent doubles player (he won 3 titles on the professional circuit).

But these individual initiatives are still very rare, and young French people who want to take up tennis are still dependent on the joint efforts of the Ministry of Sport and the French Tennis Federation.

The CSITs, of which there were twenty-one in 1946 (there would be one hundred and thirty-one twenty years later in 1967), had several missions from the outset:

1. Initiating young boys and girls aged 10 to 13

2. Identify the best players and offer them a cycle of further training with children who are members of clubs

3. Train future coaches so that they themselves can run sessions in their clubs or in CSITs as assistants, on a voluntary basis (educator).

Several issues of the *Revue Officielle du Tennis Français*, a monthly federal magazine whose first issue appeared in January 1962, give us precise information on the organisation of these CSITs, notably through the reports of the federation's general secretary, a certain Jacques Poupet.

We learn that in order to be able to benefit from teaching in these centres, which are approved by the Ministry of Youth and Sport and have the FFLT label, children have to register in advance (registration is free and certainly done by the parents) before being questioned about their real motivation!

And yes, we don't want to offer a free service to unmotivated children, and that seems perfectly acceptable.

It is also stipulated that children must be in possession of a medical certificate of fitness (for insurance purposes, as the children are not club members).

Only children who show a definite interest will have the privilege of following the introductory tennis cycle.

Physical tests are carried out first, with a twofold aim:

1. Forming level groups
2. Identifying the best elements

The aim of these tests is to assess 4 qualities considered to be essential in tennis:

1. Speed → 40-metre race
2. Relaxation → "Sargent Test" (start with feet together along a wall, the child has to jump to touch the wall as high as possible) / Long jump without run-up with start with feet together
3. Skill → Throwing balls (10 balls to be thrown into a circle two metres in diameter, ten metres away from the child).
4. Reflexes/Coordination → Catch balls alternately with right and left hands (balls thrown by the teacher to the child's right and left).

The setting up of these CSITs clearly shows that, very early on, the federation made an effort to educate young people, an effort made possible thanks to the collaboration with the Ministry of Sport, which supported this federal initiative very early on.

Financial support firstly, through the payment of indemnity fees to the federation to cover the training of PE teachers, but also material support with the loan of rackets, balls and nets (equipment remaining the property of the State).

The federation's annual budget, which at that time consisted mainly of licence fees paid by the clubs, did not allow it to be financially independent until at least 1966. But from 1968 onwards, this budget increased by almost 320% thanks to ticket sales and television broadcasting rights for the Roland Garros tournament, which was then open to professional players.

At the end of the ten-session cycle, participants are awarded a school tennis initiation certificate. The exam includes both practical exercises and an oral examination on stroke technique, and is validated by a panel made up of a member of the Ministry, a representative of the federation and the teacher who supervised the cycle.

Only the best children among those who have passed this brevet can hope to continue their training to try to obtain the brevet de deuxième cycle (on condition that they are ranked at least 30).

This is all very formal, and once again shows the self-interested side of the federation, which sees the setting up of CSITs as a way of identifying "talent"!
In the official Tennis magazine of January 1968, we read the following:

"To date, 2,256 school tennis initiation certificates have been awarded. Last year, at the same time, the figure was 703... The twelve groups selected in nine leagues for the start of the second cycle will be set up at the beginning of January 1968... Each pupil admitted to one of these groups will have a record at the federation so that he can be monitored both by the schools committee and by his league. 200 forms were drawn up for the class of 1968. The file will be increased by 400 forms for the class of 1969 (thirty groups) and 600 forms for the class of 1970 (fifty groups in the twenty-three leagues)".

The acceleration in the number of licences issued at the end of the sixties, and the increase in the number of people progressing to the advanced cycle (second cycle), shows the success of these centres and the dynamism of the federation.

The federation wants to break down the image of tennis as an elitist sport that has been associated with it for too many years, and the development of CSITs in the 1960s enabled tennis to become a physical activity that is firmly rooted in French culture.

We would like to pay special tribute to Maurice Herzog (1919-2012), who was Secretary of State for Youth and Sport from September 1958 to January 1966, as he encouraged and supported the development of CSIT throughout his term of office.

"Herzog sees sport as an ideal medium for PE for a number of reasons. The most important, in his view, lay in the moral values that sport was able to promote: perseverance, a taste for free effort, fair

play, performance, competition, success, etc... moral values that the school had a duty to promote in the 1960s, in a perspective of progress that animated all sectors of social life... Maurice Herzog's position, very widely supported by General de Gaulle, was pyramidal: democratic and broad access to sport will naturally produce an elite representing the nation in international competitions" (source: Evelyne Combeau-Mari, Revue EPS number 256, page 81, Dec. 1995)

Herzog wanted to concentrate efforts on schools and promote sport there by every means possible in order to increase the number of pupils, and our federation was right to support the Secretary of State!

For others, who are more critical, the CSITs have had only a limited impact, allowing only an introduction to tennis with no possibility of development, even for the most skilful youngsters:

"It's more a question of raising awareness of tennis than a real introduction to the sport. School sports facilities are inadequate and most PE teachers who are not qualified to teach tennis have had to make way for the federation's managers, who are too few in number to organise and supervise these young people.

Montana courses: a new approach to teaching?

Spurred on by the Montana company (perhaps to promote the brand of tennis racket?) and supported by the FFLT (which certainly saw it as a way of speeding up the spread of the sport and spotting new talent), the first tennis school opened in October 1966 at the Pierre de Coubertin stadium at Porte de Saint Cloud.

It is entirely free of charge and supervised by a national coach, Jacques Malosse, assisted by two young instructors: Alain Lambert (graduated in 1966) and Philippe Duxin (class of 1965).

"They were chosen for their belief in their profession, their technical and pedagogical knowledge and their love of children", we learn from an article in the official magazine of French tennis.

We also learn that 583 children (including 308 girls, i.e. 53% of applicants!) applied to take part in this free introductory course and that only 130 children (including 32 girls, i.e. less than 25% of applicants!) were finally selected after passing the physical tests organised at the Roland Garros stadium.

We can therefore see that, although they were in the majority among the applicants, girls were under-represented in the end. The society of the time was one in which the "weaker sex" was still struggling to assert its rights...

Everything is taken care of at this new tennis school: not only by Montana (booking the gymnasium, paying the teachers, loaning rackets to all the pupils and supplying Tretorn balls...

watch out for the elbows, sic!), but also by Fred Perry, which is providing the shirts, while the shoes will be supplied to the pupils by Spring Court!

And as soon as the school opens, the American company Tunmer will be making its new Tennis Trainer ball launcher available to pupils.

Under the direction of Jacques Malosse, coaches Alain Lambert and Philippe Duxin take turns every Thursday from 8am to 5pm for one-hour group sessions (8 or 12 children per session). As the groups are not mixed, boys and girls are of course separated, and only the best performers have access to the groups of 8.

But there's no revolution in the teaching method: we follow the principles of the Lenglen method: blank gestures, strikes on a fixed ball, ball-throwing, very few or no exchanges (not easy on the court, you might say...).

"Following a timed programme, the main basic principles of introductory tennis are studied in each lesson. One innovation is that the racquet handles are marked with the forehand and backhand grips".

"All these young people started in October; some progress more quickly than others, but they all apply themselves because they know that if their progress is insufficient, they will be replaced by young people on standby... Didn't we see a young boy walk from Place Balard to Porte de Saint Cloud one day during a strike (about a thirty-minute walk)*, so as not to miss his lesson?*

A good example of intrinsic motivation that some of today's young people would do well to take as a reference!

"Montana, Fred Perry and Spring Court hope in the near future to offer new opportunities to children wishing to learn tennis, not only in Paris, but all over France... On this Thursday 2 February, many people are crowding around the edge of the small Coubertin court. They are the CTRs on training courses at the INS, who have come to Paris for a few days to study. They all follow the two-hour course and take notes. Some of them are already thinking of setting up a similar school in their region, in agreement, of course, with the promoters of this experiment... This is the only way to find dozens of hopefuls and make tennis a mass sport".

Here again, we can see that young people are genuinely motivated and that this Montana course, sponsored by the FFLT, has four missions:

1. Initiating young people
2. Management training
3. Detection
4. Spreading the practice

The year following the creation of the first Montana course at Paris Coubertin, three other centres were set up in three different leagues: Champagne, Normandy and Orléans.

This demonstrates a real desire on the part of the FFLT to promote and disseminate tennis, but also a change of strategy, as the Ministry of Sport is not always responsive:

"It is vital that the Ministry of Youth and Sport quickly finds a solution to the tennis shortage throughout France. It would be wrong to continue to sow without being able to reap". declared General Secretary Jacques Poupet in June 1967.

René P. Pelletier: a more pragmatic approach to teaching

René Pelletier's three books: *Tennis. Style dynamique. Technique moderne* (1950), *Pour une méthode française de tennis : l'école des champions* (1951) and *Tennis moderne : comprendre le tennis moderne et le pratiquer avec intelligence* (1955) deserve particular attention as they challenge the pedagogy of the old teaching methods, particularly the Méthode Lenglen, which focused more on movement than on the game.

The author, who is not himself a technician but rather a talented writer who likes to devote himself to sports pedagogy, stresses the importance of linking technical learning to tactics:

"The technical problem is to train players who are no longer ignorant of the whys and wherefores of each tennis shot".

And when he asked Jean Borotra to preface his book "*Comprendre le tennis moderne et le pratiquer avec intelligence*" (*Understanding modern tennis and playing it intelligently*), it is natural to assume that he was aware of the portrait painted a few years earlier by Wallis Myers (1878-1939) - a British tennis player, publisher, author and journalist - who wrote of the "bouncing Basque" in the March 1930 issue *of Tennis et Golf*:

"Lacking classic means at the start, he remains a fanciful player. No coach trained him; he learned on his own without help of any kind... He cares little for the elegance of gesture; he runs at the ball, hits it, pushes it; what does it matter to him where his feet are, how he holds his racket!

His blows were often executed with the weight of his body on a foot that moved instead of being fixed to the ground... He was a great fighter, perhaps the greatest of his time. A remarkable tactician, he could see through the methods and manoeuvres of his opponents. No one is better at guessing the intentions of the player facing him, no one is better at concealing his own plans, and no one is quicker to act at the critical moment. In short, it is his psychological qualities that enable him to save difficult matches.

In his books, René Pelletier unknowingly laid the foundations for what would later be developed by PE teachers in the 1970s, before being definitively adopted by the FFT in the 1990s, namely the teaching of situationalsituations, starting with the introduction to tennis.

And he goes further:

"And why model yourself on one champion rather than another?
Will you opt for Perry's forehand or Cochet's? Lacoste's or Talbert's? Tilden's grip or Féret's? Budge's backhand or Kramer's or Borotra's? ....
One world champion triumphed with a style that contradicted the manner of another world champion...
So many world champions!
How many different forehands and backhands!

For the very first time, the author,himselfa master teacher, reminds us that each player's style is unique:

"Genres and styles evolve in sports as they do in the arts. It should never be said that such and such invented this. Every precursor has precursors".

He sees the Borotra-Cochet era as a turning point in theevolution of thegame's approach. Borotra and Cochet: before them he spoke of static tennis as opposed to their dynamic game, all movement and speed. Borotra, the bouncy Basque, develops a forward tennis style that naturally finishes the point at the net, while Cochet suffocates his opponents at the back of the court by taking the ball early.

"Cochet inaugurated the fast game, capable of outflanking the opposition. To this end, his foot placement was a real anticipation of execution, he picked up the ball very early, at the top of the bounce, sometimes even before it reached the top in order to return it even earlier; he adopted a high forehand and returned a low, spinning ball, more easily placed because it was hit higher than the net."

In his book, the author draws a parallel between teaching tennis and the school curriculum The three stages presented several years ago in the Méthode Lenglen (initiation/perfection and training) are all there.

Initiation would correspond to nursery school and primary school, improvement to secondary school and high school, while training would be a kind of transition to higher education, to university!

He also distinguishes between two types of tennis: recreational tennis and sports tennis, in other words, leisure and competition.

And René P. Pelletier doesn't pull any punches when he talks about "leisure" riders:

"Older people, such as midgets and pot-bellies, who still carry their breathlessness around the courts, may argue that sport is just a distraction. There is, in fact, a form of tennis entertainment that has nothing in common with our sport other than the use of rackets and balls.
but a prostituted use. Tennis is one of those innocent games where the senile flirts with the infantile".

As far as tennis is concerned, he is much more complimentary and, above all, he emphasises the particularities of this activity (as did Max Decugis at the beginning of the century), a sport with open skills where tactical qualities (intelligence) and mental qualities (perseverance) are at least as important as technical mastery and physical qualities:

"Sporting tennis, combat tennis, adds, even better than any other sport, the precious resource of applying the mind to trying to solve, in order to achieve the most effective style, a host of problems where the qualities of intelligence are revealed; and these steps, these incessant investigations of the mind require perseverance where character is forged and asserted".

In 1955, he contrasted static tennis with dynamic tennis, and argued that tennis would become faster and faster in the future. He insisted on the need to have excellent footwork in order to hope to play this offensive tennis. Well done, my dear René!

Finally, his assertions about racket grips were unfortunately not adopted a few decades later when the FFT's French Teaching Method was drawn up.

"With the classic grip (some call it "open" - the "hammer" grip), the grip that has done so much damage to French tennis, will we choose to imitate Cochet, who vigorously propelled the ball with his right foot, left shoulder firmly lowered, left lower limb constantly more flexed than the right?

That would be to pretend to possess his hock of steel, his exceptionally robust wrist, and above all his rare genius capable of deriving advantage and glory from playing with the difficulties or stumbling all those who pretend to imitate the choice of inconvenience and the risk-taking from which he emerges victorious... because he is Cochet, "the exceptional", "the inimitable", the "brilliant" Cochet. By copying the execution methods used by a brilliant performer, you sometimes sow the seeds of difficulty only to reap the rewards of failure.

In his remarks, René Pelletier warned as early as the 1950s of the limits of model teaching and theimportance of taking into account the specific physiological and physical characteristics of each individual: not all players are born equal when it comes to playing tennis!

And he says:

"We know that the choice of racket grips requires above all satisfying the anatomo-physiological desiderata capable of providing comfort, safety and effective robustness to the elbow and wrist joints" (Let's not forget that at the time we were playing with 450-gram wooden rackets and rock-hard, pressureless balls!)

"It's not enough for technicians and teachers to know this, the player has to understand it". The single grip," he says, *"with the hand riveted invariably immobile on the handle, is an unevolved primitive process..."*

And he goes even further, calling for deeper reflection on the way we coach:

"There needs to be a total revolution in the teaching of tennis, which can have no other basis than the primordial study of footwork, joint twists and detorsions, both of which are integrated into the total execution of strokes.

René Pelletier was the first to stress the importance of biomechanics and to take an interest in the concept of efficiency, i.e. the search for effectiveness with the least physical effort.

But at a time when the main objective of the federal authorities is to get as many people as possible playing tennis, it's better to set a model and stick to it, even if it's not, or only slightly, suitable for future students!

PART FOUR

PROFESSIONALISING TEACHING

"If France shines abroad through its thinkers, scientists and artists, it must also shine through its sportsmen and women. A country must be great because of the quality of its young people, and we cannotconceive of young people without a sporting ideal.

General de Gaulle after the humiliation of the Olympic Games in Rome (1960)

The birth of the Brevet d'Etat d'Educateur Sportif (state diploma for sports instructors)

1963 was a pivotal year in the teaching of sports disciplines, as the legislator passed a law aimed at introducing state diplomas in all disciplines - a real turning point!

The State Tennis Certificate was officially created a few years later, in 1965, at the same time as the Physical Education Certificate.

As we have seen, before this date, sports federations issued their diplomas under their own names:

"Only those who had been or were classified in the 1st series *could hope to obtain the title of* Master-Professor, *provided they had practised as a teacher for at least ten years"*.

says Georges Deniau, who himself became an instructor in 1961 - tennis was to become Open that year - at the Sporting Club de Lyon!

"When I took the exam to become an instructor, there were only a few candidates. Pierre Forget (Guy's father) and I were the only two classified in the 1st *series, the others were in the second series and one or two candidates were 15/2. The jury was made up of Jacques Feuillet, a master teacher, and Henri Cochet, a national coach - the first that the Federation has ever had, it seems to me?*

Henri Cochet's missions are manifold: he organises training sessions at Roland Garros for the best players, observing them and giving them advice. He also travelled to the regions, visiting the CREPS to develop tennis and raise its profile.

And, of course, he's an examining board!

The exam was very basic, consisting of a demonstration of all the tennis strokes, physical tests (1000 metres, shot put and high jump) and a technical talk.

According to Georges Deniau, there was no substitute for hands-on experience and confrontation with pupils (at the time, group lessons were virtually non-existent):

"What has made me progress the most in my teaching is giving lessons, trying to make the perfect gesture so that my pupil can copy".

In our sport, alongside the "official" federal diplomas, there were also titles and labels that were completely outside the control of the Federation: for example, there is evidence of holders of Suzanne Lenglen diplomas (a certain Jean Pernet in 1939) or Henri Cochet diplomas.

The latter used to organise conferences at which participants could perhaps receive an eponymous diploma, synonymous with a professional qualification?

Perhaps the Suzanne Lenglen diploma was also awarded to players who had followed a course at the Lenglen schools, or even the training to become a school teacher at the CSITs?

The first diploma making it compulsory to teach a physical activity for remuneration was created just after the First World War:

"Regulatory diplomas, a sort of state certificate before the term was coined, were made compulsory in fencing as early as 1919".

So it was through fencing, a high-risk discipline where some people improvise themselves as "weapon masters", that the legislator began to regulate the transmission of knowledge of a physical and sporting activity in return for payment.

From now on, the State, via the Ministry of Youth and Sport and in collaboration with the sports federations, wishes to exercise a right of supervision over the teaching of all sporting disciplines.

The starting point for this initiative was the summer of 1960, when for the first time the Olympic Games, held in Rome, Italy, were broadcast in colour on television. It was a fiasco for the French delegation, who failed to win a single gold medal!

Worse still, France finished an inglorious twenty-fifth in the overall medal table at these Olympics...

Colonel Marceau Crespin (1915-1988), a member of General de Gaulle's government, who had been in charge of Olympic preparation for the French national team in 1961 and who became Secretary General of the High Committee for Sport, decided to create a body of civil servants (sports teachers) to be made available to sports federations to provide better training for future athletes: These civil servants, soon to be known as CTRs (Conseillers Techniques Régionaux - Regional Technical Advisers), would be made available to the FFLT - in particular - free of charge, as they would be paid by the Ministry of Education.

It was General de Gaulle himself who gave a new impetus to sports coaching: from now on, qualifications would no longer be issued by the federations.

But in conjunction with the Ministry of Youth and Sport, the State will be imposing its directives!

The sixties were a turning point for the sporting phenomenon, which continues to grow to this day.

If the French are increasingly taking part in physical activity and sport, it is of course thanks to the creation of numerous infrastructures (particularly from the end of the war) but also and above all to a change in mentality, the world of work and free time. The latter increased with the third week of paid holidays in 1956, then the fourth in 1969, and more recently, the adoption of the 35-hour week (in 2000) and the associated RTT (reduction in working hours). All of this enabled the French to devote more time to leisure activities, including tennis.

Graduates of this first "Brevet d'Etat Tennis", awarded jointly by the Ministry of Sport and the French Tennis Federation, obtained the same titles/designations as the old federal diplomas, namely: Moniteur for the BEES 1 then Professeur for the BEES 2 and finally Maître-Professeur, BEES 3 for the most experienced and we will see that these titles remained unchanged even after the first reform in 1972.

But how was it articulated?

Gérard Valentin, who was part of the very first BE class in 1966 and later became director of the Pôle France in Reims and then co-responsible at the DTN for the Programme Avenir National (PAN) after having taught for almost twenty years at the Charleville-Mézières club, explains:

"I was granted a special dispensation to be able to take the course, as you normally had to be 21 at the time to enrol, and I was in my twentieth year... !

I spent several weeks at the Institut National des Sports (Bois de Vincennes), later known as the INSEP, where we were trained by Master Teachers (equivalent to BE3) such as Alfred Estrabeau, René Tissot and Jacques Malosse under the supervision of Gil de Kermadec, the DTN.

The exam consisted of a written test, a sports test (known as the Brevet Sportif Populaire, which was common to all BE candidates regardless of their discipline) and a sports test (known as the Brevet Sportif Populaire, which was common to all BE candidates regardless of their discipline).

These include: climbing the rope, 50m freestyle, high jump, 60m flat and 1000m flat), a one-to-one teaching session with a guinea pig and the dreaded demonstration test against another candidate.

I say 'so dreaded' because we had to respect the technical fundamentals of the time, which would be set down a few years later in <u>La méthode Française d'enseignement,</u> *in particular :*

1. *single socket (continental and/or hammer)*

2. *online support*

3. *one-handed backhand*

Having started playing tennis in Morocco on clay just before the age of ten, Gérard explains that he had to give up his natural forehand grip in order to put all the advantages on his side for the exam:

"As the demonstration test has the highest coefficient, I had to adopt a more open grip in order to give myself the best possible chance at the exam. So I spent dozens of hours hitting forehands on the training wall at theINS with a grip that wasn't natural for me. Although I got a decent mark in the demonstration test, the result was that I lost all the effectiveness of my forehand, which used to be my strong shot!"

Like Gérard, many have had to unlearn their tennis from a technical point of view in order to approach the federal model, with the sole aim of obtaining the precious sesame!

The federal managers of the time found themselves obliged to take this new state certificate in order to keep their status, and for the oldest of them, the Brevet Sportif Populaire was a real crossroads, even if none of the marks were eliminatory...

A report on the training of the instructors from the class of 1969 was published in the magazine _Tennis de France_ provides information on its organisation and the content covered.

It says that the 57 trainees (49 men and 8 women), aged from 20 for the youngest to 49 for the oldest, are supervised by 6 Master Teachers (Alfred Estrabeau, Joseph Stolpa, René Tissot, Jacques Malosse, Georges Deniau and Jean Paul Loth), under the direction of Gil de Kermadec, the National Technical Director, and assisted by Jacques Dorfmann for the refereeing courses.

The instructors had four tennis courts, a football pitch and an amphitheatre at their disposal to train future instructors over a two-week period at a single venue: the Institut National des Sports (INS) in the Bois de Vincennes, which later became the INSEP.

The first week was devoted to technique and physical preparation (court), and the second to running a tennis school and refereeing (indoor).

During the first week of training, sessions are always conducted in two stages: demonstration on the rugby pitch and work on shots without the ball (blank gestures); practical application on the courts, with each trainee taking it in turns to play the role of student and instructor. We learn that the great advantage of the training course is the unity of the method:

"A blind man _who ignored the difference in voices would think he was hearing the same teacher on every court._

The aim of this monitorat training is to ensure that future monitors have the same technique, which we hope they will be able to pass on to future practitioners. We're sure that the doors to success will be open to young talent.

Every day at around 5pm, the boys' trainees gather on the football pitch and are divided into two teams ("north" and "midday") to play a fierce match as part of their physical preparation. Couldn't this be the origin of what would later become the famous PSG vs OM Classico?

As for the 8 girls, the author of the report tells us that they were being looked after at the same time by the oldest of the trainees, André Osterberger (1920-2009), a former international hammer thrower, to prepare for the physical tests.

The popularity of tennis must be qualified, however, by the fact that at the time it was still an elitist sport, reserved for a minority, with few if any charismatic champions.

The French are more passionate about the cyclists Anquetil and especially Poulidor, "the eternal runner-up".

Opposite photo taken during the BE training course in October 1969 on theINS courts in the Bois de Vincennes. 57 trainees, 6 instructors: "Six masters who spoke the same language supervised the future instructors. In a short time, all French children will learn to serve in the same way" (Source Tennis de France, December 1969).

Tennis, a team sport", says the National Technical Director (DTN) Gil de Kermadec in an article in the EPS magazine number 110 of July-August 1971: "The newly implemented teaching method is resolutely oriented towards team teaching", says the DTN (the photo above, which illustrates the article, comes from the Tennis de France magazine and shows the extent to which the instructors apply the training they have received to the letter!

The Abdesselam plan, a first attempt to professionalise coaching

When former French number two Robert Abdesselam (1920-2006) became chairman of the FFLT's sports commission in 1963, he was saddened by the state of top-level French tennis:

"only one player in the first series, Pierre Darmon, is really able to compete with the greatest players of the time, while several countries with fewer players can boast a number of great champions in their ranks...French players lag behind other countries when it comes to training, athletic preparation and

healthy living, difficulties that are all the more worrying given that young hopefuls in French tennis are not known for their sense of discipline" (sources, Éric Belouet and Michel Dreyfus, Robert Abdesselam, une vie criblée de balles, 2009).

Between 1946 and 1963, most of France's best players, particularly those who represented us in the Davis Cup, were regularly mocked in the national press, and not just in the sports press. Our representatives are often criticised for their lack of preparation, particularly in terms of physical fitness. And the federal authorities are not spared from criticism either. Looking through the archives of the newspaper *Le Monde*, dating back to its creation in 1944, I was able to read, here and there :

"The defeat of our Davis Cup players at the hands of the Yugoslavs prompted some bitter comments. The Yugoslav player Puncec, who defeated Yvon Petra, said: "It was good physical condition that your champions lacked most; training here is more thorough and tougher... and when I say training, I mean physical preparation" (article by Olivier Merlin, Le Monde, 18 June 1946).

"We have had enough of seeing pretentious stylists with cocky calves or out-of-shape guys who have never wanted to take part in physical training linger around the courts [...] It is inconceivable that we should not be able to set up an organisation similar to the one that has so brilliantly enabled the development of our competitive skiing" (Article by Olivier Merlin, Le Monde, 29 July 1947).

It is important to note that Olivier Merlin (1907-2005), the author of these articles, was a keen sportsman and a great sports connoisseur.

He was a senior editor at *Le Monde* for almost forty years (1945-1984). And not only did he criticise, he also proposed solutions through his articles.

And what he suggested to the federation in one of his papers written in 1946 shows what a connoisseur he was!

"We had to draw up a rational fitness programme for our Davis Cup players and impose a strict lifestyle discipline under supervision. We should try to improve them in an attractive way, by doing things that are appropriate for tennis: working the hand, the arm's motor muscles, making the kidneys and back muscles more supple, maintaining the abdominal muscles, - more or less advanced exercises depending on the shortcomings observed on the court. Their relaxation should be cultivated (100-metre start, firm jumps), they should be put on their feet, and their breath should be maintained by running almost every day. This training should be monitored by a sports doctor, who is as invaluable for tennis players as a vet is for thoroughbreds. Rational training, then, but also a strict lifestyle [...] A considerable amount of sleep, regular working hours, a very healthy diet: these are the principles of hygiene which, in addition to appropriate physical training, give the champion perfect physical and nervous balance".

Robert, also known as Bob Abdesselam, was well aware of all this and put in place his eponymous plan shortly after his arrival at the federation, as explained by Messrs Belouet and Dreyfus, the authors of his biography:

"This plan will be built around two main observations: firstly, the era of volunteer managers is over and secondly, the efforts of the players need to be coordinated.

He selected twenty male players (including Barclay, Barthes, Beust, Chanfreau, Contet, Jauffret and Goven) and fourteen female players, known as the "national players", aged between 15 and 24, for the national teams.

Abdesselam believes that players over the age of 24 *"know, or should know, what they have to do, and most of them have reached their peak".*

It also sets out the specifications to be met by these players and is uncompromising in the eventofnon-compliance:

"Anyone who refuses to follow the specifications will automatically be excluded from the group of national players and will never again be selected for a French team, even if he is the strongest".

The programme or specifications that the so-called "national" players were called upon to respect covered six areas as follows:

→ Training consisting of sixteen hours of tennis and four hours of physical preparation per week (for those who were busy with their studies or work, this was an option). early morning and/ or late evening sessions).
→ Undertake not to miss any training session without good reason.
→ An individual fitness test once a month under the s u p e r v i s i o n o f a doctor at the Institut National du Sport.
→ Monthly participation in a weekend training course bringing together all the national players as well as sportsmen and women from other disciplines.
→ Pay particular attention to your healthy lifestyle
→ It is essential that you keep up another activity, such as school or work, outside tennis.

Robert Abdesselam was very attached to the last point, having himself successfully combined top-level sport with brilliant studies. Above all, he did not want to jeopardise the future of young players in the event of sporting failure, especially as tennis was still, officially at least, an amateur sport in 1963.

There had indeed been private initiatives to try and form training groups and to coach the most promising youngsters in the best possible way, I'm thinking in particular of the initiative of a certain Jean Pierre Bergerat in the early 1960s.

He came up with the idea of bringing together a number of promising youngsters at his school (the Bergerat school), including a certain Jacques Renavand, on whom Racing relied heavily, as well as Stade Daniel Contet (1943-2018), and offering them daily training under the guidance of some very good players.

A veritable training centre with the stated aim of producing champions, Bergerat's initiative initially led to a sharp rise in technical standards, but unfortunately it was not to be followed up.

Perhaps this initiative was too avant-garde at a time when it was more desirable to think about one's future professional life than to try and make a career in amateur tennis, which, let's not forget, didn't bring in a penny!

Through his charter, Bob hopes to bring French tennis out of its isolation and probably draw inspiration from the Australian model, which dominated the international scene in the 1960s: *"Those who have agreed to be part of the 'Nationals' category know what they are signing up for. There are honours, but there are also constraints. Outside of training, they will have to observe a very strict rule of life, without abuse of any kind, and follow a carefully studied diet, not ingesting anything at any time."*

To implement his plan and ensure that the troops are well led, Abdesselam will rely on four men:

➤ Jacques Dudal (1926-2013 was in charge of physical preparation (he ater became the National Technical Director of the)French Athletics Federation between 1976 land 1978).
➤ Jacques Iemetti (1922-1969) coached the French national teams.
➤ Pierre Darmon, French number one and recent Roland Garros finalist (1963), will be responsible for the tactical training of the national players.
➤ Gil de Kermadec, former French number three and editor-in-chief of *Tennis de France* magazine (the only magazine available in newsagents dealing exclusively with tennis news), will be responsible for overseeing and coordinating the whole operation, becoming the federation's first national technical director.

More than thirty years before the creation of the future CNE (Centre National d'Entraînement, created in 1986 within the grounds of the Roland Garros stadium and then relocated to Porte d'Auteuil in 2016 following the in-depth renovation of the Roland Garros stadium), it can be said that Bob Abdesselam was the first man, the first elected official of the federation to attempt to professionalise coaching within the federation.

Unfortunately, he was dropped by some of the national players and also by the chairman at the time, Robert Soisbault (1902-1985), because of his intransigence and excessive rigour:

"As long as we control and monitor them, they are angels of obedience. But as soon as we relax our vigilance, they start eating too much, drinking too much, getting up too late, engaging in competitions that exhaust them, training foolishly, slacking off and listening to themselves. Listening to themselves,

thinking about their nerves, their defeats, about everything and nothing, is a very French fault that is very difficult to combat".

Even if the Abdesselam plan was abandoned soon after it was put in place, we can say with certainty that it contributed to putting an end to the 'amateurism' of French players in the way they trained and behaved, and ushered in a new era for French tennis.

In 1963, the federation had a technical and sporting director in the person of Gil de Kermadec (who we'll talk about later), as well as a team of specialists in the following areas: physical, technical and tactical.

And it can count on the financial support of the Secretary of State for Youth and Sport, who has helped set up this technical organisation for French tennis by allocating operating subsidies to the federation every year.

With just over 1,000 affiliated clubs in 1963 and just under 90,000 licence-holders, the association alone cannot meet its needs.

In a report by Jean Noury (1904-1983), Senator for Ille-et-Vilaine (1959-1971), concerning the 1966 Finance Bill (Senate opinion), we learn that the salaries of the National Technical Director, the national coaches and the Regional Technical Coordinators were paid in full by the Secretary of State for Sport.

The latter, nicknamed "Messieurs Tennis", will be responsible for spotting young hopefuls and ensuring their development during regional and national training courses, again subsidised by the Secretary of State.

In return, Gil de Kermadec has made every effort to facilitate contact between our young hopefuls and the best foreign hopefuls.

In 1966, a team of French players took part in the Orange Bowl, an American competition that brought together the world's elite young players in sunny Florida during the Christmas holidays.

In this way, the state-supported federation gave itself the means to train an elite by taking into account all the aspects linked to performance, with the exception of the mental approach, which was not yet considered an essential component in the 1960s in France.

Infact, Patrice Hagelauer was one of the very first French coaches to raise this issue in 1974, the day after theFrench junior team lost to Spain in the Valerio Cup (the equivalent of the Davis Cup for under-18s) played in Vittel. Hagelauer, the team's captain, explains:

"We were eliminated because in the two matches on which everything depended, our players showed themselves incapable of overcoming their stage fright. I'm convinced that the habit of overcoming fear

is only acquired through competition [...] Young Americans play at least 150 matches a year, and in this respect the Spanish, Italians, Swedes and Germans are also well ahead of us.

I think it's above all this shortcoming that has caused us so many setbacks, because technically, we were rather superior (more complete) to the Spanish. But we only have practice players, whereas they have seasoned players with all the automatisms of competition (mental attitudes, concentration, relaxation, reaction to fear, etc.) which are totally different from the technical automatisms [...] Let's prepare ourselves first like those who beat us by producing players and not little coaches" (sources: Tennis de

France number 258, October 1974, pages 37 and 39).

Patrice Hagelauer argues that it is by 'matching' more that fear will fade and mental strength will eventually develop.

It wasn't until the mid-1980s that the French Tennis Federation really began to take notice of the situation, which was instigated by a certain Alain Cassaigne, then a federal coach:

"I remember being contacted by a literary agent, in this case a lady, at the end of the seventies, whose job was to introduce American books toFrench publishers so that they would be willing to publish them in French.

This lady, who knew that I knew English and that I was coaching the best young players at the FFT at the time, asked me if I could read a book written in 1972 by a certain Timothy Gallwey and entitled The inner game of tennis to see if it might be worth translating into French and publishing it here?

Overwhelmed by the revelations in this book, which dealt with the mind and what would later be called neuro-linguistic preparation (NLP), which I had never heard of before, I told this lady that the book would be of interest to the public. So she asked me if I would translate it into French, which I did.

This led to the publication of Tennis et psychisme in 1977, which I renamed Tennis et concentration in a second edition in 1985.

Alain Cassaigne was the first coach in France to bring a sophrologist to the INSEP in 1984-85, a certain Nelly Michelin, who had received American training on the subject. Unfortunately, the federation did not support him in his endeavours, and for almost twenty years, the mental approach was sidelined by the FFT.

In an interview I had with Nelly Michelin in November 2020, she explains :

"For ten years I specialised in top-level sport, helping athletes to manage their emotions. Alain Cassaigne asked me to help the young players he was coaching at the time. Unfortunately, it was very difficult to convince the other coaches, who were closed to any outside intervention.

I know that Yannick Noah tried to convince the DTN managers in the mid-1980s, but to no avail. For my part, I didn't insist too much, as at the time I was already doing a lot of work with other sports and was being approached by both business executives and politicians.

Today, mental preparation is an important component of training and it can no longer be said that French players are not prepared for it, yet every time one of our representatives falters, commentators and journalists do not hesitate to wave the mental flag as the main reason for the failure.

For Sam Sumyk, a seasoned coach who has taken two foreign players (Victoria Azarenka of Belarus and Garbine Muguruza of Spain) to the top of the WTA rankings, the notion of mental is too broad and not specific enough:

"In France, we use the word 'mental' all the time. I think that when we don't have an explanation for a particular poor performance, we blame it on the mental state of our players.almost makes you think they're mentally retarded! In my opinion, the three hundred best players in the world are all very strong mentally. What makes the difference between players is their state of mind, their attitude, their way of thinking, their logic and their courage".

So Sam Sumyk doesn't like the word 'mental', which in his opinion is an ugly word used primarily by journalists and TV consultants when they have no rational explanation to offer -in short, a catch-all word!

Having had the chance to talk to Sam and watch one of Muguruza's matches at the 2018 Hong Kong WTA Open with him, I realised that a great deal of technical confidence in a shot can give a player peace of mind and therefore mental solidity and a clear mind. On the other hand, if the player is not confident in his or her technique, then he or she will not attempt the zone that would be the most appropriate to play given the opponent's characteristics: the logic of the game versus the logic of the player, a permanent battle of wits in tennis!

Professional tennis teacher or sports educator?

We saw earlier that very early on, in 1929, tennis teachers organised themselves into a corporation by creating the Association Française des Professeurs - in the professional sense of the term - de Tennis (AFPT) on the initiative of master teacher Martin Plaa.

But fairly quickly, and more out of a desire to develop the sport than toharm the professionals, we saw that the federation created the unofficial status of educator in 1947 to deal with the shortage of teachers, a status which was made official in 1975.

In my opinion, this could and should have been rectified back in 1963, when state diplomas were introduced for all sports, but unfortunately we chose to name these diplomas "Brevet d'Etat d'Educateur Sportif" and forgot to include the word "professional".

This shows once again the lack of recognition by the public authorities in general for those who choose a career in sports teaching, and I'm not just talking about tennis here, as sport has long been considered in France as a related activity, and a teacher of a sporting discipline as a volunteer amateur, and unfortunately this image still persists even today in our country!

For many years, and this is still not the case today, professional teachers (holders of a state diploma) and 'volunteer' teachers (holders of a federal diploma as a sports educator, even though this is recognised by the French tennis federation!

Remember that in 1970, according to FFT sources, there were more federally qualified teachers (780) than state qualified teachers (531)!

The former were not obliged to regularise their situation, and rightly so in my view, since they had already demonstrated their skills for many years!

Very early on, at the very beginning of the 1970s, state-qualified tennis instructors tried to get together, first on the Côte d'Azur, with the creation of the Union Nationale des Professeurs de Tennis (UNPT) in 1970, then in the Syndicat National des Brevetés d'Etat de Tennis (SNBET), created in Paris the following year, but to no avail.

In 1974, this organisation became the Fédération Nationale des Enseignants Professionnels de Tennis (FNEPT), whose primary mission was to defend and represent tennis teachers in their dealings with the federal authorities.

In practice, it mainly brought together self-employed workers for whom it offered various types of insurance at preferential prices and defended their interests in the face of potential conflicts with the clubs (the employers).

When the FFT made the status of federal educator official in 1975, to cope with the influx of people wanting to learn tennis, it was very difficult to distinguish between professionals and volunteers.

And it will be even more so in 1979 with the arrival of the 2nd degree federal educator diploma. At the outset, the FNEPT was intended to be a platform for the exchange of teaching methods between professional teachers from all over France and from all backgrounds (self-employed, employed, etc.).

In my opinion, this was a very good initiative, but one which may have been viewed very negatively by the DTN, who probably saw this organisation as a counterweight?

In fact, Philippe Brossard, Director of the FNEPT, told me in April 2020:

"In the 1980s, the FNEPT launched a training centre for the state tennis certificate. But this was gradually scaled back and then abandoned, due to a lack of human resources and also because, at the time, the DTN was putting pressure on the Ministry of Sport to give it a monopoly on training in France.

It's a real shame, because when the FNEPT was set up, it took up Martin Plaa's initiative by organising an annual French Tennis Teachers' Championship. Unfortunately, this event disappeared in the early 1990s due to a lack of participants.

It's not easy to bring together all the players involved in tennis, in the clubs and on the fringes of our powerful federation!

So in the early 2000s, the organisation refocused on defending the profession and social benefits, then from 2005 on ensuring that clubs and their managers complied with the National Collective Agreement for Sport (CCNS).

Personally, I think that FNEPT should not have changed its name.

By becoming the Fédération Nationale des Moniteurs et Professeurs de Tennis (National Federation of Tennis Instructors and Teachers) and abandoning the term *"Enseignants Professionnels" (Professional Teachers)*, it has perhaps sown some confusion? Shame!

It has to be said that in seeking to professionalise sports teaching through the 1963 law, the Ministry actually sowed the seeds of trouble by adopting the term "sports educator" in its diploma, a term which is not strong enough, in my opinion, to define professional teachers who hold a state diploma.

The profession has long suffered from this shortcoming, and suffers even more today with the proliferation of statutes which, once again, confuse both practitioners and professionals: educators, initiators, activity leaders and assistant tennis instructors are often confused with state-qualified teachers, and the boundary between these statutes, which are quite different, is not clearly defined...

A National Association of Tennis Educators (ANET) was even set up in 1994 to sow a little more doubt, an association that was disbanded in 2012.

But most clubs need so-called 'educators', all of whom have received training and most of whom do an excellent job with the children.

Originally, most of these federal educators were PE teachers and this was a godsend for the FFT because, thanks to their initial generalist training, these men and women have added value to tennis schools, particularly in their ability to manage groups and introduce new teaching methods.

Some of these instructors have even become CTRs, notably Alain Mourey (Burgundy) and Jean-Claude Marchon (Paris), both of whom have contributed to the development of teaching methods: Alain Mourey was the author of the book *Tennis et pédagogie,* published in 1986, while Jean-Claude Marchon recorded his research into mini tennis in a book entitled *Mini-Tennis, Tennis, Maxi-Tennis*, published the same year.

Two great men to whom we must pay tribute!

I don't think we should abolish this status today, but I do think we need to put safeguards in place and control it better: why not restrict this activity to students, young retirees and/or part-time employees?

I think it's very important to better protect professional teachers (those who hold a state diploma and a professional card issued by the Ministry of Youth and Sport).

Indeed, the current organisation of teaching is reminiscent of the situation before the Open era, when brown amateurism reigned... In short, an unhealthy situation...

Personally, I think that the BEs and other DEs are to some extent responsible for the situation. Most of them are abandoning the beginners/improvement groups, and are only interested in training outside the clubs, three-quarters of which are made up of members - young or adult -whose primary objective is relaxation and leisure.

So haven't the professional teachers left the field wide open for the initiators/AMT/CQP to deal with the majority of club members?

A new body has recently come into being, the Premier service union, created in July 2021 by Clément Griffon, whose aim is to defend the rights of professional teachers, particularly in disputes they may encounter with their employers, the clubs, represented by their chairmen. Affiliated with the CFDT, Premier Service is a genuine union specialising in legal issues and is keen to work hand in hand with the FFT to help teaching professionals better manage the legal disputes they encounter with clubs during their careers.

Premier Service is set to become a key partner for both practising French teachers and foreign coaches wishing to set up in France.

In exchanges I had with its Chairman in April 2022, he said:

"Our role as a social partner affiliated to the CFDT (Confédération Française du Travail) is to ensure compliance with sports legislation, to defend the interests of teachers and to inform our partners of the laws in force.

Few people know this, but the profession of tennis instructor is regulated by the French Sports Code, which came into being in 2004. So it's not a diploma that makes you a sports instructor, but rather the possession of a professional card. And it's quite possible to hold a professional card without actually holding a state diploma (e.g. CQP/AMT).

Finally, it should be noted that it is the government services (via the prefectures) that decide who has the right to work in France, whatever the profession. So, in absolute terms, foreign teachers, whether or not they are nationals of the European Union, could quite easily obtain a professional card and come to work in France, without the FFT being able to object.

For its part, President Moretton's new team has taken an excellent initiative by creating, in March 2021, a representative council of teachers within the federal bodies, but the title given -Conseil National des Enseignants - does not seem to me to be strong enough (what about the notion of Professional?) and, above all, very vague and unrepresentative (almost 45% of its members are women, when we know that only around 15% of professional teachers are of the "weaker" sex...). Don't take this as misogyny on my part, just an observation!

Isn't the purpose of this national council to raise issues relating to teaching rather than the legal problems encountered by teachers?

So why not include all the problems encountered by teachers in the field in a three-way game - FFT/National Teachers' Council/Premier Service union - so that we can work together to find solutions and prevent future conflicts?

There are certainly divergent interests: the FFT is naturally more on the side of its affiliated clubs, represented by the various presidents, while the teachers' council and the Premier Service union would naturally have an interest in supporting each other?

But just as important as the president/teacher pairing within the clubs, I believe it is essential for the federation to have a trio of FFT/National Council of Teachers/Union to be able to implement its policy and ensure that everyone works together.

The pioneering role played by some PE teachers

In this section, we will see the extent to which certain PE teachers have played a decisive role in the development of tennis, its teaching methods aimed at the very young and its spread throughout the country.

These initiatives began well before the official rapprochement between the FFT and the Ministry of Education (1994 agreement signed by President Bîmes and Minister François Bayrou).

At the end of the Second World War, when the French Tennis Federation was short of teachers, it encouraged its good club players to come to Paris for training, so that they could then teach tennis to young people in their clubs on a voluntary basis.

Subsequently, some PE teachers began to take an interest in the sport and in teaching it to young people.

Tennis has always been an essential part of the courses run by the Amicale de l'ENSEPS (Ecole Normale Supérieure d'Education Physique et Sportive), for two reasons:

1. Tennis is seen as a complementary leisure activity that can complement the basic training of PE teachers.

2. Tennis was presented as a way for PE teachers to earn extra income during the school holidays (and it officially became one in 1975 with the creation of the Federal Educator diploma by the federation).

In the summer of 1956, the leaders of the Amicale ENSEPS offered tennis training during their annual course at the CREPS in Montpellier.

In order to register for the tennis course, trainees must "respond positively to any request from the Jeunesse et Sport (Youth and Sport) to run tennis schools at overtime rates", according to one trainee.

Tennis is initially taught in the traditional way by PE teachers, i.e. in accordance with the methods used in federal clubs: the various strokes of the tennis (forehand, backhand, volley, service, smash) are approached separately, using the ideal technical gesture as a model.

But very quickly, these generalist teachers moved away from the principles of federal teaching to focus on the very essence of tennis: the game of ball, which enables pupils to assimilate the notions of partner and opponent, but also to learn to move around in a well-defined space, to run, to jump...

Back in 1963, a certain Louis Dutertre, then a PE teacher in Tananarive (Madagascar) - a nod to my wife - was already wondering why tennis was one of the few sports not played by schoolchildren (*Revue EPS* number 66 of July 1963).

For Professor Dutertre, tennis is a mass sport in that "*girls and boys, adults and veterans can play*".

For him, tennis is an educational sport that promotes the physical development of the individual.

Given that the 'ball on the wall' was one of the very first school sports (training on the wall being the basis of tennis), Professor Dutertre wonders why tennis should be excluded from the school?

Noting that tennis teaching in 1963 was essentially private, Louis Dutertre suggested that PE teachers should be trained to teach tennis: "They already teach all the other sports, so what would be different about tennis?

At the time, the training of future tennis teachers was a cottage industry: apprentice teachers were grouped around a Master Teacher who provided them with training before taking a national examination.

Louis Dutertre mentioned the possibility of ENSEP training future PE teachers in tennis during their 4 years of training, so that they can become good players and good school educators.

An average tennis player, Mr Dutertre was put in charge of a CSIT in Bandol in the Var by the local council, which could not find a tennis teacher. To do this, he decided to divide the 40 students into 3 groups according to age and ability, with lessons on Thursday mornings from 8.30am to midday.

René P. Pelletier's book, _Précis de tennis moderne_ (which we mentioned earlier) served as the theoretical basis for his teaching, using his experience as a PE teacher for the practical part by crossing the skills required in ball and throwing sports, for which he had received training at the Ecole Normale Supérieure.

Relations between PE teachers and the various sports federations, including the FFLT, were rather good because PE was still under the authority of the Ministry of Youth and Sport (this will no longer be the case from 1981, when they will be attached to the Ministry of National Education). But there has always been this difference, which consists of saying that the federations train while the Ministry of Sport executives initiate.

As far as the Tennis Federation was concerned, it was not until the 1970s that we saw the beginnings of collaboration between the two bodies: Gil de Kermadec and Jean Paul Loth for the Federation, and Gilbert Omnes, Bernard Pinon, Alain Mourey and Jean Claude Marchon for the Ministry of Education, who played a very important role in the development of tennis in France.

We find traces of this rapprochement in the archives of the EPS journals (numbers 104, 110, 121, 131 and 136) published between 1970 and 1975.

It was PE teachers who were the first to succeed in transforming the sport of tennis, with its strong focus on technique and movement, into a playful activity by developing what has come to be known as situation-based teaching.

From the early 1970s onwards, PE teachers believed that technique, high-level sport and children did not go together, and that receptive methods did not allow pupils to discover, invent and create. They wanted a new kind of education and were interested in so-called active teaching methods.

To achieve this, we had to find ways of simplifying the sport, both because of the lack of tennis courts and because PE teachers themselves felt that the approach was too technical. These same teachers were quick to point out the flaws in the model pedagogy set out in the famous French teaching method, notably through a certain Bernard Pinon, then a professor at the University of Paris Lacretelle, in a dossier published in issues 131 (January-February 1975) and 132 (March-April 1975) of the magazine EPS and entitled

Teaching or enabling learning? Réflexions sur la pédagogie du tennis:

"Kept out of school, ignored by PE teachers (with rare exceptions), tennis teaching could only be taken in hand by former players whose level of practice allowed them to be considered competent".

The implication here, according to him, is that a good player does not necessarily make a good teacher!

It is symptomatic to note that in France, the only two 'teaching methods' were decreed by federations (Ski and Tennis) that trained teachers in a short space of time, with 'succinct' pedagogical information.

Bernard Pinon raises the problem of the training of professional tennis teachers who, before the 1972 reform, could obtain their diploma after a fortnight's training culminating in a short examination....

But is the avowed aim of unifying teaching from the outside really desirable? For beginners, the model is often, for a time, the teacher's or the expert's execution, but gradually they are led to discover the gesture methods which enable them to make the most of their possibilities. In fact, there can be no "model" movement or sequence, because a behaviour that is effective in one situation may no longer be effective in another".

In his speech, Bernard Pinon spoke of the particular nature of tennis, an open-skills sport that requires a constant ability to adapt: as the player is constantly in a state of uncertainty, he must be able to adjust his response according to the situation.

And for him, teaching by model is more akin to 'training', whereas teaching by simulation is more about adaptability:

"On the one hand, technique is coercion (model pedagogy); on the other, it is adaptive expression". Technique is therefore not primary. It becomes the means chosen to concretely solve a given task.

I think it's very important to stress that Bernard Pinon's comments about the French tennis teaching method published by the FFLT in 1972 are not in any way an indictment of the Federation. Indeed, he is pleased to point out that the FFLT made the following recommendations when the document was published:

"The fundamental principle which should guide the teacher in the choice and order of the exercises he uses (...) is to try to make it easier for the pupils to discover tennis for themselves, so that their progress is not obtained by "training" but is the fruit of successive awareness, the causes and consequences of their motivation".

My friend Éric Bory, sports director of my training club, the Tennis Club de Saint Germain Lès Corbeil, since 1991, has been very familiar with this transition, having himself started taking tennis lessons in 1971 at the age of 10 and having completed a STAPS course between 1979 and 1982.

Eric completed his CAPEPS in 1982 with a dissertation on tennis training, after having had the opportunity to interview some of the best French players of the time, including Régis Brunet, Gilles Moretton, Pascal Portes and Yannick Noah:

"I started in 1971 at the Yerres club in Essonne with a certain Jacqueline Leneuf, whose teaching rigorously followed the principles of the French method: empty strokes, ball-throwing machine fed by the students themselves. And as we were playing on a parquet floor and with extremely hard balls, there was absolutely no possibility of rallies. A real frustration! At the time, no tennis school accepted children under the age of ten because the equipment was totally unsuitable for young players and, as many people wanted to try their hand at tennis and there weren't enough courts, you could only play doubles.

I began to discover another approach to tennis when I entered the STAPS programme at Lacretelle in Paris in 1979.

At the time, tennis wasn't one of the sports options you could choose, but I was lucky enough to have one of my trainers, a certain Bernard Pinon, who took a huge interest in the sport.

He came from an athletics background and when he found out that I played tennis quite well -I was ranked 4/6 at the time - he asked me to come and help him in the summer in Avoriaz, where he was already running tennis courses for the 'children's village' set up by Annie Famose, a former ski champion who had developed a sports course concept (skiing in winter and tennis in summer) based on an Austrian method that aimed to teach through games and role-playing.

So it was with Bernard Pinon that I discovered the "mise en situation" teaching method: the aim was to make the sessions more fun, to add more volume by concentrating less on the technical input and more on the intentions.

There was more of a laissez-faire approach than the ultra-rigid teaching I had experienced in my early days with Jacqueline Leneuf and the French method.

The idea was to give the child a goal and to see how he managed to achieve that goal before giving him any advice whatsoever".

Whereas the federal approach was very formal, very directive and very analytical, the university approach was much more global and uncluttered.

Bernard Pinon, for example, described the forehand as a set of shots played to the right and after the rebound for a right-hander (to the left for a left-hander).

Although he wasn't a specialist in the activity, he managed to make it interesting for beginners".

Bernard Pinon's thoughts and writings have set off a whole movement among PE teachers. They were the first in France to come up with the idea of adapting space, equipment and rules to the morphology of primary school children.

A long process of research and experimentation carried out in particular by Jean Claude Marchon, Christian Rieu and Pierre Larcade - three men from the French education system -was documented in a book published in October 1986 entitled "Mini-tennis, tennis, maxi-tennis". We'll be talking about all this in more detail a little later!

PART FIVE

THE DE KERMADEC / CHATRIER ERA

"There's no question of trying to get everyone to play in the same way. It's about instilling essential knowledge from the outset".

Gil de Kermadec, 1969, as a prelude to the <u>French teaching method</u>

The creation of Tennis de France magazine and the role played by technicoramas

1953 was an important year for the development of tennis in France, with the creation of *Tennis de France* magazine, the first independent monthly devoted exclusively to tennis.

It wasn't until 1976 and the initiative of a certain Jean Couvercelle, then a sports journalist for the daily *France-Soir*, that a second monthly hit the newsstands, the famous *Tennis Magazine,* but more on that later!

It is important to note that *Tennis de France* was created in the same year as the American magazine *World Tennis Magazine*, and that from the outset these two monthly magazines were highly politicised, each with their own objectives:

➢ Philippe Chatrier, the founder of Tennis de France, wanted to open up the Grand Slam tournaments to professionals. Subsequently, Chatrier and his team put all their energy into to making the tournaments accessible to professionals.protect the Roland Garros tournament and make the 4 Grand Slams the mainstay of the tennis season.

➢ promoting and defending the interests of women's tennis for Gladys Heldman (1922 - 2003), the founder of *World Tennis Magazine,* whose daughter Julie was ranked number 5 in 1969. Gladys and her daughter supported the American player Billie Jean King at the end of the 1960s in setting up a parallel circuit to defend the interests of women players ("Virginia Slims" circuit, named after a brand of women's cigarettes belonging to the American Philip Morris group). This circuit became known as the WTA (Women's Tennis Association) in 1973. All this is very well recounted in the film *Battle of the Sexes,* released in 2017.

In France, there had been other magazines covering tennis news before that: such as *Tennis* magazine, which was created in 1910 and became *Tennis et Golf* magazine in 1913, and *Tennis Sports* magazine, which appeared every Thursday between December 1929 and February 1930, followed by other monthly magazines dealing more broadly with all racket sports and all attached to the FFLT, with, in order of appearance, *Tennis and Badminton magazine* (1924-1939), then the *French lawn tennis, badminton, ping ball and table tennis magazine* from 1939 onwards, better known as *Smash magazine.*

Finally, in 1950, the FFLT decided to distance itself from other racquet sports and focus solely on tennis with the launch of *Coup Droit* magazine (December 1950).

This self-proclaimed *"Lawn-tennis Français, revue de diffusion et d'information de caractère général, organe officiel de la FFLT"* (*French lawn tennis magazine for general distribution and information, official organ of the FFLT)* and the magazine's director was none other than René Mathieu (1899-1960 - Chairman of the FFLT's press and propaganda committee) and husband of the champion

Simone Mathieu (1908-1980) - double Roland Garros champion in 1938/1939 - whose name the court, so decried because it was built in the Auteuil greenhouses, bears.

René Mathieu is a man worth taking an interest in. He was a journalist and an accomplished sportsman, and in particular a good badminton player, a sport he knew so well that he became president of the young federation in 1934.

The son of one of the founders of Stade Français, he is a highly influential figure who has some very good friends who are journalists at Le *Figaro* and L'*Auto.*

He contributed to the development of badminton and praised it in the various official magazines of the FFLT, of which he was director.

In the January-February 1943 issue of Smash magazine we read:

"In all the countries where badminton is played, we find that tennis players are often very good badminton players, provided they have the stamina to last twenty minutes of non-stop wrestling, because badminton involves far fewer stops than tennis: the shuttlecock rarely leaves the court surface. it's not a feminine game, nor outdated as I hear here and there".

In fact, Henri Pellizza (1920-2001), French junior tennis champion in 1938 and ranked in the French top 10 in singles for ten consecutive years, was also number one in badminton from 1940 to 1956, never losing a single game to a French player!

René Mathieu wasted no time in presenting badminton as a complementary activity to tennis, mentioning the possibility of transferring learning and pointing out that he wanted to achieve this:

"To draw everyone's attention to this game, which is an education in tennis, a school of volley play, the very volley that our tennis players lack. Tennismen, play badminton!

This information can be found in Julie Grall's excellent doctoral thesis, defended at the University of Rennes II in March 2018 and entitled: *Histoire du badminton en France de la fin du XIXème siècle à 1979, pratiques et représentations (History of badminton in France from the end of the 19th century to 1979, practices and representations).*

A visionary, René Mathieu also understood very early on that badminton could be a preparatory activity for younger players, when he declared in the March-April 1942 issue of *Smash magazine:*

"Thanks to the lightness of the racket - about the same length as the lawn tennis racket - and the shuttlecock, it is possible to get very young children to play without excessive effort and to teach them the essential principles that will make them skilful tennis players when their muscular strength enables them to handle the lawn tennis racket, which is twice as heavy, and to withstand the impact of the ball".

Without really realising it, badminton is presented as a form of tennis suited to children's morphology!

But badminton is also presented as a way for tennis players to keep fit during the winter at a time when indoor tennis courts are in short supply.

As _Smash_ magazine reported _in_ August-September 1950:

"The opening of the badminton season, which coincides with the closure of the outdoor lawn tennis courts, is just around the corner. We advise clubs that don't have covered surfaces for the winter to look for a covered place to play badminton. That way you can keep in touch with your mates and make progress on the volley."

But let's get back to Philippe Chatrier, the founder of the independent monthly _Tennis de_

France! Like René Mathieu, Philippe Chatrier is a professional journalist and a great connoisseur of tennis.

He was an excellent player himself, winning the French junior championship in 1945 and the French number six ranking in 1952, having been selected on several occasions to represent France in the Davis Cup between 1948 and 1950.

But at the time, he was opposed to the federal vision, which he felt did not allow his sport to develop as he would have liked: in 1953, Philippe Chatrier was already a visionary who thought that the Grand Slam tournaments, including Roland Garros, should be opened up to professional players, otherwise tennis would gradually die out...

For its part, the FFLT remained very attached to the principles of amateurism dear to Baron Pierre de Coubertin, and many players chose to join the troops of the American Jack Kramer, himself a former player who became a promoter of professional tours, first in the United States and then in Europe.

The players want to be able to make a living from playing tennis, and Jack Kramer, like Philippe Chatrier, wants tennis to open up and become a universal sport by breaking down the boundaries between 'pro' and 'amateur'.

The status of French players has always been a divisive issue within the FFLT, as far back as 1926, when Suzanne Lenglen decided to move to the United States to play in exhibitions and receive a substantial salary in return.

In a statement, she raised a number of issues:

"Since tennis is a lifetime's work, if we have to spend our lives learning to play for nothing, why isn't there a gallery of amateurs watching for nothing?"

So for two years, the French champion was banned from the FFLT, an anomaly for some when you consider how much tennis has gained in popularity across the Atlantic and also on the other side of the Channel, thanks to the French player.

"The aim was not to play tournaments but to organise exhibitions that would allow spectators who were unable to travel to the venues where the major events took place to see in action some of the best players, whose names and exploits they knew from the press but had never had the chance to admire. The players would go to the spectators because the spectators couldn't go to the players".

Jacques Feuillet tells us on page 554 of the excellent book he co-wrote with Henri Cochet and published in 1980 by Editions Stock under the title *Tennis du jeu mondain au sport athlétique.*

These exhibitions were an excellent way of promoting tennis, an objective which is dear to the hearts of the national federations, and in particular the French federation!

But the latter wanted to reap the financial rewards of organising the competitions, and there was no question of paying the players, who were the guarantors of the spectacle! In short, an Ubuesque situation...

This was all the more absurd given that the French federation oscillated between tolerance and intransigence towards its own members and according to its own interests: Lenglen was rehabilitated in 1929 and encouraged in her initiative to open a tennis school in Paris.

The same was true of Henri Cochet, who was reclassified as an amateur in 1942, enabling him to take part in the French Open held every year at Roland Garros during the German occupation and until the Liberation of Paris.

This is the same Cochet who turned 'pro' in 1933, and surfing on his fame, succeeded that same year in getting an international professional match between France and America held at Roland Garros stadium, with the exceptional consent of the lawn tennis federation.

A sort of Laver Cup before its time, with Tilden and Barnes for the USA and Cochet and Plaa for France!

Philippe Chatrier is to set up his own monthly *Tennis de France* magazine in an attempt to impose his own vision of tennis, a sport he wants to develop not only in France but also internationally, a development he believes will involve opening up all tournaments to all players, including professionals.

As soon as the magazine was created, the editor-in-chief decided to cover all the latest international tennis news: amateur tournaments (the four Grand Slam tournaments being the most recognised) and professional tournaments (US Pro, Wembley Pro and French Pro being the most financially endowed).

The magazine is therefore frowned upon by the federal authorities, who are only interested in amateur tennis.

It's an era that's hard to grasp for people like me, who only knew the Open era!

Between 1930 and 1967, the Roland Garros stadium hosted two very different tournaments:

1. The grand slam we all know (reserved for amateurs during the period)

2. The Championnat de France International Professionnel ("French Pro Championships")

It's worth mentioning that this 'French Pro' was organised by the French Tennis Teachers' Association (AFPT), founded by master teacher Martin Plaa in 1929, and that it was open to all French and foreign professional teachers, as well as professional players from all backgrounds!

This French Pro, which did not take place in the 1940s, has seen its last five editions played not at Roland Garros but indoors at the Pierre de Coubertin stadium and on parquet!

Fatally, the federation quickly found itself at odds, which Chatrier did not hesitate to denounce in his magazine.

Very early on, he also turned _Tennis de France into a_ highly technical magazine, enlisting the services of a certain Gil de Kermadec.

The latter, who was passionate about images and cinema and was himself a leading player, having been France's number three in 1954, set about dissecting the moves and movements of the champions using the most sophisticated means available at the time, making them accessible to everyone in the new magazine. And with his Leica camera, he would immortalise, as he had done in the past, the best of the best.

The atmosphere that reigned on the Roland Garros courts from the 1950s to the mid-1980s was like no other.

In 1956, he broke down the service movement of Australian Lewis Hoad into six phases: Start / preparation / loop / rotation / release / strike and adds arrows to analyse and explain the snowshoe's path.

This is recalled in the work of researchers Jean Michel Peter and Caroline Martin, under the title *L'apport des technologies dans l'analyse du mouvement du service en tennis*, published in January 2017 in the journal *Science et motricité.*

And the two researchers affirm: "*de Kermadec's description of Lewis Hoad's service remains fairly close to that developed by the Lenglen method back in 1942*".

Gil de Kermadec's work was one of the first technicoramas and was published in *Tennis de France* magazine n⁰ 40 in August 1956.

He also made a number of films for the federation and set up the FFT's audiovisual department.

The first of these films, entitled *Les bases techniques du tennis (The technical basics of tennis),* was made in 1966 during the French internationals, when Gil de Kermadec asked the players on the court just before the start of their match to assume fixed positions to demonstrate a forehand, a backhand and a serve, all without moving and without a ball.

And every month, in the new issue of *Tennis de France,* readers can discover the techniques of the champions of the day, using highly detailed photographs.

These images are dissected and analysed by the director himself, so won't many practitioners draw inspiration from these models totry and learn the movements and gestures themselves?

The purpose of technicoramas was to allow us to see everything that we couldn't see with the naked eye.

At a time when group lessons were virtually non-existent, not everyone could afford private lessons with a teacher. Alain Moreau, vice-president of the FFT, gives an interesting account in the July 2019 issue *of Tennis Info*:

"*Very quickly, I subscribed to Tennis de France. In that magazine, there was Gil de Kermadec's technicorama, which broke down the different strokes: the forehand, the backhand, the serve. I had a good friend who also played. We made progress together by dissecting the technicoramas! We used to practise our strokes in his room for hours on end.*

Many young people have learnt to play tennis by copying a model: the best player in the club, a champion with whom they identify, ignoring their own style, etc.
!
Even today, mimicry is still very much a part of the game, even if it does present a few risks for young players: it seems difficult and very risky for a young player in training to systematically hit forehands in lasso mode like our friend Rafa before he has solid support and anchoring.

The role of television accelerated the pace of change, particularly during the two-week French Open at Roland Garros, from the late 1970s onwards (the matches were televised live on public channels).

In fact, all the youngsters remember playing their best tennis every year around the time of Roland Garros! For those of us lucky enough to go to Porte d'Auteuil every year to see the players 'in real life' and so 'drink in' their technique, our big game was to come back to the club as quickly as possible to try and reproduce the game of our favourite champions in a real situation.

And often our first ten minutes on the pitch were like a dream: we hit the ball perfectly because our brains had recorded all the images and were able to retranscribe them to us, even if only for a very short time...

Above is a technicorama by Gil de Kermadec, illustrating the smash after the rebound. You'll recognise German champion Steffi Graf

I think it's important to stress that although Philippe Chatrier became President of the French Tennis Federation in 1973, he never tried to turn *Tennis de France* into an antechamber of the federation - quite the opposite.

At the very time when the French teaching method is coming out, the monthly magazine shows a certain open-mindedness, as technical sections that do not necessarily go in the direction of the method are written each month by teachers and/or professional players with very different visions. And the magazine doesn't shy away from discussing how teaching is done abroad.

From June 1974 onwards, Éric Loliée, a teacher at the CASG (Club Athlétique de la Société Générale) Jean Bouin, wrote a column entitled: La technique américaine d'apprentissage rapide.

Éric Loliée, who has closely examined American techniques during his stays in the United States, informs the reader each month of the recommendations made across the Atlantic, always using photo montages, rather like technicoramas:

"Although there is no national method in the United States, the systematic search for simplicity of gesture has ultimately created a unity of teaching" we read in the preamble.

Tennis de France also never hesitates to go and meet the champions of the day to get technical advice for its readers. And the magazine never hesitates to mention technical works published abroad, in the interests of keeping its readers informed, whether they are professionals, amateurs or amateur players.

So, even though its founder became president of the federation in 1973 (he remained president for twenty years, holding the posts of president of the French federation and president of the international tennis federation for fourteen years, from 1977 to 1991), the monthly magazine cannot beconsidered a stakeholder.

1968: a saving grace for tennis in France, the "May 68" of Tennis International

Few people are aware of this, but the tournament and the Roland Garros stadium were threatened for a time and owed their salvation to the initiative of Philippe Chatrier, then a member of the French Lawn Tennis Federation.

The latter is doing its utmost to open up the competition to professional players, with the sole aim of ensuring the tournament's continued existence.

The 1966 edition of the French internationals attracted just 25,000 spectators, while in the same year South African Owen Williams, director of the professional tournament in Johannesburg, succeeded in attracting more than 62,000 spectators over the course of his event, something that Chatrier is sure to appreciate.

Owen Williams is an important figure in world tennis. A former South African player born in 1931, he is considered to have been the first full-time tournament director when he took over the organisation of the US Open in 1969.

And he did a great deal to promote the universalisation of tennis, encouraging the arrival and participation of the Afro-American player Arthur Ashe in the Johannesburg tournament in 1973, at the height of the apartheid policy.

In particular, he helped Arthur Ashe to create a foundation to make tennis accessible to black children in South Africa (Black Tennis Foundation), a foundation that he personally supported.

The keys to Owen Williams' success in organising his tournaments are quite simple: he takes advantage of the event to create an exhibition for advertisers (village), in return for a site and therefore visibility.

In this way, the brands agreed to pay a fee to the organiser, who in turn managed to attract a large number of spectators by charging affordable rates: people came to see some very fine tennis played by the best pros and at the same time to discover new products... A visionary, then, who was later hired (1981) by Lamar Hunt as General Manager of the WCT!

At the same time, the Roland Garros tournament was increasingly abandoned by the public, who were tired of not seeing the best players who had turned professional... The tennis world of the time was divided in two: on the one hand, there were the professional players - who did not all have the same status - and, on the other, there were the players who were not professionals.

They are divided into players under contract to promoters, 'independent' or 'itinerant' players and 'teaching' players - who compete in the biggest cities and in front of large crowds for ever-higher fees - and amateur players, who are the only ones with access to Grand Slam tournaments, for the prestige and a few dollars in bribes ('brown amateurism' ....).

In short, it was a completely unhealthy situation that Philippe Chatrier and his colleagues put an end to in March 1968 at a General Meeting of the International Tennis Federation, when they succeeded in getting a vote to open twelve tournaments to all players, amateurs and professionals alike! As a result, the 1968 Roland Garros was the first Grand Slam tournament open to 'professional' players.

The final pitted the two best Australian players of the time, Rod Laver and Ken Rosewall, against each other, the latter winning brilliantly.

The events of May 68 also had a lasting impact on the Roland Garros tournament and helped to popularise tennis in France: students on strike were passionate about tennis, not hesitating to cross the gates to enjoy the spectacle offered by these players magnificently dressed in white.

Even though ticket sales were virtually nil that year (due to the revolution, people entered Roland without paying their ticket because "it is forbidden to forbid"), 1968 marked a turning point at Porte d'Auteuil and a new era began for the FFLT.

Chatrier, president and guardian of the French internationals

As soon as he was appointed head of the FFT in 1973, Philippe Chatrier, an inflexible president and a great defender of his Grand Slam tournament, did not hesitate to launch an arm wrestle with the American Lamar Hunt and his right-hand man, the Welshman Mike Davies, who were both trying to organise a circuit for the best players on the fringes of the international federation:

"We are the guardians of a heritage that we have no right to abandon to the pimps of sport," warned Chatrier as soon as he took up his post.

By 'guardians of a heritage', Chatrier is asserting the precedence of the four Grand Slam tournaments and the Davis Cup over the other competitions, or rather exhibitions, that are springing up here and there. Promoters grouped together in an organisation called the WTT (World Tennis Team) have in fact created intervals across the Atlantic and decided to sell franchises to major American cities in order to organise mixed team matches there, every year between the beginning of May and the end of August.

Chatrier rightly saw this as a threat to the future of the Paris Grand Slam, which at the time did not enjoy the same prestige as it does today...

In fact, in 1972, when he was still only vice-president of the French Tennis Federation, Chatrier was forced to accept that the tournament that year would be sponsored by a brand of beauty products - Vanaos, a subsidiary of L'Oréal - in exchange for the princely sum of 522,000 francs. In a crime of lèse-majesté, the 1972 event was even called the Vanaos French Open! But Chatrier never wanted to perpetuate this 'naming', and the decision was taken above all to save the federation's finances at a time when the tournament was still finding its feet!

It was a time when most tennis was still played on natural grass, so the very best players of the moment were reluctant to come and play in Paris, on a clay court that required time to adapt and where their game, built around the serve-volley, suddenly lost its effectiveness ...! As a result, the President used _Tennis de France_ magazine _for_ political ends, not hesitating to have articles written that took a swipe at the Intervilles:

"Tennis de France does not publish and will certainly never publish the results of the American Intercity Championship. Have wrestling results ever appeared in a judo magazine?" This was the response given by the magazine's editors in October 1974 to a reader who was surprised not to find in _Tennis de France_ the results of Intervilles, where great champions such as the American Connors and the Australians Newcombe and Goolagong play.

"As we have seen many times before, Intercities is not only a sports show that makes a mockery of tennis, but also a direct attack on the major European season, which runs from May to July.

July" explains Paul Haedens in his editorial published in October 1974 (cf. _Tennis de France_ number 258)

As a result, President Chatrier was inflexible with all the big names who signed contracts with the WTT: all of them were banned from taking part in the 'French' in the 1970s.

Borg in 1977 and Chris Evert-Lloyd between 1976 and 1978 - to mention only the most charismatic champions - will not be able to take part in the French internationals.

Philippe Chatrier's intransigence may well have cost the American Jimmy Connors a calendar Grand Slam, as he was excluded in 1974 and subsequently decided to skip the tournament. And the exclusion of Connors encouraged the emergence, that year, of the first great star of world tennis in the person of the Swede Bjorn Borg, who won his first Grand Slam title, at just eighteen years of age and to everyone's surprise!

But Chatrier eventually won his arm wrestle with the tournament organisers and by the dawn of the eighties, all the top male and female players would be at Porte d'Auteuil, and not just for shopping!

However, it is worth remembering the very important and pioneering role played by Lamar Hunt and Mike Davies, because if top-level tennis is what it is today, it owes a great deal to these two men who took strong and courageous decisions at a time when international bodies were still very rigid:

1. Adoption of the tie-break, created by a certain Jimmy Van Alen (1902-1991) in 1965 and adopted for the first time in a Grand Slam match at the 1970 US Open (played in nine points with sudden death at four points all round in its original format, which had the particularity of being able to give both players a match point simultaneously)!

2. Adoption of coloured balls (first orange then yellow) to make the game more visible on television

3. Installation of chairs for the players with a compulsory 90-second break every odd-numbered game (in order to be able to broadcast advertising spots, a source of additional revenue).

4. Application of the 30-second rule between points to ensure continuity of play (and put an end to the antics of Romanian player Ilie Nastase)

All this is formidably well recounted by my colleague Chris Davies (son of Mike, executive director of the WCT, and therefore Lamar Hunt's right-hand man) in his book *Balles neuves* published in April 2019 and which I have already mentioned previously.

It's worth remembering that the American Jimmy Van Alen, who first came up with the idea of shortening matches by introducing the tie break, was above all a lover of tennis, the game and its history.

It was this man who created the International Tennis Hall of Fame Museum in Newport in 1954 (on the very spot where the first tennis court was built in the United States) and who donated it to the US Tennis Association.

Once accused of distorting the counting system in tennis, we must pay a heartfelt tribute to Jimmy Van Alen for what he has done both for the continued existence of the game and for the duty of remembrance of the champions, and also of all those who have made tennis history (272 people from some thirty nations have been inducted into the Hall of Fame to date)!

But let's get back to our president Chatrier, who, by approaching the head of the sports department of what was then known as ORTF (Office de Radiodiffusion Télévision Française), managed to get French Open matches broadcast live on television from 1974 onwards.

Chatrier's stroke of genius was that these broadcasts brought tennis into people's homes and very quickly made it the leading individual sport in France.

What's more, it will boost the budget of the FFT, which, in addition to ticket sales, will now be able to collect TV rights and sign increasingly lucrative advertising contracts every year! It's worth remembering that it was BNP (the longest-standing sponsor of our Grand Slam, after Lacoste, which has been involved in the tournament since 1971) that helped finance the construction of the boxes on centre court back in 1973. More than 50 years later, BNP is still one of the main sponsor of the tournament!

And what about the Perrier company, sponsor since 1978, and its famous bucket hat that we've all worn, less for its sexy side than to protect us from the sun when we could sit on the centre court or the annexes for hours on end to admire our champions!

From the mid-1970s onwards, and still today, the Roland Garros tournament has been a key part of baccalauréat revision and exam preparation for all students in France, whether they're laymen or not!

Roland Garros became the annual sporting event not to be missed on television, in the same way as the Tour de France cycling race - the Grande Boucle - and the French quickly became passionate about the little ball that had turned yellow in the meantime, with Sweden's Bjorn Borg - the Nadal of the time - and his revolutionary technique: excessive top spin and two-handed backhands being no strangers to the game....

When Chatrier became President of the International Tennis Federation in 1977, he set about unifying professional tennis and bringing the parallel circuits to heel.

He also worked for the reintroduction of tennis to the Olympic programme, which was achieved in Seoul in 1988.

Philippe Chatrier's vision is to be applauded: while the prestige of the Roland Garros tournament is well established today, the same was not always true in the past, and Chatrier's actions were decisive.

And then it was Chatrier who revolutionised team training in France by remaining very open to what was being done in the dominant countries of the time, led by the United States and Australia:

"He was good friends with the American players Tony Trabert (1930-2021) and Donald Dell and asked them to come and look after the best young French players when we were on tour," Jacques Thamin, a Wimbledon Junior finalist in 1969 and 137th in the ATP rankings, told me.

"And he ended up getting the agreement of Australian John Newcombe, who signed up with the FFLT for two years in 1969! I have fond memories of him because he followed me to Wimbledon when he was playing in the main draw, and it was really a great learning experience for me to be able to get advice from a great champion like him!"

It was also our President who contributed to the universalisation of tennis.

By getting our sport back into the Olympic Games, he has helped to develop the sport both in the emerging countries of South America, Asia and North Africa, and in the new nations (particularly those that have emerged from the dismantling of the former USSR and the break-up of the Yugoslav republic).

With governments giving priority to supporting sports on the Olympic programme, the Olympic Games have become a showcase for all nations, and tennis is set to benefit greatly from this...!

So I don't agree with those who would like to rename our centre court the "Rafael Nadal court", even though I have a great deal of respect for our Spanish friend, a formidable ambassador for clay-court tennis with his stratospheric record at Porte d'Auteuil, boasting fourteen singles titles and 112 matches won since his first appearance in 2005. Why not have an 'allée Rafa Nadal', but frankly, renaming the Philippe Chatrier court would be tantamount to erasing our memory?

The history of our sport and our stadium belongs to us!

The French teaching method (1972)

It was conceived and thought out in 1963 by one and the same man, Gil de Kermadec (1922-2011), whom we have already mentioned, when he became the Federation's first National Technical Director.

And it was the arrival at the federation of a new management team made up of former players (the trio of Marcel Bernard - president -, Philippe Chatrier and Robert Abdesselam - both vice-presidents) in 1969 that enabled de Kermadec to set up a plan to renovate French tennis. This renovation plan has two main focuses:

1. Putting each person in the most effective place
    → Chatrier will be in charge of the French teams
    → Abdesselam in charge of international issues

2. Create a teaching method similar to that used by the ski federation
   → The work must be collective and no competent personality should be left out of the equation

Although he was a PE teacher and a top-ranked player, de Kermadec never taught tennis or even coached.

He was a pure theorist with a passion for images and photographs of movement, and by 1969 he already had a database of over 10,000 negatives representing all the greatest champions to have played Roland Garros since 1953.

So he came up with the idea of using his materials to support the recommendations made by technical and educational experts, as the executives of the French Ski Federation had done before him as early as 1956 (*Source, George Joubert, <u>Ski technique moderne,</u> 1956*).

From 1969 onwards, all practising tennis teachers (just over four hundred nationwide) were asked to put forward their suggestions.

The following year, in 1970, de Kermadec organised two seminars:

→ An educational seminar attended by twelve PE teachers
→ A technical seminar attended by the main master teachers, including Estrabeau, Stolpa, Tissot and many others.

The method is therefore the fruit of four years of intensive work (1969-1972) during which Mr de Kermadec approached the technicians of the time to draw up a teaching document, the primary aim of which was to agree on the stages of learning and the use of a common vocabulary for all teachers.

It's a bit like what the executives of the French ski federation did, particularly a certain Georges Joubert, who said of his method:

"There has been talk in recent years of the possibility of generalising a training technique, in a way internationalising skiing. It's not normal for a tourist or holidaymaker to be given different advice depending on whether he's taking ski lessons in France, Italy or Austria [...] each country is jealous of its own methods, and it's difficult to reach an agreement with a view to unification. There is, however, a common ground: teaching is based on a synthesis of what the best competitive skiers are doing at the time and this teaching evolves according to these references [...] In our ambitions to codify, so to speak, ski teaching, between the fundamental concern not to separate ski touring from ski racing, we are moving towards simplification and efficiency [...] one champion will simply go faster than the other, will undoubtedly have a different style, but the base will be identical. Incidentally, the problems posed by ski teaching can be compared to those of other sports, such as tennis and swimming, where pupils have been taught false and useless movements for decades [...].

From 1952 to 1955, Jean Vuarnet played a decisive role in the efforts we made at Grenoble University to develop a teaching method. Today, we are the only organisation in the world capable of offering the complete alphabet of skiing, from base to summit (Sources, <u>Le Monde</u>, 13 February 1970, comments collected by François Jannin from Georges Joubert about his book <u>Ski technique moderne</u>, published in 1956).

So we can say that the DTN wanted to follow the example of the ski federation.

The aim of the French method is to unify the fundamental teaching of tennis and to broaden the pool of beginners by encouraging the development of group teaching.

The aim was to modernise the Lenglen method, which had also attempted to provide basic instruction, as mentioned above.

In an article published on 24 July 1971 in the national daily <u>Le Monde,</u> de Kermadec warned on the eve of the method's release:

"There's *no question of trying to get everyone to play in the same way. It's about instilling essential knowledge from the outset. It's agreed to limit the number of blanks, to get everyone playing straight away so that they can enjoy the fun of the game, bearing in mind that on the other side of the net there's a partner to whom you're throwing the ball, not an opponent to be beaten*".

As we shall see, Gil de Kermadec's starting point will soon be shattered...

For those who have never had the chance to consult this document, it is very precise and extremely detailed, with many drawings and photos.

When it came out in 1972, this book was intended to be a support tool for all teachers (it was republished in 1978) and very quickly fulfilled its role, especially in helping affiliated clubs to set up their tennis schools, which would enable them to welcome more players.

From the mid-1970s onwards, clubs needed to organise their activities (demand was outstripping supply!) and the method was going to help them do just that!

This method is organised around four main headings:

1. Organisation of t h e tennis school (levels, operation, structure, tests, equipment)

2. Suggested exercises (to develop <u>fundamental skills</u> - attitude, balance, dissociation, coordination - <u>control of trajectories -</u> juggling, throwing, catching - to develop <u>control of the</u> <u>racket -</u> gripping and juggling - <u>control of movements -</u> movements with blanks, with a fixed ball, with a presented ball, with a thrown ball, on the wall, with a ball-throwing machine -<u>control of game situations</u> and <u>corrective </u>procedures for each shot).

3. Tactical principles: when to do what, where to play

4. Technical principles: the theory is explained for each shot with the help of drawings, and practice is studied using technicoramas of the champions, including the Australians (Emerson, Rosewall, Laver and Roche).

On the technical side, the experts who worked on the French method chose to draw inspiration from the players they considered to be the most technically accomplished for each of the different shots:

★   Ken Rosewall (Australia) → waiting forehand, waiting backhand

★   Rod Laver (Australia) → approach with carioca steps, flat serve

★   Tony Roche (Australia) → volleyed forehand from half-court

★   Roy Emerson (Australia) → backhand volley mid-court

★   Andrés Gimeno (Spain) → slice forehand, uphill in stride

★   Pancho Gonzales (USA) → backhand volley, flat serve, jump smash

★   Jan Kodes (Czechoslovakia) → top spin forehand, top spin and slice backhand

Note that return of service is not covered in the method, which is somewhat surprising.!

As for "holding the racket with both hands", this is presented as a shortcoming, a fault that we advise you to watch out for:

"It is therefore advisable: not to teach it systematically; to choose equipment that is appropriate for the child (racket with a light head, handle that is not too big, etc.). It should be noted that children who tend to play with both hands are often the most gifted, as they frequently play against older opponents without having enough strength to control a ball that is too fast with just one hand. We must therefore avoid letting them play in conditions that are too uneven.

At the time of the method's release, the Australians had already been dominating tennis for many years. Although they played little on clay, the Aussies had won Roland Garros ten times, with seven different players, between 1953 and 1969. And over the same period, they won the Davis Cup final twelve times, missing out on the last step only once, in 1969!

The Australians are home to many champions, including Ken Rosewall, Lewis Hoad, Mervyn Rose (1930-2017), Rod Laver, Roy Emerson, Fred Stolle, Tony Roche... and all observers, whether sharp-eyed or not, envy their technique.

Given that de Kermadec made his first films during the French Open and from 1966 onwards, it is fair to assume that he was so influenced by the Australian players that he used them as models for his method.

If Kodes and Gimeno (1937-2019) are also featured in the 'practical theory' section, it is almost certainly because they won at Porte d'Auteuil on the eve of the method's release (in 1970 and 1971 for the Czechoslovak player, in 1972 for the Iberian).

As for Pancho Gonzales (1928-1995), de Kermadec could not fail to make him a role model. After turning professional in 1949, he was unable to play at Roland Garros but was considered the best professional player between 1952 and 1961.

From the outset, the method, even if it is intended to evolve, is based above all on the pedagogy of the model!

The problem is that Ken Rosewall, Rod Laver and all their acolytes (note that there is absolutely no mention of women) come from a country where sport, or rather sports, are practised from an early age, which means that Australian players are very early on, accomplished athletes, highly coordinated and capable of adapting very quickly to any situation.

In an interview with me in March 2022, Trevor Allan, a Franco-Australian who taught at CSM Tennis Marseille for many years, explained:

"I was born in the suburbs of Sydney in 1955 and, like all young Australians, I started by swimming. In those days, all young people in my country had to be able to swim 50 metres before they could play other sports. After that, of course, I played rugby, football, cricket and, of course, tennis. My father was a very good tennis player himself, but he never put himself in the position of coach. I started out with a woman, there were twelve of us on the court and the sessions consisted of blank strokes and hitting fixed balls. Of course, there were returns with ball boys, rather like those that were done in France at the same time? Naturally I hit my backhands with both hands, perhaps because I was playing cricket? In any case, I took up tennis seriously at the age of thirteen, before that I played all sports for fun. Contrary to popular belief, we didn't just play on natural grass, but also on a surface that I think was unique to us, which consisted of termite mounds (see illustration below). These courts were very common in the Australian outback. It's a surface that's similar to clay in terms of sliding and bounce, but it's still faster. It was Ken Rosewall who suggested that I abandon my two-handed backhand when I was sixteen or seventeen and opt for a more direct preparation, which I did very quickly. I think I had a very solid foundation in Australia, even if it was when I arrived in France that my tennis really took shape, thanks in particular to the advice of Monsieur Stolpa. He had a very good eye and strengthened my backhand by advising me to turn my shoulders earlier and accentuate my follow-through. Later, I trained with his group and made it up to the first series in 1980 at the age of 25!

I played on the professional circuit for a few years before moving to Marseille, where Mr Stolpa offered me the chance to replace him as coach, an offer I naturally accepted!

Above, a termite mound, and on the right, the Bundaberg Tennis Club courts in Queensland (Australia).

Based on Trevor's comments, I can say that the French method was inspired by the Australian models, while overlooking the fact that the sporting culture of young French men and women is still much weaker than that of our Australian friends, for a number of reasons, in my opinion:

→ The school timetable does not allow you to take part in sport
→ Attitudes at the time did not yet attach any importance to sporting activities
→ When young French people do sport, they engage in just one activity
→ Sports infrastructure in France in the 1970s was still very poor, whether at municipal level, in schools and/or within clubs.
→ The capricious weather in most of mainland France means that sports cannot be enjoyed all year round, as is possible in Australia.

During the winter, most of France's top players give up tennis in favour of team sports (football, basketball, handball, hockey) to keep fit.

And with the spread of the French method, they abandoned badminton, which was considered to be 'harmful' because wrist play was considered too important and in opposition to racket gripping techniques, which recommended a firm wrist. Times are changing...

Knowing that the work of Gil de Kermadec and his advisers was bound to follow the evolution of the game, the fact of taking the best players of the time as a starting point should not have been a problem, but certain members of his entourage appropriated the method to make it a universal dogma, which had the effect of creating a split between the old master teachers who were very attached to individual lessons, The younger teachers, represented by Jean Paul Loth and Georges Deniau, were more interested in developing the practice and therefore in group lessons, a source of greater income.

But this battle between 'old' and 'new', 'elitists' and 'egalitarians' or 'craftsmen' and 'industrialists' seemed to have been lost in advance to the last-mentioned: isn't the aim of every sports federation to increase its membership?

As we have already seen, we are still very attached to model teaching, to the "beautiful player", to "playing beautifully", to "clean technique", to beautiful gestures, and the French teaching method will be impregnated with this typically Franco-French tendency!

In the sixties and seventies, in France, the focus was more on the manner than the result, not just in tennis but in all sports: in cycling, Poulidor, the eternal runner-up is more appreciated than the champions of his time, first Anquetil and then later Eddy Merckx…

In fact, Yannick Noah himself confirmed this trend in comments made several years after his victory at Roland Garros:

"I couldn't stand this loser attitude any more, we're good, we lose and then we're happy all the same".

But let's get back to the method, a teaching document that was bound to evolve in line with new developments in the game of tennis, but which unfortunately was taken at face value from the moment it came out, in 1972, not only by the teachers themselves but also by a large number of federal officials at the time, who made it their 'bible'.

The document confirms the idea that tennis was considered to be a highly technical sport, and the conception of the game was also very strict at the time: the gestural part of the game was predominant, if not exclusive, and the question of whether the game could be played differently was not asked…

Some teachers, notably Alfred Etrabeau, were very opposed to the single style and the single grip, even accepting the use of the two-handed backhand, but they were soon marginalised by the federation.

This meant that the BE candidates had to unlearn their forehand (even if it was effective) in order to be able to demonstrate the "federal" forehand during thedemonstration test, as Gérard Valentin confirmed to us earlier!

This was the perverse effect of the French Method, because it led several generations of players and teachers down a path that they would not necessarily have taken naturally, and even if it has to be acknowledged that the application of the method enabled tennis to develop by facilitating collective learning, it left a certain number of players who did not meet the criteria by the wayside…

In the November 1974 issue of <u>Tennis de France </u>magazine, Joseph Stolpa, a master teacher of Hungarian origin (who coached, among others, the French number one Françoise Dürr and some of the best French players of the time), working in Marseille, declared:

"The first hold that beginners are generally taught is the shake-hand hold, also known as the hammer hold. This grip, which I personally prefer to call the waiting grip, is taught to you in order to execute a straight punch. In my opinion, this is a serious mistake.

Joseph Stolpa, who first met Françoise Durr in Oran (Algeria) in 1958 and remained her sole coach for the rest of her career, did try to change her unorthodox grip (see illustration), as Françoise Durr confirmed to me in an interview in April 2020:

"Joseph became my coach when I was fifteen or sixteen. I already had my own game, with my bloody backhand grip, which he tried to change by putting plaster around my hand and the racket handle, but to no avail. So he tried to understand my game a bit, to improve what I could do. My backhand along the line was my best shot, even though my grip was a bit strange! He gave me a lot of serenity and motivation.

This example confirms that one of the great qualities required of a coach is the ability to adapt. It's better to be pragmatic than too rigid.

And it has to be said that Joseph Stolpa got the best out of the Frenchwoman (winner of the women's singles at Roland Garros in 1967, world number three in singles the same year and world number one in doubles in 1969).

Opposite, France's Françoise Dürr and her famous backhand catch

It's also worth looking at the comments made by the Anglo-Saxon experts at the time about Ms Durr's setback to see just how different the approaches are between France and the United States, where pragmatism is the order of the day!

In the book entitled '*Strokes & strategies*', published in New York in 1976, which is a compilation of advice collected between 1972 and 1975 in the very serious *Tennis Magazine US,* we read the following in an article written by the Australian player John Alexander (number 8 in the world in 1975):

"Many top players compensate for their unorthodox grips by developing their own skills (e.g. Connors, Goolagong). The strangest grip of all is that of the Frenchwoman Françoise Durr, who uses an eastern forehand grip for all her shots. Although her wrist and elbow remain below the racket, her backhand

is extremely effective despite a very strange-looking grip [...] but she moves and positions herself particularly well, sets very early and always manages to keep the ball very close to her."

Remember that the term "forehand" literally translates as "front of the hand" whereas "backhand" means "back of the hand", so it is perhaps more obvious to Anglo-Saxons that they need to change their racket grip, as the forehand and backhand are played with the opposite sides of the hand: palm against back!

Very early on, some teachers opposed the method, in particular a certain François Lacaze, who believed that the single grip recommended in the method would in no way enable the player to develop an effective forehand:

"For a right-handed player, theright shoulder attachment is behind the body on the forehand and in front of the body on the backhand, so a change of grip is essential.

This same François will try to alert the DTN to this point:

"Our masters have lost their heads, all the ingredients are present in the method for a bad forehand" he said, but he was not heard, as he was criticised for wanting to call everything into question...

Convinced of his convictions, he undertook in-depth research into the racket grips of various champions from the greatest tennis nations at different times:

"I began my research in 1973 by going several times a week to the French National Library, which was next door to my home in Versailles. All the tennis magazines from all over the world were available for consultation, so I didn't hesitate to make photocopies of articles that seemed interesting to me in order to build up a very rich and well-documented file. I came to the conclusion that all the federations, and not just the FFT, have been wrong in their approach throughout the ages," he told me in an interview in February 2022.

François Lacaze will show that racket grips have evolved over time, along with the equipment (balls/rackets/strings) and playing surfaces.

And he will highlight the most effective and least effective forehands for all eras, concluding very early on that the FFT's choice of method is not the most judicious!

Talking to Gail Lovera, who is Australian by birth and whose father, Ross Sheriff, was one of Australia's top ten players before becoming a coach, she explained:

"I started playing tennis on my own at the age of nine and when I picked up the racket for the first time, I put my hand flat on the handle, which naturally gave me a western forehand grip. My father never intervened to change my grip because it allowed me to give a lot of top spin with my forehand, which very quickly became my best weapon.

But tomorrow's technology is not necessarily yesterday's or today's!

Young players with "unconventional" techniques and/or two-handed backhands, such as my friend André Toumieu, have also come up against federal intransigence:

"With *your two-handed backhand, you'll never get past the 15/2 ranking*," he was told by a federal official when he was 15 in 1976.

André still climbed to -30, thanks to his coach at the time, Pol Guillemin (1919-1997), a master teacher who firmly believed in his two-handed backhand.

"Maître' Guillemin, as he was known in the Essonne region where he taught for over thirty years at ES Viry-Châtillon, is said to have been one of the first teachers in France to take an interest in teaching the two-handed backhand.

This information was revealed to me by Mme Guillon-Schutze, who knew Pol Guillemin well when she was a boarder at ES Viry-Châtillon, and she added:

"Pol was a very inquisitive teacher; he had taught for a year in the United States (California) before joining ES Viry. As well as being an excellent player - he was ½ finalist in the French tennis teachers' championship - he was an excellent trainer.

He has taken over two hundred and fifty players into the second series.

I remember that he wasn't satisfied with what he was teaching on the forehand, so he asked a physics teacher friend to calculate for him the trajectory of a forehand ball that would have maximum effectiveness with minimum effort.

And some time after receiving his friend's report, Pol's pupils began to have a phenomenal forehand!"

In fact, shortly after the French method was finalised and distributed in 1972, players with a technique that was the opposite of the one set out as a model in the method arrived on the circuit and "cannibalised" a large number of Grand Slam tournaments: Jimmy Connors and Chris Evert with their surgically precise two-handed backhands!

As for Sweden's Bjorn Borg, he shattered the method: open stance and very closed forehand grip, use of the wrist, the hand and therefore the top spin to excess.

He, too, had a hybrid backhand: two-handed preparation and shot, one-handed accompaniment! The backhand was no less destructive, especially for anyone venturing into the net against the Swede!

Between 1974 and 1981, Borg won Roland Garros six times (losing to just one player at the Porte d'Auteuil throughout his career, the Italian Adriano Panatta) and Wimbledon five times in a row (1976-1980), completing three successive Roland Garros/Wimbledon doubles (1978, 1979 and 1980), a major achievement given that at the time there was virtually no transition between the two tournaments and that the English grass was very different from today's, with a very low bounce that did nothing to encourage exchanges from the baseline...!

This anecdote underlines the fact that we must never jump to conclusions or make definitive statements!

So when the "method" was republished in 1978, Gil de Kermadec himself warned in his preface:

"The most serious mistake, and unfortunately also the most common, is to confuse what is said or advised to teachers with what the teachers themselves should say or advise their pupils. For example, the "theoretical technique", which is a fairly strict median technique for the personal use of people in the field, does not necessarily have to be taught to students, at least not at all levels or to all students.

Indeed, a teacher needs to be able to demonstrate a median style, i.e. one that is as far away as possible from all the extremes, so that it can serve as a valid visual example for students of all types.

But the quality of his teaching will be reflected in the way he guides each student to find his or her own personal style, enabling them to make the most of their natural gifts.

And the greater these gifts, the greater the risk that an imposed median technique will be nothing more than a straitjacket resulting in only average - not to say mediocre - exploitation of all his potential".

We have to recognise and acknowledge that the widespread use of the French teaching method has led to a considerable increase in the popularity of tennis across the country: it's the era of blank strokes and fixed ball shots.

It was not uncommon, for example, to be able to accommodate up to twelve pupils per pitch and per teacher!

The method was based on assimilating movements and discipline before being allowed to play a few balls.

It's a bit like swimming, where for a very long time children learnt to breaststroke on their stomachs on a stool!

"A good quarter of an hour of each lesson will be devoted to repeating the 4 main strokes -drive (forehand and backhand), serve, smash and volley - with the pupils moving all over the court. These movements are necessary to embed the strokes in the muscle and also to warm up the child.

Another 15 minutes of the session will see the pupils working on fixed balls or performing specific movements".

The big advantage of the method is that it makes it very easy to create groups: there's no need to worry about the age of the pupils, or even their sex or ability, because there's very little room for play in the sessions and most of the rare balls hit by the pupils are either with the teacher or in front of the ball-throwing machine, which was widely used at the time.

"The method specifies how the teacher should conduct his lessons:

➢ *teach all the tennis strokes in the same lesson*

➢ *review every shot, from the blank demonstration to hitting a moving ball, in every lesson*

➢ *first teach shoulder orientation and preparation to the right and left at the back of the court*

➢ *plan written or oral assignments asking students to describe the previous week's lesson"*

The French method helped to accelerate the spread of tennis in France from the early 1970s, and in that respect alone it has been extremely useful!

But it must also be acknowledged that in terms of technical contribution, it has had perverse effects, symbolised in particular by the success of DDL...

This plastic support - better known as the 'fix finger' - bears the initials of its three designers, Deniau, Delage and Loth, and was designed to ensure that all pupils could use the 'correct grip', i.e. the official grip. For many years, it was believed that there could only be one racket grip and not several...

In an article entitled "*Tennis and me*" published in the January 1984 issue of *Tennis Magazine*, the artist Hervé Cristiani (1947-2014), himself a former hopeful and tennis enthusiast who made short films during the French internationals, warned :

"What if this style of play that was imposed on everyone wasn't the absolute rule? Today the single technique seems almost monstrous, but at the time it was an almost compulsory fashion."

It has to be said that the method has had perverse effects: by trying to make everyone play in the same way (remember that this was not what Mr de Kermadec was aiming for), we have wiped the slate clean.

However, the history of our sport is very rich in terms of technique. As early as the 1930s, some players innovated by hitting their backhand with both hands with great efficiency, notably two Australians:

1. Vivian McGrath (1916-1978) Australian singles winner in 1937 and quarter-finalist at Roland Garros in 1935

2. John Bromwich (1918-1999), twice singles winner in Australia (1939 and 1946).

McGrath was one of the first players to hit all his shots with both hands on both sides, which could be explained by the fact that he played both cricket and tennis for a long time!

In France, as far back as the 1960s, it was said that a player who played with both hands on both sides had no future in tennis.

The case of a certain François Pierson is fairly symptomatic, as although he won the Critérium (French second series championship) in 1968 at the age of 22, he was never promoted to the French first series, as his style of play did not fit in with the standards of the time.

It's a pity, because this man who started out playing hockey managed to make a learning transfer when he took up tennis, and quite successfully at that, but it seems that federal ideology prevailed over reason as far as he was concerned!

In fact, it wasn't until the 1980s in France that two-handed backhands began to flourish in tennis schools and then, quite naturally, in youth tournaments, with the early detection system. Today, we face the opposite problem, so much so that in tennis schools we find it difficult to teach the one-handed backhand, a stroke that takes much longer to become effective but which offers those who master it perfectly a much more complete range.

This finding is perhaps linked to the fact that it is less easy for a child to support the racket with the opposite hand on models that are certainly lighter than before but all have a double stick, which makes itmore difficult to spread the fingers at the heart of the racket.

On the left, master teacher Jacques Malosse gives his pupil instructions on gripping the racket and arm position: on the right, young girls practising backhands on a fixed ball (a ball held in place by stretchers). The two photos were taken at Coubertin during sessions of the Cours Montana in October 1966 and February 1967.

Above, an illustration showing young boys hitting backhands on a fixed ball during a guided session using the French method. Jacques Malosse was a member of the steering group that devised the method with the National Technical Director, Gil de Kermadec.

Opposite, the grip of the racket according to the French method

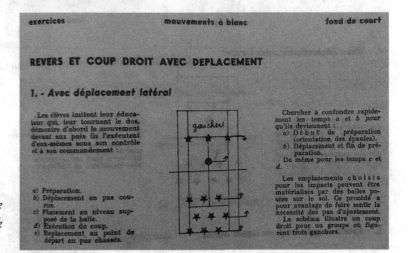

On the right, an extract from the French method, section blank movement exercises

On the left, a number of fixes proposed in response to defects detected on the reverse side.

Tennis Magazine launches a second specialist monthly magazine

As we said, the development of the French teaching method will enable more people to play tennis, as teachers are now able to take on groups that have been trained in group teaching.

As a result, from the mid-1970s onwards, club membership grew, both among adults (men and women) and children.

It was a time when the sports section of the daily press was beginning to take on greater importance, and it was with great foresight, anticipation and lucidity that Mr Jean Couvercelle, then a sports journalist with the newspaper France-Soir (a daily with a circulation of one million), decided to launch a new all-tennis monthly: *Tennis Magazine*, whose first issue came out on 1 April 1976 - and that's no joke!

"I started my career as a sports journalist for the France-Soir newspaper almost during the Open era, taking over from a certain Alain Bernard, a former tennis player from the Musketeers era. I covered rugby, golf and tennis, which I quickly fell in love with, to the point where I wanted to create a new magazine, the one I wanted to read. Having worked for Tennis de France in the past, I naturally told Philippe Chatrier about my project. Above all, I wanted a very friendly magazine with a lot of complicity between the reader and the editorial team. Of course, the early days were difficult because we couldn't sell our magazine inside the Roland Garros stadium, as Tennis de France had exclusive rights there.

From 1976 onwards, tennis became the only individual sport to have two monthly magazines on newsstands, demonstrating the great enthusiasm in France for the little ball that had turned yellow (the first yellow balls arrived on the French market in 1978). And very soon there were even three, with the arrival of the monthly *Le Monde du Tennis* at the very beginning of 1980, bearing witness to the tremendous growth of tennis in France at that time!

Tennis Magazine will further popularise tennis in France at a time when the world professional circuit is still under construction. From the outset, the magazine was aimed more at the general public, with sections that differed from *Tennis de France*, which focused mainly on the big Parisian clubs and social tennis.

Through *Tennis Magazine*, Jean Couvercelle is going to give a voice to as many people as possible: top players as well as amateur players, coaches, tournament directors, club presidents, doctors, etc. But above all, he is going to cover all the latest news in international tennis, which was not always the case in President Chatrier's magazine.

And he doesn't hesitate to invite himself to the homes of the stars of the day (Vitas Gerulaitis, Bjorn Borg, Jimmy Connors, Tracy Austin, Chris Evert...) for interviews, always with a view to popularising tennis and its players.

From 1976, Jean Couvercelle enlisted the services of technician Georges Deniau to write the technical sections:

"I started at the France Soir newspaper with Georges and I noticed straight away that he was a passionate person with an extraordinary eye. It was really Georges who gave me the desire to play tennis myself, which I started a little late at around the age of twenty, twenty-one. So, quite naturally, when I started the magazine, Georges became the technical adviser and he remained so for forty years!

It is important to note that Mr Couvercelle managed to climb to the top of the second series (15 to be precise) by playing very little and without really seeking the advice of a teacher:

"Covering the weekend events, I didn't really have time to take lessons or play many tournaments, so I mainly learned by mimicry, as I was lucky enough to see all the champions play in front of me almost every week".

It will ensure that readers have access to advice from both professional teachers and top players, addressing both beginners and experienced players.

Pierre Barthes, supported by Francis Rawsthorne, as well as Patrice Hagelauer, Yannick Noah and the iconic American coach of the eighties and nineties, the famous Nick Bollettieri, had their say in the magazine.

So it's fair to say that *Tennis Magazine*, like *Tennis de France*, has brought tennis into as many homes as possible, and not just by allowing young teenagers to wallpaper their bedroom walls with the central poster they loved discovering each month!

Well done, Mr Couvercelle.

The 5,000-court operation: a plan to meet the very high demand for tennis practice

Riding on the growing popularity of tennis, the federal authorities, led by President Chatrier, who was also Chairman of the ITF, obtained substantial funding from the public authorities for the construction of tennis courts throughout the country.

Aware of the extent of the needs, the then Minister for Sport, Jean-Pierre Soisson, agreed during a visit to Roland Garros in 1980 to launch a five-year plan to build 5,000 tennis courts in addition to those normally built each year.

This 'Operation 5,000 Courts' will be financed by the FNDS (Fond National de Développement du Sport), a government body recently created to help develop sports infrastructure throughout France.

And aid can only be paid if there is a link between the local authority and the club: the local authority undertakes to sign an agreement with the club for the use of the pitches for a minimum period of fifteen years. The club receives exclusive use of the facilities!

This will make it easier for local authorities to promote club facilities, while the federation's clubs will be responsible for promoting the teaching, running and practice of sport.

Once again, a win-win agreement between the FFT and the French government.

And for the FFT, it's also a way ofconsolidating its power over the clubs and thus gaining a better understanding of the French tennis landscape.

This 5,000-court operation will make it easier for people to play tennis, because soon there will be tennis courts all over the metropolitan area.

It therefore contributed to a steady increase in the number of licence holders until the early 1990s.

PART SIX

TOWARDS EDUCATIONAL EXPERTISE

"I've come to believe that the only knowledge that can influence an individual's behaviour is that which he discovers himself and makes his own".
Carl Rogers (1902-1987) Personal Development, 1968

Motor preferences and the importance of using the free arm: a new approach

At the same time as the French method was being reissued, Odile de Roubin went against the grain by focusing not on the technical gesture but on what she called motor preferences, which for her should be considered as fundamentals.

In her 1983 book, *Le guide du tennis naturel*, Madam de Roubin warns in her introduction:

"If tennis is a difficult sport to play, it's not, contrary to popular belief, because of its complex and meticulous technique. Tennis technique is simple. It's based on a few fundamentals that we'll call the 'basics'.

And she goes even further, saying that the search for the ideal gesture so dear to the French method is futile in her opinion:

"There is no need to struggle to learn the ideal gesture: there isn't one, or rather each one is ideal insofar as it is effective".

Here, Odile de Roubin joins René P. Pelletier, whom we mentioned earlier, in explaining that, like Pelletier, the teacher must first and foremost take account of the individuality of his or her pupil(s):

"There are so many different styles, all equally valid. So which one is best?

So, rather than starting from the gesture, Odile de Roubin suggests staying focused on the fundamentals, i.e. the common points found in all top-level players: movement, positioning, balance when striking, when the ball is taken, strike plan, transfer, etc:

"Rather than a precise forehand or backhand movement, etc., it's the fundamentals that you need to start by acquiring: all tennis movements depend on them".

To achieve this, she explains that learners need to be able to play with their whole body and that teachers need to be able to take into account the physical and psychological characteristics of their pupils.

And she was one of the first to talk about the impact of laterality (eye/foot/hand), of motor preferences, on the way we play: having worked with the Swede Bjorn Borg during his career, she quickly realised that if he played with semi-open or even open support on the forehand, it was above all because he had a right directing eye, which is rather rare for a right-handed player, and so he didn't need to turn to keep his attention on the ball.

Personally, I'm sorry I didn't discover Odile de Roubin's book sooner, and I can only recommend it to all my teaching colleagues, because it's so logical!

When, more than forty years later, Gilles Simon talks about the Federer obsession and the 'federalisation' of minds within the FFT in his book, "*Ce sport qui rend fou : réflexions et amour du jeu*", he is merely denouncing this very risky phenomenon, which for a very long time has consisted of setting up one player as a model: Ken Rosewall in 1972 through the French method, Roger Federer today.

However, like Gilles Simon - whom I don't know but whom I respect immensely as a player -I wouldn't dare denounce this attitude as a uniquely French phenomenon: Here in Hong Kong, where I've been living and teaching since May 2011, many players, especially recreational players, ask me to 'teach' them Federer's forehand after buying their champion's complete outfit, including, of course, the famous 340-gram anvil bearing the no less famous W ('Woman or Man', the Hong Kongers like to ask during the famous 'toss' at the start of the game!) and strung with a luxilon at a prohibitive tension ...!

It is interesting to note that a few years after the release of the French Teaching Method, an American teacher, Dennis Van Der Meer (1933-2019), made the same initial observation as de Kermadec and therefore proposed a "universal" teaching method for the United States by creating the PTR organisation in 1976.

Van Der Meer built his method by focusing more on biomechanics than on the technique itself: we can see a difference in culture here, which we still see today between the French system, which is very attached to technique (form, gesture) and the American system, which is more pragmatic and focused solely on efficiency while respecting each individual's style.

To illustrate this point, it is unlikely that a boy like Jim Courier, whose backhand stroke in particular is more reminiscent of a baseball batter than of our model, would have made a career in France (see illustration on page 116)!

Closer to home, geographically speaking, the Swedish school and its emblematic coach Percy Rosberg has been able to adapt to the personalities of its players, accepting both types of backhand very early on and, above all, not hesitating to juggle between one and the other in order to find the gesture and racket hold that suits each player best.

Stefan Edberg, for example, switched from an inefficient two-handed backhand to a particularly sharp one-handed backhand that proved much more suited to his attacking 'chip and charge' game (see illustration on page 115).

But let's get back to the international organisation called PTR, created by the American coach Van der Meer.

This organisation is little known to teachers and/or future teachers, yet it has been represented in France for twenty-five years now by my colleague Thierry Lamarre.

A former top-level rower (he represented France at the junior world rowing championships in 1976), he discovered tennis by chance during his military service in the Joinville battalion, where he made friends with another top-level sportsman in the battalion, a certain Gilles Moretton, current president of the FFT.

After working as a rowing coach and holding a BEES 2nd degree, he obtained his BEES 1st degree in tennis at the age of thirty in 1987.

He then decided to resign as a rowing coach to teach tennis exclusively at the Compiègne and Noyon (Oise) clubs, and very quickly became interested in the American approach:

"When I looked through the tables of the various Grand Slam tournaments, I noticed that almost 60% of the players in the main draws at the end of the 1980s were American. So, in 1991, I decided to go to the United States to find out more about training methods, and I made my first trip to Florida while I was there.naturally. When I went to the various training camps/academies, I discovered training methods where the physical and mental dimensions were paramount, influenced most certainly by the Australian Hopman".

In 1996, Thierry returned to the United States, to Hilton Head (South Carolina), headquarters of the USPTR:

"I met the founder there and offered to set up a PTR branch in France. He was very attracted by the proposal and, as he had no teaching materials in French, he asked me if I could translate the supporting documents, which of course I agreed to do, although it was a long-term job.

So I stayed there for ten months, with my wife and children, to be able to translate the documents but also to immerse myself in their method, as I was also able to teach at the Van der Meer World Class Tennis during this period".

The PTR France agency was officially opened in 1997 and to date Thierry has trained over a thousand people in the American approach to coaching:

"There are BEs and DEs, but also people who don't hold a state diploma, ranging from club players in the early second series to negative and/or numbered players who have tried their hand on the circuit before turning to teaching. Although not recognised by the FFT, the PTR enables its holders to find jobs abroad, where the diploma is accepted in more than 120 countries. The PTR certification can be used to obtain a work visa as a professional tennis coach in almost any country.

On the left, the very special backhand of American champion Jim Courier, born in 1970 (photo taken in 1984). A two-time winner at Roland Garros in 1991 and 1992, he became world number one in 1992. Above, on the right is that of my friend André Toumieu, born in 1961 (photo taken in 1983 when he was ranked - 30). André never received any support from the federal authorities, which is a shame...!

Opposite, Sweden's Stefan Edberg at the 1980 European Under-18 Championships in France. A few weeks after this competition, he changed his backhand for a one-handed grip. His coach Percy Rosberg wanted to try something new, and he was a great success!

Opposite is an illustration that appeared in Sports Illustrated magazine in 1958 and was then used a second time to illustrate learning transfers in a technical book on tennis (Sports illustrated book of tennis published in 1960).

This illustration shows the similarities between the swing of left-handed American baseball player Ted William (1918-2002) and the backhand swing of American tennis player Donald Budge (1915-2000), the first player to win the calendar grand slam (1938).

Sources: William F. Talbert & Bruce S. Old, Stroke production in the game of tennis, USA, 1971

Two photos that illustrate the learning transfers that can be made between baseball and tennis, two sports where the throwing movements are similar, even if the tools are different: bat or racket, the same battle for the German player Sabine Lisicki or the American player Jim Courier!

To return to the French method, it was curiously by moving away from it at the start of the 1990s that top-level French tennis regained its pedigree with, in particular, the emergence on the international scene of the new 'Musketeers' (Simon, Gasquet, Tsonga, Monfils), who had been put on the map by the previous generation (Pioline, Grosjean, Clément), whose technique on the right-hand side was closer to the American model (use of more closed grips, enabling you to hit harder and create more spin, in particular by mobilising the following three segments: forearm/wrist/hand): forearm/wrist/hand).

But it's also because the French method has brought thousands of young people into the game that we've been able to train tennis players capable of competing with the best again, as in the days of the Musketeers.

In the wake of Odile de Roubin's study of motor preferences, mentioned above, I would also like to make a special mention of my friend Didier Masson, a teacher-trainer whose work, published in 1984, on the role of the free arm (and/or the opposite hand) has proved subtle and particularly useful, as it concerns all practitioners, whatever theirlevel, technique and/or style.

Like Odile de Roubin, Didier focused on one particular element, and was the first teacher to devote a book to it: the free arm.

And he's going to come up with a summary that is, I believe, very timely and full of common sense: it's in the detail that the difference is made.

The central point of his demonstration is that the free arm should help to relax the forearm muscles between shots: if the free arm is used incorrectly, the dominant hand (the one holding the racket) will tense up and the blood supply will be interrupted, leading to aches, cramps, pain, lack of flexibility and fatigue.

Didier will show, with pictures and demonstrations, that :

→   The free hand helps with the grip change.
→   The free hand guides the racket for preparations (forehand, backhand).
→   At the net, the free arm makes it possible when the player is in the waiting position to maintain the orientation of the racket screen perpendicular to the ground.
→   On the backhand, the free hand must be used to mask bunted balls.
→   When serving, the free arm helps to place the ball correctly and maintainbody balance.
→   In the smash, the free arm helps with the cocked position, fixing the ball and guiding it as it descends quite naturally in the direction of the shot played.

And, of course, Didier Masson does not overlook the two-handed backhand, which he considers to be a stroke in its own right:

"Historically, the two-handed backhand is not new; it has always existed. Although there has been a lot of talk about whether or not it should be used, it cannot be neglected in tennis instruction."

In conclusion, it has to be said that between its development in the early seventies and the early nineties, the French method swept all before it.

The result is a stereotyped technique, centred on a model that takes no account of the specific characteristics of each individual.

In my opinion, the work of Odile de Roubin and Didier Masson in particular could have been taken into consideration a little earlier, as they constituted a very interesting addition to the method, but to no avail!

At present, my colleague Pierre Garnier, based in La Roche sur Yon (Vendée), is the reference on motor preferences, a theme on which he offers training courses. I would urge anyone who is interested to get in touch with Pierre, whose expertise in this field is well established.

The reform of the BE and the 1984 law: towards more professional teaching and better regulation

The first reform of the brevet d'Etat took place in 1972, with the creation of a core curriculum common to all disciplines.

Our BE Tennis retains its three different degrees corresponding to the three titles: instructor, teacher and master teacher, but future candidates will now have to pass two groups of tests to be able to obtain their BEES and be officially recognised as a professional teacher:

1. a core syllabus common to all sports, and this is what's new (knowledge of anatomy, physiology, biomechanics and psychology)

2. a tennis-specific exam (a demonstration test, an individual session and a group session with adults and/or children, a written test and an oral).

And as soon as this reform was introduced, the FFT showed itself to be very intransigent, including with regard to foreign coaches: the case of Sever Dron, a member of the Romanian Davis Cup team in the 1970s, confirms this.

Although he had graduated from the Bucharest Sports Institute after four years of study and had been a professional tennis coach for several years, Sever, who was granted political asylum in France in 1972, was obliged to pass his BE in order to be able to teach here:

"The training I received in Romania was extremely specialised, because for four years we learned about physiology, the biomechanics of strokes, anatomy, motor skills and muscle chains. In short, as in all the Soviet bloc countries at the time, sports trainers received comprehensive training.

But even though I was a graduate of the Bucharest Sports Institute and had several years' experience as a tennis coach in my home country, my qualifications and experience were of no value to the FFT, so I had to pass the BE1 exam to be able to work legally for the Melun club (Seine et Marne, Paris League), which immediately took me under its wing.

After a three-week training course at a centre in Montpellier, I graduated in October 1972. The examiners included Jean Paul Loth, Georges Deniau and Jacques Dorfmann. And my partner for the demonstration test was Pierre Darmon, former French number one. Two years after obtaining my BE1 (instructor's qualification), I obtained my BE2 (teaching qualification)".

Sever Dron went on to work with Henri Leconte and Julie Halard-Decugis (ranked number one in the world in doubles in 2000), before opening his own private clinic in Ris Orangis in the Essonne region of France.

A lot of people will claim to be professional teachers, even though they only hold the specific BE1 exam. And this situation is going to create a lot of tension and jealousy with teachers who have validated both groups of tests.

The FFT didn't pay too much attention at first, too busy riding the wave of the great tennis boom of the early 1980s!

The case of player-teacher-coach Trevor Allen, an Australian who arrived in France in 1974, is very unusual, as he explained to me in an interview in March 2022:

"I came with 2 Australian friends to play tournaments on French Riviera and never left. I met Mr Stolpa, a master teacher in Marseille. He gave me some very good advice, which enabled me to move up to the first French series. I went on to play on the circuit and then, in the mid-1980s, Mr Stolpa asked me to replace him, which I of course accepted. Not being a BE and of Australian nationality, it was very difficult for me to regularise my situation. I tried several times to take the diploma, but each time at the last moment I was told that there were administrative problems with foreign coaches, without knowing which ones? In the end, I was able to benefit from the FFT's high-level training programme in 2000, the year I became a state-certified coach, even though I had been teaching at club level full-time for over fifteen years.

But very quickly, regulations were needed, especially as the problem of federal educators, who also had a troubled status, arose in parallel with these BEs that were not completely validated...

127

In 1984, there were 16,099 federal instructors (first or second level) compared with 2,176 state-qualified instructors, i.e. one professional teacher for just over seven "volunteers", which considerably weakened the profession...

The famous law of 1984 strengthened the system by stipulating that *"no-one may teach physical and sporting activities for remuneration (...) unless they hold a diploma attesting to their qualifications and aptitude for these functions. This diploma is a French diploma defined and issued, or issued by equivalence, by the State".*

In 1986, "only" 12,089 federal instructors were listed by the FFT, compared with 2,641 state-qualified instructors (one for every four and a half).

The FFT took advantage of the 1984 law to redefine the 3 levels: the instructor was designated as a general teacher, the professor was defined as a coach and the master-professor as an expert researcher, a title that was used less and less and eventually disappeared.

But with the 1984 law, the aim of which was to protect BEs, the problem arose of the status of Federal Educators, whose title of "educator" led to confusion.

This will put many clubs at odds with the Ministry of Youth and Sports on the one hand and the Ministry of Labour on the other...

The 1992 law will govern the field of action of these instructors, who will hold a federal diploma issued by the leagues after training, the content of which will vary from one league to another.

It has to be said that, at present, nothing is clear-cut in the landscape of tennis teaching in France and it is difficult to set the cursor on the professionalisation of teaching.

And what about teachers from the European Union who have qualifications in their country of origin and who, in my opinion, should be allowed to teach in France without having to take the DE course?

On the one hand, we are allowing 'non-professional' teachers to work as professionals, while on the other, we are blocking teachers from the European Union, even though they have qualifications!

It has to be said that European harmonization will still not be complete by 2025, but will it ever be?

The structure of the BEES was maintained until June 2008, when it was renamed the Diplôme d'Etat Jeunesse, Education Populaire et Sports (DEJEPS), with only two levels: DE and DES.

The development of tennis camps and the influence of Australian training methods

Two men with very different profiles were behind the establishment of the first tennis camps in France in the early 1970s: Georges Deniau and Pierre Barthes.

Georges Deniau was already an experienced trainer when, in 1973, he launched the eponymous courses in France at two separate locations: Flaine (a resort in Haute Savoie) and Hauts de Nimes.

Coach of the French Davis Cup team from 1969 to 1972, his skills as a teacher and coach are well established, and it was President Chatrier himself who suggested that he organise camps for young people and adults.

Philippe Chatrier sees this as an excellent opportunity to accelerate the development of the sport in France.

Pierre Barthes, meanwhile, will be relying more on his status as French number 1.

Having chosen to turn professional at a very early stage in his career, he met all the great champions of the day and, thanks in particular to his travels to Australia and the United States, was introduced to different training methods that were not widely used in France at the time.

He moved to Cap d'Agde somewhat by chance in 1972-1973, where he set up a 'tennis camp' that soon became the first tennis training centre in Europe: the Club Pierre Barthes.

But let's take a look at the history of this tennis centre, because it's a rather unusual story!

In 1962, General de Gaulle himself decided to turn part of Languedoc-Roussillon into a 'French Florida'. He was convinced that France's economic future lay in its tourist potential. But Pierre Barthès's grandmother, who owned land between the sea and the pine forest in the commune of Agde, absolutely did not want to be expropriated by the State.

She's saving them for her grandson Pierre!

"She kind of forced my hand", Pierre Barthès later said, adding:

"If I could have chosen a place for a tennis camp, I would have done it in the Paris region... But they came looking for me".

In 1966, while on a professional tour and playing an exhibition match in the Béziers arenas against the rising star of the day, Australian Rod Laver, the town's mayor suggested that he build a few courts not far from there, in Cap d'Agde, at the same time as building the future tourist resort.

Pierre Barthes agreed, and the Cap d'Agde tennis centre was inaugurated in July 1973.

Pierre Barthes, who was more of a tennis player than a teacher, had the foresight to enlist the services of a real coach in the person of the South African Francis Rawstorne, who was technical director of his centre for fifteen years.

It is important to note that it was the Australians who first developed tennis camps back in the 1960s, when their players dominated the amateur circuit and fed the professional circuit every year.

But why Australians? There are many reasons:

1. As a continent blessed with vast open spaces, tennis courts have sprung up very quickly.

2. A particularly favourable climate, allowing outdoor sports to be played almost all year round, particularly lawn tennis.

3. Young people educated on the British model, with a strong emphasis on sport (Australia is a member of the Commonwealth)

In a report broadcast on 20 June 1962 on RTF (Radiodiffusion Télévision Française) as part of the programme Les coulisses de l'exploit, with commentary by a certain Thierry Roland (1937-2012), who needs no introduction, we can see how one of the most famous Australian coaches of the time, Vic Edwards (1909-1984), operates with all his pupils (young people aged between twelve and seventeen) in the western suburbs of Sydney.

A blend of the Lenglen and French methods:

1. Twenty young people on a court performing blanks shown by coach Edwards

2. Workshops where you hit fixed balls hanging from gallows

3. Playing on the wall

4. And Vic Edwards explains:

"I make sure that the player is able to centre the ball perfectly on the brackets before moving on to the next stage, which is to successfully return the ball using the ball thrower. Only the most gifted players will be able to take part in the inter-school cups, mixed competitions played with 4 players over 6 matches (4 singles and 2 doubles). Individual work will then be carried out on each player, without forgetting to improve their physical condition. The tournaments will do the rest, meaning that a natural selection will take place. Only one in ten thousand of them will be able to claim a career, the others will remain club players".

The report shows that tennis was a very popular sport in Australia in the early 1960s. And unlike in France, everyone played and it was very easy and cheap to join the many clubs where you could improve your game every day.

Tennis is a religion here. And it's interesting to note that one of the players featured in the report, described as one of Vic's best, hits all her backhands with both hands!

In fact, it was these same Australians who exported their model of tennis camps to the United States, with Harry Hopman leading the way in 1969, followed by Vic Edwards in 1972.

And it was on theother side of theAtlantic that the Hopman method came to the fore for many years. It's a training method that gives free rein to technique and focuses on the physical aspect and discipline, both of which are central to the game:

"I am in favour of a change of grip and the freedom to develop one's own style, but I am adamant about physical commitment and discipline" (cf. Harry Hopman, *Better Tennis*, 1972).

Georges Deniau and Pierre Barthes were the first in Europe to draw inspiration from the Australian model, a few years before the opening of the famous Bollettieri Academy in Florida (1978).

They both benefited from Philippe Chatrier's foresight and support at a time when tennis still needed to become more popular in France.

As I write these lines, it is important to emphasise that after two decades of suffering (1996-2016), the Cap d'Agde site is back in the limelight with a new brand: the French Touch Tennis Academy, represented in particular by Charles Auffray, to whom I can only wish success.

In the meantime, other private tennis centres have sprung up, notably Patrice Hagelauer's Sophia Country Club, created in 1984 on the Sophia Antipolis site (Alpes Maritimes), a veritable 'tennis Mecca' in France in the 1980s.

All of France's greatest tennis champions have played here and used the facilities to train, either regularly or occasionally: it has to be said that the weather in this southern part of France favours outdoor play!

After passing through the hands of the Contet/Lambert tandem between 1990 and 1996 (Team Daniel Contet, created in 1977), the site was taken over by Charles Auffray and Régis Lavergne between 1998 and 2015 (ISP Academy) with one of the objectives, which was very innovative at the time, being to place young French players in American universities by offering them training in 2 areas: tennis training and preparation for the TOEFL (test of English foreign language).

After playing sixteen Davis Cup matches between 1961 and 1969, the late Daniel Contet (1943-2018) was one of the very first teachers to set up a private Tennis-Etudes programme with placements in American universities (1998) as part of his eponymous Team, which was founded in 1977.

To do this, he has drawn on several generations of great players he has worked with during his career, not hesitating to take advice from American, Australian and Czech coaches, proposing a method that respects the balance of life: education (behaviour), studies (success) and tennis (performance).

Taken over by Patrick Mouratoglou in 2015 when he chose to move his academy from Thiverval (Yvelines, south-west of Paris) to the Côte d'Azur, the Sophia-Antipolis site is now known as the Mouratoglou Tennis Academy.

It has always been a great pleasure for me and my wife to go there every year since the summer of 2015 and the start of our collaboration with the management as the official representative for the Hong Kong market through the company we set up in 2014, Sehenoland Ltd.

To date, all the Hong Kong residents we've sent to Patrick's house have come back delighted with their stay!

It has to be said that the atmosphere and ambience that reigns here is one that encourages emulation at all times, whatever the level or profile of the trainees!

France, which is not, in principle, a country of 'academies' (unlike our Spanish neighbour), is seeing more and more initiatives flourish, so it seems to me that the FFT cannot ignore the phenomenon any longer, even if former president Bernard Giudicelli never hid his desire for a rapprochement!

However, in my opinion, and quite rightly so, he was more concerned with renovating the Roland Garros stadium, an issue of particular priority for the French Tennis Federation, which has been battling with the public authorities for many years.

President Giudicelli will always be remembered as the man who won the arm wrestle and successfully modernised our stadium.

He also succeeded in making Roland Garros an internationally recognised brand and, above all, a Grand Slam tournament par excellence at a time when the status of the Parisian major was beginning to be seriously threatened.

I realised this right here, when I arrived in Hong Kong in May 2011, because when I spoke to my young students about the Roland Garros tournament, they didn't know what it was, or rather they did, but for them it was the 'French Open'.

Today, they're all talking to me about Roland Garros!

This change in mentality is to the credit of the Jean Gachassin/Bernard Giudicelli duo, who have both managed to ride the wave of Li Na, the first Chinese player to win a Grand Slam singles title at Porte d'Auteuil (2011).

In 2012, the French Grand Slam launched the "Roland Garros in Beijing" operation, as explained in the article "Land of China", published in the *Roland Garros 2019 Magazine*:

"During the fortnight, the Chinese capital will vibrate to the rhythm of clay courts, giant screens and activities of all kinds, all set up in a replica of the famous Village, right in the middle of the city's biggest shopping centre, The Place".

In September 2015, the federal authorities even decided to recruit an official Roland Garros brand representative for China, a territory that currently has nearly twenty million regular players and represents a very large market for the Roland Garros brand.

And the gamble seems to have paid off, as confirmed by Argentine Carlos Rodriguez, who has been based in Beijing since 2012 (ex-coach of Belgium's Justin Henin, a three-time winner at the Porte d'Auteuil, as well as China's Li Na, with whom he won the Australian Open in 2014):

"The special magic of Roland Garros works very well with the Chinese; they love clay courts and the Paris Grand Slam is the tournament with the greatest reputation here".

So I think we should pay tribute to them for this initiative, because even if the Covid pandemic has put a brake on all this during three years, the fact remains that the FFT is one step ahead of its competitors!

It's up to President Moretton's team to take up the baton and usher in a new era by agreeing to collaborate with the various private structures that currently dot the region, in an agreement that I believe can only be a win-win situation!

All in Academy, Elite Tennis Center, Tennis Club Hauts de Nimes, Mouratoglou Tennis Academy, and I'm forgetting some, aren't all these private structures working for the good of French tennis and allowing the French system to shine internationally, thereby serving the interests of the FFT?

More on this later.

The training wall: the most important teaching tool

For several generations of French and foreign players alike, the wall was the first training partner, the only way to learn to play at a time when not only were tennis courts scarce, but so were teachers, and access to clubs, where children were not welcome, was reserved for an elite.

In the post-war period, the FFLT also obtained subsidies from the regional and departmental units of the Ministry of Physical Education and Sport for its affiliated clubs to build training facilities, and specified in its official bulletins published every two months :

"We strongly advise all club leaders wishing to build a wall, which is so useful for teaching tennis to young people and for training adults, to apply to their Departmental Director of the Directorate General of Education and Sport for a grant which could cover up to 50% of the expenditure incurred" and to specify that

The *number of players who can train together in front of the wall is naturally determined by its length. A 10 to 12 metre wall easily allows 4 players to practise simultaneously."*

Suzanne Lenglen practised on a wall of exposed stones, the bounces being random, so she was able to develop her eye for detail, her ability to read trajectories, her anticipation and her balance - all essential qualities for a tennis player!

Closer to home, Françoise Dürr and Odile de Roubin have also spent long hours at the wall developing their skills.

Mr Paul Jalabert, born in French Algeria in 1928, told me a few years ago that he had learned to play on the wall and that he had never taken a single tennis lesson during his entire career (he was ranked in the French first series and played in the final draw of Roland Garros 17 times between 1946 and 1966, after having been French Junior Champion in 1946) - another era!

In the seventies and eighties, it was still very difficult for young people to get access to a tennis court, as these were reserved primarily for adults in affiliated clubs.

So I remember those matches on the wall at my training club, the Tennis Club de St Germain les Corbeil, when I took out my first licence there in June 1982!

Everything could be worked on: consistency from the baseline, of course (alone or with others, with each player hitting his shot one after the other at a pre-drawn target), but also the smash, serve and volley. The 'little shots' were never forgotten, even if it proved difficult to hit decisive drop shots against the wall! The training sessions were

Mixed, U10, U12, U14 and U16, the wall didn't discriminate!

So for a lot of children, the club wall was the main playing area, the place where we could try out new shots, try out new ball effects that we put into practice on the court with our friends as soon as a court became available, even if only for a few minutes. Sometimes we played with 6 players on each side, so we had to elbow each other, but we didn't lack for imagination.

Personally, I think it's important to let children give free rein to their imagination. Getting them to play with each other on a large pitch, allowing them to bounce the ball several times in order to get it back into the opposition's half of the pitch, and observing how they manage seems to me to be an important step in learning, assimilating and understanding the technical fundamentals:

1. Reading trajectory / displacement

2. Timing of ball pick-up / placement

3. Balance / support

4. Strike plan / zones

5. Effects (flat, lifted, cut, sliced)

6. Trajectory (taut or rounded)

7. Replacement

Tennis is above all a dual sport: learning techniques is pointless if they are not linked to the game.

And I do mean techniques, because there is no single way of playing: I often remember my first steps in the activity at the age of 10/11 in the early 1980s at my club in St Germain Les Corbeil: Jacqueline Leneuf, my first teacher, who could have been my grandmother at the time and for whom I've always had a great deal of respect, was very directive and her teaching was not at all open to fantasy: we were forbidden to hit the ball with anything other than our feet in line, and wrist strokes and other racket grips that deviated from the hammer grip were severely punished by Madam Leneuf.

With Jacqueline, it was 'sink or swim', and my two brothers preferred to give up tennis, not accepting to be called 'stupid' even though they both seemed to be, racket in hand, sic!

Moreover, Jacqueline was only interested in children she judged fit for competition, and she had the honesty to shout it loud and clear: recreational tennis wasn't for her, and 'puppets' and other 'clowns' weren't welcome in her class. A different era!

Her selection criteria were physical qualities, determination, commitment and resilience. That's what immediately drew me towards competition and gave me the chance to follow her teaching!

As for me, I was certainly more docile, or at least more passionate, because even if I sometimes came home from the lesson crying, I couldn't help going back, the love of the yellow ball - which was sometimes still white at the time - won out over reason.
!
My colleague Alain Cassaigne, who is now retired and has held just about every conceivable position in French tennis, confirms that the Cochet lessons (the very first group lessons in France, given at the Racing Club de France and following on from the Suzanne Lenglen Schools) were

organised along the same lines: physical tests first, then tennis tests, in order to identify possible future competitors. In this way, teaching, even collective teaching, was always designed with a view to achieving performance.

The focus is first and foremost on the competitor, and much less on the leisure player, the Sunday player, who represents 85% of licence holders...!

Nowadays, training walls have unfortunately disappeared from clubs, but perhaps they are coming back into fashion?

As I write this chapter, in the midst of a worldwide lockdown due to the Covid-19 epidemic, players, professionals and amateurs alike, have no option but to hit the ball against the wall in their basement, against the garage door or even in their hotel room for those who have remained under strict quarantine for the 2021 Australian Open!

Another tool is also making a comeback: the good old Jokari, revived in 2007 under the name 'Planeto' and available in a variety of versions from the big sports brands we all know.

The principle remains the same: you can kick a ball anywhere as long as the ground surface allows the ball attached to the other end of the rubber band to bounce: in your street, in a car park, in your home and/or why not on your terrace!

Although very interesting, this tool has its limits: it's difficult to play with two people, as it only allows forehand and/or backhand shots after the rebound! But when you don't have a choice, as when you're in confinement, it's a tool that has the merit of allowing its user to 'keep the upper hand'.

So the wall was the only way to play tennis and hit balls.

But the wall also has its pernicious effects, as many young players have built their game with unorthodox grips and techniques, which has not prevented some of them from winning Grand Slam tournaments - Françoise Dürr springs to mind. Despite the best efforts of her coach, the famous Joseph Stolpa, who has trained many top players, Françoise told me that he had never managed to change her grips (see illustration). Perhaps it was a blessing in disguise, because rather than focusing on what he had identified as a weakness, he preferred to concentrate on his player's strengths (determination, courage, a very powerful forehand) by regularly setting her targets to achieve.

Gail Sherriff, who started playing tennis on her own in 1954 at the age of 9 in the suburbs of Sydney, Australia, her country of origin, explains that she naturally held her racket in a 'western' forehand grip and that her father (Ross Sherriff, considered to be one of the greatest Australian coaches of the time) let her.

This is a positive effect of the wall: finding your own solutions to a given problem, which is the very essence of the game of tennis!

But let's not kid ourselves either: the youngsters looked at the tennis courts with sparkling eyes and the hope of being able to walk on them, even if only for a few moments, to be able to exchange ideas in a real-life situation.

The FFT and its emblematic president at the time, Philippe Chatrier, were quick to understand this and launched a major campaign: the 5,000 courts operation in 1981, but more on that later.

Before that, in some clubs, it was possible to play on a real court provided you were good enough to be in the first team, which of course wasn't easy...

The softball, "made in France" and a revolution in the teaching approach

1986 was a landmark year in the teaching approach to tennis, seeing the birth of what was then known as the "soft" ball or "mini-tennis" ball, now known internationally as the "orange ball". !).
We must pay a heartfelt tribute to three men who were at the origin of this formidable "revolution" - the word is not too strong, as there were many holdouts at the time, including among the federal executives.

The three men were Jean Claude Marchon (a PE teacher with a background in athletics), Olivier Letort (a young tennis instructor at the time) and Philippe Sautet (a second-series player and Managing Director of Nassau France at the time, who later founded the Nestea Cup national ranking tournament with his half-brother Christophe Lesage).

Jean Claude Marchon (1933-2020), who was CTR of the Paris league at the time, set up mini tennis throughout the schools in the Paris region. We'll see that his work was later taken up by the FFT, which made it its very first federal programme at a time when tennis was losing momentum, but we'll come back to that later.

So Jean Claude and Olivier Letort were looking for a way to develop a ball that, when dropped from a height of 2.54m (ITF standard), would bounce at hip level with five- and six-year-olds.

At the time, it was customary in tennis schools to puncture balls that had already been used, but these were still very heavy for the children and therefore not easy to return...

It was while talking to the late Philippe Sautet, who had already been the French managing director of the South Korean company Nassau for a number of years, and who himself was having the worst difficulty getting his three/four-year-old daughter to play, that our friends decided to work together on developing a new ball that would be easier for youngsters to master! After several attempts, a new tennis ball was born, called a soft ball and then a mini-cool ball: the first mini-tennis ball!

Yellow in colour, the stitching on these balls was sometimes green, red, pink...

So, as Olivier Letort explains, they will very quickly become part of children's imagination, with strawberry balls, mint balls, etc.

At the same time, the Tennis Club de Fontenay aux Roses (Val de Marne, 94) will be starting work on what will be known as progressive tennis. Used on small courts, the mini-tennis ball, which resembles a real tennis ball, allows children aged five or six to hit the ball freely without fear of making a mistake, and to quickly discover sensations similar to those of an experienced adult.

A little later, in 1990, Philippe Sautet had the genius to invent a ball designed both to enable adults to start playing and to make it easier for 'less gifted' teenagers to do so: the cool ball, better known today as the green ball (FFT) or green ball (ITF).

All teachers who worked in clubs in the late 1980s and early 1990s, which is my case, remember the buckets of Cool and Mini-Cool balls from Nassau, which at the time was the only brand to sell these balls and which were widely used in clubs throughout France and the rest of the world.

The Nassau "soft ball", the very first mini-tennis ball, was named a little later,

Mini Cool" balls after the introduction of the intermediate "cool" ball

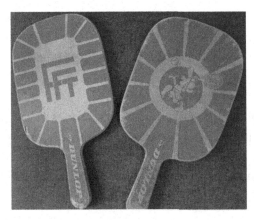

Opposite are the wooden pallets used for mini tennis sessions. The paddles first appeared in Swedish primary schools in the 1970s, and later in our tennis schools.

It should therefore be said that it was French educators who made it possible to open up tennis to a younger audience (5-6 years old with the adoption of the soft ball) but also to convert teenagers and young adults with little experience of the sport with the introduction of the intermediate ball, which is easier to tame when you have no experience. Even today, many clubs that don't have indoor courts are loaned multi-purpose sports halls by their town halls, where the discovery of tennis would not be possible without the use of these slower-moving intermediate balls!

However, it is important to remember that the idea of adapting tennis to be played by as many people as possible was not exclusive to French teachers. Tennis was already being played with wooden pallets in primary schools in Sweden in the 1970s.

This is undoubtedly one of the reasons for the sudden, unexpected and rather surprising rise of Swedish tennis in the 1980s: 18 players in the final draw of the 1987 French internationals, a record that is unlikely to be beaten given that Sweden had a population of just under 8.5 million at the time!

But thirteen of the sixteen finals played between 1974 and 1989 also featured a Swedish player:

➢ Bjorn Borg, 6 finals, 6 titles (1974, 1975, 1978, 1979, 1980, 1981)
➢ Mats Wilander, 5 finals, 3 titles (1982, 1985, 1988)
➢ Mikael Pernfors, 1 final (1986)
➢ Stefan Edberg, 1 final (1989)

By shortening the striking tool, the hand is brought closer to the strike zone, making it easier to distance the ball, tame the bounce and centre the ball.

And then this movement was born in the United States, in the 1960s and 1970s, where the idea of reducing the size of pitches to make the game easier emerged under the impetus of the American Dennis Van der Meer (founder of the PTR organisation in the United States) and the Canadian Peter Burwash (1945-2022), founder in 1975 of Peter Burwash International (PBI).

It's worth pausing for a moment to consider the latter.

The man nicknamed "The FlyingCanadian" started out as an ice hockey professional player before turning to tennis after a terrible accident.

He became Canada's number one player in 1971 and represented his country several times in the Davis Cup at a time when it was very difficult to make a living as a professional tennis player.

Like other players of his era, he did not hesitate to give tennis lessons in the hotels where he stayed and on the sidelines of the tournaments he played in.

And very quickly, he came up with the idea of bringing quality tennis to every corner of the world.

My colleague and friend Éric Thorel, who taught at TC Revel (Midi-Pyrénées league) as a federal educator in the late 1980s, joined the PBI company in 1990 and never left.

Currently based in French Polynesia, he taught for several years at the Hong Kong American Club and of course worked alongside Peter Burwash:

"I took the BE course at the CREPS in Toulouse in 1988, but I couldn't see myself teaching in a club, so I didn't get my diploma. Having always had a taste for travelling, I went to the United States, where I first took the USPTA course, the equivalent of the BE in the USA, before obtaining the Bollettieri diploma, which at the time had a great reputation.

It wasn't long before I heard about the PBI organisation and the opportunity to travel the world while teaching tennis, which fitted in perfectly with my aspirations!

So I contacted Peter and signed my first contract with them in 1990.

Having very quickly put an end to his playing career in 1975 at the age of thirty, Peter had the idea of setting up his own company, the aim of which was to approach luxury hotels to offer quality teaching to all guests.

It was a time when there were few, if any, tennis instructors in these hotels, even though they were equipped with beautiful tennis courts. And in the few places where there were teachers, they weren't any good, so there was no continuity for guests wishing to indulge in their favourite sport during their holidays and/or business trips.

Peter recorded his method in his first book, <u>Tennis for Life,</u> published in 1981, and like all new teachers who join PBI, I took the in-house training course, an intense and very dense 450-hour course over four weeks.

A training programme where interpersonal skills are at least as important as know-how and where the central idea is to adapt teaching to each individual according to his or her needs, an approach that was different at the time from that advocated by the FFT, which is still very attached to model teaching.

Peter's motto was very clear on this point: "looking good doesn't win matches".

Peter Burwash's book <u>Tennis for Life</u>, which Éric refers to, is absolutely remarkable and shows just how avant-garde this teacher/pedagogue was.

In fact, he was behind the creation of a number of programmes that were later taken up by our federation: baby tennis, tennis for the deaf and hard of hearing, for the blind, the physically and mentally disabled, prisoners and delinquents, etc.

The highly pragmatic PBI method is based on the same fundamentals for both forehand and backhand strokes:

1. Striking zone
2. Balance
3. Using the free arm

And he insists on the triple dimension, the triple vision on which all tennis players, whatever their level, must focus their attention, just like anyone driving a private car:

1. The ball
2. The opponent
3. The court/playing area

I remember that after my first driving lesson, my father suddenly seemed like a mutant, able to hold the steering wheel, turn up the volume on his car radio and shift his manual gearbox all while smoking his cigarette and chatting to us!

How was he able to do all this without thinking?

Quite simply because, like any self-respecting motorist, once he was behind the wheel of his car he had a permanent overview of what needed to be done, which was not the case with his racket in hand!

The motor programme takes weeks, months or even years to automate!

In his remarkable book, Peter Burwash warns against the risks of tennis elbow, explaining what can cause it and why (remember that in the early 1980s, people were still playing with wooden rackets weighing around 400 grams...):

➢ Piston" backhand where the thumb is positioned behind the racket handle: the player pushes the ball from the elbow, which becomes the centre of rotation to the detriment of the shoulder.

➢ Hitting straight shots in a hammer grip and/or with your arm straight also puts a lot of strain on the elbow.

➢ Serving with the elbow extended: the biceps and shoulder no longer play their role as shock absorbers, leading to a risk of inflammation of the elbow.

Finally, Peter Burwash doesn't forget to warn about the risks of injury that can affect all practitioners, whatever their level, and here again his recommendations are extremely pertinent.

Wrists, ankles and abdominal muscles are particularly important, he says:

➢ As the wrists connect the racket to the rest of the body, they are particularly important to strengthen.

➢ Ankles are also pronerto injury because they are the joints in direct contact with the ground. So they need to be strong and flexible at the same time.

➢ It's important to strengthen thel abdominal muscles because .all tennismovements are initiated from these muscles (the nave being the centre of gravity)

And as far as physical preparation is concerned, the Canadian Peter Burwash stated as early as 1981:

"To get into shape for tennis, I don't recommend jogging (which was very popular in North America in the late seventies and early eighties)*, but rather shuttle runs in different directions over short distances. As well as skipping rope and playing mini tennis."*

For my part, I can only recommend reading this book, which has been published in eight different languages, including French.

In fact, more than forty years after its publication, the points made in this book are still relevant today and help us to refocus on the basics!

SEVENTH PART

ATTEMPTS TO REVITALISE TENNIS IN FRANCE

"Rather than preparing trainees for an exam, we prefer to train them to take action in their future careers to turn them into passionate instructors, competent coaches and enthusiastic leaders".
Jean Claude Massias on the black folder, November 1997

Federal programmes: a means of building loyalty among members

The king sport of the eighties, tennis went into 'crisis' at the beginning of the nineties, losing more and more members each season to golf, which is becoming more fashionable, particularly among the higher socio-professional categories who always want to stand out more or less.

Interviewed in June 1995, Jean Paul Loth, ex-DTN of the FFT (1977-1989), describes a paradoxical situation:

"Tennis has never been played as much as it is today in France (one million members compared with just 200,000 twenty years earlier in 1975). And the number of non-licensed players is estimated at 4 million, despite the fact that there are 10,000 clubs in operation... The problem is that many of these clubs, around 50%, have no facilities (club house, changing room, toilets, social area).

And among the largest structures, which were the main venues for players in the 1970s, the courts are beginning to age and their renovation is posing budgetary problems...".

For these reasons, some fans see no point in paying an expensive annual subscription fee for a service they consider mediocre.

In fact, even in the heyday of the FFT, in the mid-1980s, there was always a high turnover of members, but the FFT never paid any attention to it: there were always more people coming in than going out!

In my opinion, this turnover could be explained more by the fact that teaching is considered to be too rigid, too difficult and not much fun, so many players who are not naturally predisposed to playing tennis end up giving up, even though the activity remains fashionable! And then perhaps the first ball tests mentioned in the French method back in 1972 didn't do enough to hook children because they were too focused on technique and, above all, too elitist?

In fact, these tests were originally designed first and foremost for detection, or rather selection purposes: in fact, they turn out to be real exams, with each test having a corresponding eliminatory mark!

There are six of them: 1st ball, 2nd ball, 3rd ball, bronze racket, silver racket and finally gold racket. They are supposed to take pupils from the beginners' level to the first classification of the time (30), which will allow holders of the gold racket to have access to 'competition' training.

All teachers are expected to be able to organise these tests in all clubs as stipulated in the method:

"To make them accessible to all educators, the tests, as they have been regulated, require nothing more than a court, balls and rackets".

These tests are designed to test the six qualities that the method's creators believe are essential for good tennis play:

1. Physical qualities

2. Address

3. Technical expertise

4. Knowledge of tennis

5. Team spirit

6. Combativeness

The tests for the 1ˢᵗ, 2ⁿᵈ and 3ʳᵈ balls are organised within the club itself, during the session, with the instructor being the only person in charge, as is currently the case in clubs. This is not the case for racket tests.

These must be examined by a jury, and what a jury it is, since the jury must, in principle, include :

→ The president of the league or committee
→ The regional or departmental director of Youth, Sports and Leisure
→ The CTR
→ The director of the tennis school in question
→ The educator (i.e. the teacher)

Most snowshoe tests are therefore taken at departmental or even regional level. A certificate is issued by the chairman of the jury to successful candidates, entitling them to wear the corresponding badge issued by the FFLT.

These tests therefore left no room for fantasy, as the child had to reproduce the federal model, so there was no possibility of detecting the hidden qualities of the pupil which, in my opinion, should have been a priority objective for the federation, but the mentality of the time was very different...

So, very quickly, these tests are going to have the opposite effect to that intended: how many kids are going to leave tennis schools because they think the assessment system is too restrictive?

Especially at the time of the Ecole des fans programme, broadcast every Sunday on TF1 and during which all the children in the running systematically emerged as winners: *"the children are formidaaaaables [...] under your applause"* liked to remind the presenter of the time, the famous Jacques Martin (1933-2007).

Of course, this is not something that could have been said by the National Technical Delegation!

145

It should be pointed out, however, that these first federal tests were not systematically implemented in all clubs.

Having started tennis in 1982, I never took a single one of these tests, whereas my cousin, who was at a tennis school in Paris at the same time, was very proud to tell me that he'd got his orange ball... Moreover, these tests were more a means of creating homogeneous groups for the teachers than a guarantee of the pupils' know-how!

We now have to react to this downward trend in the number of licence holders, and this is how the federal programmes came into being under the presidency of Christian Bimes (1993-2009) and the impetus of successive national technical directors Daniel Dominguez (1994-1996) and Jean Claude Massias (1996-2005), with a threefold objective:

1. Attracting new members
2. Keeping existing members
3. Improving the framework for practice

And for the first time, the federation is going to take an interest in the well-being of its members in the clubs, by trying toinstil a new dynamism that is less focused on performance than on the enjoyment and conviviality of club members.

Obviously, the federation's primary objectives remain, in order: competition, spotting young talent and developing its membership.

The idea is to adapt tennis to the different categories of players we want to attract, so that tennis comes to the public and not the other way round!

The Mini-Tennis programme in 1994, the Junior Club in 1996, the Adult programme in 1998, as well as grants to clubs to help them build a clubhouse for their members, renovate their playing surface, acquire teaching equipment to make playing easier, and so on.

In short, the 1990s were a time of questioning at federal level, and it has to be said that there were many proposals and actions on the ground: it is the strength of a major federation that it can adapt to changes in society in general and in sport in particular.

And with the introduction of all these programmes, the status of the teacher is going to change somewhat, and in a positive way: whereas the profession had an image of a "dilettante", the tennis instructor is going to become an expert, the person on whom the club is going to have to rely if it wants to develop and open up to new audiences, as we can read in an article in the *Revue STAPS* from spring 2002 entitled *Le jeu de rôle des moniteurs dans les clubs de tennis* (*The role-play of instructors in tennis clubs*)
:

"When, at the beginning of the 1990s, the FFT was faced with a drop in the number of members, it decided to revive the practice of tennis and stepped up its efforts to improve the structure of tennis teaching within clubs. To do this, it created and proposed new projects to clubs... As part of this overall development, instructors became essential cogs in the clubs' operation, as they were the main disseminators of the federal objectives at local level...In order to respond to federal policy guidelines, instructors can no longer be satisfied with simply providing tennis instruction, but must become involved in club life as a whole, combining personal interests, club interests and federal interests... And since the introduction of federal programmes, tennis instructors are seen as experts, on whom the development of clubs depends to a large extent.

And this is how the FFT is creating, whether voluntarily or not, the famous president/teacher pairing that should become the driving force behind clubs.

We will see later that, although they are better trained than their predecessors, vocational teachers will suffer an erosion of their pay and a deterioration in their working conditions, which are now perhaps reaching their peak? It's paradoxical!

But let's now try to go into a little more detail about these programmes, without going into a complete catalogue: Mini-Tennis, Tennis at School, Adult Initiation Centre, Junior Club, To each his own match and, closer to home, Tennis Santé and Baby Tennis are programmes that have fundamentally changed the way tennis is taught, with the common objective of adapting the activity to all audiences.

As a result, tennis was to become *"A sport for everyone"*, as the slogan that appeared in the federation's advertisements during the French Open at the end of the nineties recalls.

And indeed, in the 21st century, tennis is now played by everyone: girls and boys, men and women, working people and retirees, able-bodied and disabled, from the age of three to ninety.

➤ *The Mini-Tennis programme (1994)*

It's important to note that the Americans were the first to try and adapt sports for younger children (basketball, skiing, etc.).

As far as tennis is concerned, didn't Dennis Van der Maer already give exhibitions on small courts and with small rackets back in 1955?

It's true that the idea came to him first but, for once, it was on the other side of the Atlantic, on the Old Continent and more specifically in France, that things really started to happen, and here again it's worth highlighting the driving role played by PE teachers.

In fact, in the 1970s, some of them very quickly saw the advantage of introducing their primary school pupils to tennis and, as great enthusiasts, began to think about how to set up the activity:

reducing the length and width of the playing area, lowering the net, reducing the size of the rackets (wooden pallets), using old balls (pierced and/or punctured) to limit the height of the bounce but also to reduce the risk of accidents, etc.

Pierre Larcade (National Education Pedagogical Adviser, Poissy district in the Yvelines) in an article entitled Mini-Tennis published in Revue EPS number 152 of June 1978, tells us the following:

"You don't have to be a tennis champion to explain to the children that the game consists of passing the ball with the racket over the obstacle, which could be a net, a bench, a string or a bungee jump.

Later, his colleague Gérard Jaquet (Vitry sur Seine district, Val de Marne) stated in the November 1982 issue of EPS magazine, in an article entitled "Le mini-tennis à l'école" ("Mini-tennis at school"):

"Tennis is now the second most popular sport in France after football. The media have made a major contribution to the popularity of a sport that, until recently, was considered expensive and reserved for the elite.

Beyond the passions, the figures and the tremendous commercial stakes represented for some by a sport that has become a consumer commodity, schools cannot remain on the sidelines of a social phenomenon.

The negative aspects of tennis, due to its excesses, are well known: championships, stardom, the collusion of sport and money; but these are not sufficient reasons to deprive children of a rich, enjoyable and motivating physical activity. On the contrary, isn't it an act of education to tackle them in order to denounce them more effectively? With a minimum of equipment and a simple tarmac courtyard, schools can take the initiative.

Initially reluctant, the FFT jumped on the bandwagon, so to speak, taking inspiration from the work of Jean Claude Marchon and his fellow PE teachers to enable its affiliated clubs to broaden their membership base by introducing mini-tennis in all clubs. As a result, we will be able to welcome younger children to all tennis schools: five- and six-year-olds.

It's true that mini-tennis was introduced a few years ago, but without the benefit of federal support.

From 1994 onwards, all clubs were encouraged to open a section for their youngest members.

Subsequently, the federation and clubs began to take an interest in mothers, with the development of introductory tennis centres for adults, particularly women, but we'll talk more about this later.

> *Tennis at school (1994): official democratisation of the sport*

Already encouraged just before the First World War by the federation itself, at a time when it had little control over the clubs, this movement came into its own in the early 1990s,

A number of teachers in the Education Nationale, who were themselves tennis players, were very soon attracted by the idea of getting their pupils to play tennis as part of their PE lessons, and this was already happening in the 1960s. At the time, tennis was seen as a "bourgeois activity" with no place for it in schools. But very quickly, and as we have seen with President Chatrier's initiatives in particular, our sport was democratised in the seventies and eighties and finally became an essential sport for our young people and across all social classes.

Also, the work of JC Marchon, at the time CTR of Paris, and his acolytes Philippe Sautet and Olivier Letort, to make tennis easier to teach, particularly to the youngest players, would later facilitate the rapprochement between the FFT on the one hand and the Ministry of National Education on the other, leading to the signing of a National Agreement between the two parties in 1994: Tennis was now officially included in the programme of physical activities taught in primary schools and, above all, tennis instructors and other teachers were able to visit schools via agreements between town halls, schools and clubs.

I sincerely believe that, more than Yannick Noah's singles victory at Roland Garros in 1983, the French team's success at home against the formidable Americans in the 1991 Davis Cup final helped to facilitate this agreement between the FFT and the Ministry of Education.

This collective victory, fifty-nine years after the famous Musketeers, may well have helped the public authorities to realise that tennis was part of the Republic's sporting and historical heritage, and that as such there was no reason why it should not be taught in schools?

Also, but that's another subject, as I was lucky enough to follow this Davis Cup final live on television (on the channel that was still called FR3) and to have kept indelible memories of it -I was twenty years old in 1991 - I think we have to give a lot of credit to our tennis players who took part in this campaign.

Indeed, as I stated in my BE2 dissertation, defended in June 2005 at the CREPS in Châtenay-Malabry and entitled *En quoi et comment le tennis en milieu scolaire peut-il dynamiser les écoles de tennis?* :

"By winning the Davis Cup against the "untouchable" Americans, Noah's team gave French sport a new lease of life, enabling other disciplines to assert themselves on the world stage, particularly team sports, with numerous continental and world titles at both club and national level (basketball, handball, football, volleyball, etc.)".

It is undeniable that the official introduction of the Tennis in Schools programme has enabled the FFT to revitalise the sport and, above all, to recruit and retain new young members.

➢ *The Junior Club (1996): A new organisation for the tennis school*

The reform was based on a very simple observation: in the majority of clubs affiliated to the FFT, young people have one hour of lessons a week at a fixed time of the week, whereas in other sporting activities they can train several times a week (team sports such as football or basketball, for example), so there is greater flexibility! The original idea behind the Junior Club was to enable children to spend more time at the club, by offering slightly longer sessions (an hour and a half or even two hours) and incorporating a variety of fun activities aimed at developing their motor skills and coordination.

This has led to the development of workshop sessions in clubs, but gradually the tennis session has been transformed into a "fair" with football / hockey workshops, motor skills courses, all without even needing to use the primary object of our practice: the tennis racket!

In the end, the student was no longer playing tennis, or at least was no longer learning anything directly related to the activity...

The Junior Club was revamped in 2006 to better adapt to the activity in which parents enrolled their children, beforebeing completely supplanted by Galaxie Tennis in 2014.

➢ *CIT Adult (1998): for family tennis*

Once again, the idea is to be able to adapt the teaching to different categories of players: sportsmen and women, non-athletes and women, by offering a 'tailor-made' approach. And this has been made possible by the arrival on the market of "cool" balls (our actual green ball). These balls came into being after the mini tennis ball ('soft' ball) and were originally designed to enable players with no motor skills and no previous sporting experience to succeed in making exchanges as soon as they started playing.

I think that many teachers, like me, have also had to deal with the difficulty of getting adults to play in multi-sports gymnasiums lent by town halls to clubs that don't have indoor courts. The 'taraflex' surface, an ultra-fast surface, prevented adult beginners from being able to play even once or twice, so the use of intermediate balls proved to be essential and made it easier to develop introductory tennis centres, particularly for women.

Once again, it will be overhauled in 2005 to incorporate the new game formats (Tennis Evolutif / A Chacun son Match).

➢ *A chacun son Match, Tennis Evolutif (2008)*

After introducing new teaching programmes based on evolutionary pedagogy: widespread use of soft balls (created in 1986) in sessions with young children, then intermediate balls (actual green balls) with teenagers and adults, the FFT looked for a way to gradually bring all newcomers into official competition. Thus was born the "To each his own match" concept.

Noting that official competition is generally too high a level for new players and that most young girls and women are not attracted by official competition, the federal authorities decided to encourage clubs to set up competitions by level of play on adapted courts and with adapted balls.

It's worth remembering that although it was the French who invented softballs and intermediate balls and introduced their widespread use in clubs for teaching purposes, adapted competitions first saw the light of day on the other side of the northern border, in Belgium to be precise, at the end of the 1980s!

My Belgian colleague Philippe Rome, who taught at the Leopold Club in Brussels in the early 1980s, recalls:

"I remember Jean-Pierre Collot (who trained Justine Henin and Olivier Rochus, among others) invited Jean-Claude Marchon to Brussels to present his concept, which was not yet known as mini-tennis.

Jean-Pierre was immediately charmed. For him, it was the future of tennis. So we set up mini-tennis sessions at Leopold at the end of the 1980s, well before the programme was institutionalised in France and extended to all clubs by the FFT.

The French invented the concept, but it was first developed in French-speaking Belgium by Walloon teachers. And very quickly, in 1989, our National Technical Director Jacques Leriche introduced a new experimental format for under-10 interclub competitions: matches were played on an eighteen-metre court with soft balls. Each match consisted of two singles and a double, and the teams had to be mixed. And Jacques, who didn't care about the final result of the matches but wanted above all to see the game being played and the children becoming independent, introduced special rules:

→ *2 points for winning volleys*
→ *Parents gathered in an enclosure*
→ *Ban on discussing arbitration decisions*

The success of this format of play was such that in the summer of 1991, the Association Francophone de Tennis (AFT) made it compulsory to organise individual tournaments and team competitions for under-10s using this format of play in its territory (Brabant/Hainaut/Liège and Namur-Luxembourg).

The Belgians were bold and daring very early on, and their initiatives were soon crowned with success, with the emergence at the highest level of two champions from the same generation and trained in the same way: Justine Henin in the women's event and Olivier Rochus in the boys' event.

➤ *Adapted Tennis (2010)*

The idea here is to enable people with mental and/or psychological disabilities to play tennis. Adapted sport tennis is different from disabled sport tennis in that it works by level of understanding of the rules, unlike disabled sport tennis which works by type of disability.

The FFT's objective here is to be able to welcome a new audience by offering guarantees to each player. From now on, we will adapt the sport to the specific characteristics of the target audience.

➤ *Tennis Health (2017)*

Sport as therapy has become a public health issue in the 2010s and therefore a priority for the Ministry of Sport. The FFT positioned itself very early on in this field by developing its Tennis Sport Santé bien-être programme.

I can't help but give a little nod here to my colleague and friend Benjamin Bouhana, who was one of the first in France to take an interest in this aspect by setting up a very comprehensive programme along these lines back in 2014: Fitennis.

Its programme, based on shadow tennis and postures found in the game, had the advantage of being able to bring all the players together at the same time, whatever their level, because no ball was struck.

This Fitennis programme is in fact an improvement on the famous American-Canadian Cardio-Tennis programme, which had its limitations even though it had some very interesting points: integrated physical preparation based on workshops, but with constraints, particularly in terms of safety...

A BVA study carried out in 2014 revealed that for 25% of tennis players, the main motivation for playing tennis is health and well-being.

For the federation, this is a real development challenge, aimed at recruiting new audiences (women, senior citizens, companies) and improving the loyalty of certain categories of members, particularly non-competitors and women, in the wake of the 'women's school'.

From 2017, the federation is also creating a "Tennis Santé" label, the aim of which is to offer clubs educational programmes aimed at people suffering from certain pathologies: breast, prostate and colon cancer, metabolic diseases (obesity, diabetes) and cardiovascular diseases, the benefits of tennis for these pathologies having been validated by the medical community. Tennis Santé aims to contribute to the physical, mental and social well-being of patients, the three components of the definition of health.

Tennis Sante is all about tennis instructors and doctors working hand in hand.

From a psychological point of view, the fun and friendly aspect of tennis appears to be a decisive factor in improving the condition of patients, who are often undermined by the disease.

And from a physiological point of view, the use of progressive teaching methods, which are already widely used in clubs, makes it possible to introduce adults who are beginners to the sport and who have pathologies that could be contraindicated to practising sport!

However, as I write these lines, this new way of playing tennis is sorely lacking in visibility: although 122 clubs have obtained this label after having trained one or more teachers in this specific activity, it would seem that doctors don't know about it.or, even more embarrassingly, that they are simply unaware of the existence of this new programme?

Communication between leagues, departmental committees, clubs and doctors' surgeries or hospitals is still needed.

➢ *Galaxie Tennis (2015)*

Once again, the tennis school has been reorganised.

This reform, known as the "under twelve reform", is based on the following observation: Every year, tennis schools lose 40% of their young girls and 30% of their young boys. This worries the federation, because even if these losses are partly offset every year by the influx of new members, it notes that it is now in competition with a number of disciplines that are increasingly accessible to younger players (mini-basketball, baby gym, baby swimming, etc.). With Galaxie Tennis, the FFT wants to focus teaching more on the game and the match, whateverthe size of the court the youngster is playing on.

We will also be developing age-group competitions to ensure that everyone has the same chance of success.

In addition, all tennis schools began to cater for the very young with the adoption of the "white" court (lane by lane, without a net and playing with a straw ball): this was the era of "baby tennis".

Galaxie Tennis wants to adapt to the expectations and evolution of society: younger and younger players and fun at all costs. It's right up there with the times!

➤ *From the courtyard to the court (summer 2019)*

A project that began in the Val d'Oise (Paris League) in cooperation with Patrice Lesellier, an educational adviser from the French Ministry of Education specialising in PE.

The idea is to use tennis as an educational tool during school time. A potential support for cross-curricular learning, independent practice in the playground during breaks. Ultimately, the aim is to ensure that school teachers are fully capable of delivering the programme in their own schools, whether in the classroom and/or the playground, even if they've never held a tennis racket in their lives! The programme has 3 main strands: general learning, motor skills and free practice in the playground.

The leagues are putting together a special kit containing all the teaching materials suitable for 3/5 year-olds. Volunteer schoolteachers will be able to attend training sessions in the leagues and committees, racquet in hand, to immerse themselves in the world of the very young. Tennis as an Olympic sport, the history of tennis, the history of the Roland Garros stadium through the tournament posters produced every year since 1980.

In addition to the federal programmes that have helped to revitalise tennis throughout the country and put clubs and, above all, teachers back at the heart of the game, an individual initiative has helped to democratise the game: the Fête le Mur association.

Fête le Mur, when tennis comes to disadvantaged neighbourhoods

Following on from his association *Les Enfants de la Terre,* which he set up with his mother in 1988, Yannick Noah set up the *Fête le Mur* association in 1996 *to* help children from disadvantaged neighbourhoods discover the joys of tennis.

Fête le Mur, an association under the law of 1901, benefited from the Federation's support to officially become the FFT's operator in priority neighbourhoods in May 2017.

The solidarity of the Noah family, who for nearly thirty-five years have been doing their utmost to help children from disadvantaged neighbourhoods find their place in society, deserves a special mention. The Fête le Mur association has embarked on a mission of education and integration through tennis: for over 25 years now, almost 42,000 disadvantaged young people (from 72 towns, 15 regions and 134 priority neighbourhoods) have benefited from free tuition. Each participant is expected to respect the seven values promoted by the association: Respect, Solidarity, Combativeness, Tolerance, Self-esteem, Discipline and Willpower.

Some of these young people have gone on to become club instructors themselves, while others have become referees. In short, it's been a great success, made possible by the essential adaptation of the coaching staff.

Adapting to the environment first of all: the sessions don't necessarily take place on a tennis court, but most of the time on a car park, a lawn, a gymnasium or in the street. And then we had to adapt to the audience and build young people's loyalty by adapting our teaching methods: the need to move, to have fun, to be active, to play, to exercise, to make friends, to get to know others better and to get to know ourselves better!

So today, thanks to all these federal and/or private initiatives, tennis is widely accessible to everyone, whatever their social background. And yet, at the dawn of the 21st century, tennis is once again in crisis, a crisis that could be explained more by changes in consumer society than by a lack of interest in the sport and the activity itself?

The "black book": updated training guidelines

This is a real revolution at federal level: a committee of experts has been set up to work for several months on the production of an educational guide to better reflect club activity: "when to do what and with whom".

This committee, originally composed exclusively of men - parity was not yet on the agenda -(Jean Claude Massias, Bernard Pestre, Dominique Poey, Alain Mourey, Dominique Roy & Alain Kronenberger) was to create a document whose content, divided into seven modules, would serve as a basis for training future professional teachers:

→   Module 1: Mini-tennis, levels 1, 2 and 3 (for children aged 5-6)
→   Module 2: Introduction
→   Module 3: Training
→   Module 4: Management training (leading educational meetings with your team)
→   Module 5: Club development
→   Module 6: Managing your business
→   Module 7: Preparing for the exam

The original idea was to help trainers prepare their trainees for the BE exam, with a dual mission: to help them teach better and to enable them to think about the development of their clubs.

It should be noted that this document was intended solely for the use of BE trainers and FFT managers, leagues and committees. It preceded the creation in 1997 of the FFT's Training and Teaching Department, headed by Bernard Pestre, a department whose role would be to help practising teachers who wished to update their skills, particularly with regard to federal programmes and the use of new teaching methods.

The "black binder" is a very large document, containing over four hundred pages!

It has been regularly updated by the DTN in line with the development of federal programmes and changes in the legal framework.

I would like to mention in particular the only two women to have been involved in this project: Florence Lamoulie, a lawyer, and Nathalie Delaigue, who was responsible for employment management issues.

In its 1999 version, the seven modules covered in the document account for approximately 520 hours of training.

But how was it built,you might ask?

This comprehensive document is based on three areas of teaching modules:

1. Actions
2. Skills/Abilities
3. Theoretical knowledge

Each sector is fed by what the DTN's experts have seen fit to focus on. Every theme is addressed and dealt with, from getting to know the child at his or her various stages of development, to organising a session, respecting the teaching approach, observation, the coach-trainee relationship, the relationship with parents, the use of teaching tools, the technical basics, the tactical basics, programming a tennis school year... in short, nothing is left out, and above all we're starting to talk more about skills than knowledge!

Importantly, links are provided to sources that can help you develop your knowledge (federal documents, videos, bibliography, etc.).

The black folder is a prelude to the DTN's opening up to the outside world, which will be reflected in the organisation of the first national colloquiums, aimed at bringing together all the teachers in France for a day or morning of exchanges.

But little by little, these conferences were to be held less frequently: 4 seasons between the sixth in Lyon (in 2000) and the seventh at the Carpentier stadium in Paris in 2004. The eight took place seventeen years after the seventh, in 2021, but in a brand new Roland Garros stadium, with the participation of many experts in their fields (Olivier Letort Tarek Francis in particular).

These will be supplemented by annual conference reserved for teachers who are members of the Club Fédéral des enseignants professionnels (an organisation set up in 1997).

These mornings of exchange, which will take place every year during the Roland Garros tournament and not far from the stadium, will once again be a way for the DTN to get its messages across to its teachers on themes chosen in advance and based on the federation's primary interests.

Having attended several of these conferences, I have to say that these meetings were very useful and gave me the opportunity to reboost my teaching approach!

Before that, the federation was very inward-looking, which is not always a good thing...

The black binder is also a document that focuses on the training of instructors and will be used by all league managers in the Federal Instructor training sessions.

MODULE 1

Animer le mini-tennis avec des enfants de 5/6 ans

Actions	Savoir-faire/Attitudes	Connaissances théoriques
NIVEAU 1 :		1. De l'opération mini-tennis faite par la FFT, des objectifs du mini-tennis. page 3
<u>Objectifs à atteindre</u> : *Dirige et anime un atelier du mini-tennis*		
- Accueille sur le court un groupe de 4 à 6 enfants.	• Capter l'attention. • Parler simplement.	2. De principes simples de communication avec des enfants et de conseils simples aux parents page 4 Annexe.2a « Principes simples de communication avec des enfants de 5/6 ans » page 5 Annexe 2b « Conseils aux parents »page 7 3. De l'enfant de 5/6 ans. page 8 4. De principes simples d'accueil. page 9 Annexe 4a « Accueil hebdomadaire (à chaque séance » page 10 5. De règles simples de sécurité. page 11 Annexe 5a « Règles de sécurité » page 12
- Assure la sécurité.	• Garantir la sécurité. • Faire respecter les règles de fonctionnement du groupe.	6. Du matériel. page 13
- Utilise un matériel pédagogique adapté.	• Placer le matériel.	7. Des ateliers. page 14 Annexe 7a « Evolution des ateliers du mini-tennis » page 15
- Met en place un atelier et l'anime.	• Mettre en place les différents ateliers. • Dans l'atelier tennis, déterminer et mettre en place les conditions de jeu permettant aux enfants de faire des échanges.	8. De principes simples d'organisation de groupe. page 16 Annexe 8a « Travail en groupe » page 17
	• Animer le groupe avec enthousiasme. • Etre patient, compréhensif et disponible.	

NB : Les numéros dans la 3ème colonne correspondent à la pagination figurant au bas des fiches "connaissances théoriques" qui suivent

Actions	Savoir-faire/Attitudes	Connaissances théoriques
NIVEAU 2 :		
<u>Objectifs à atteindre</u> : *Dirige et organise une séance de mini-tennis*		
- Accueille un groupe de 10/12 enfants et leurs parents.	• Communiquer collectivement et individuellement.	
- Prépare, anime et dirige une séance de mini-tennis.	• S'assurer de la cohérence des ateliers.	1. De la pédagogie spécifique au mini-tennis.
- Met en place des exercices de pré-initiation.	• Choisir les exercices adaptés. • Organiser l'espace et le matériel. • Répartir les rôles.	2. D'exercices simples de pré-initiation.
- Observe, évalue.	• Vérifier les progrès. • Repérer les aptitudes.	3. De moyens simples d'observation et d'évaluation
- Travaille en relation avec un initiateur.	• Organiser le travail en binôme. • Orienter l'action de l'initiateur.	
	• Etre créatif.	

NB : Les numéros dans la 3ème colonne correspondent à la pagination figurant au bas des fiches "connaissances théoriques" qui suivent

Above, one of the 400 pages of the famous black binder, the training reference framework at the end of the 90s.

PART EIGHT

WHAT KIND OF TENNIS FOR 2050, AND HOW SHOULD IT BE TAUGHT?

"The sliced backhand has no place in modern tennis, we have to stop teaching it". Statement by Patrice Dominguez (1950-2015), during his second term as National Technical Director (2005-2009), during a tour of the DTN, visiting the Essonne Tennis League in 2007.

Training bodies: towards a delegation of powers by the FFT and the Ministry

Following the development of the black book (training guidelines) and the development of federal programmes, the FFT will gradually delegate the training of its future teachers to the French Tennis Federation.the regional leagues and departmental committees to train instructors (currently known as AMT or CQP Tennis).

From the early 1990s onwards, training became more professional and new actors appeared on the federal scene: private organisations, whether or not approved by the State, i.e. the Ministry of Youth and Sport (approval will become compulsory from 2000).

Little by little, the leagues are abandoning their efforts to train future teachers and concentrating solely ontraining the best youngsters and retrainingtheir instructors.

As a result, new actors will emerge and gradually take over from the leagues and the CREPS when it comes to training for the BEES Tennis.

In the Paris region, the two main operators are ACTJ, a private organisation which organised its first training courses in 1992, and Trans-Faire, which was awarded the "official Ile de France training" label in 1993.

By entrusting training to approved centres, the FFT is in no way relinquishing its 'control' over training, since the training content still comes from the black book.

And trainers at non-accredited private centres are invited to follow the federal guidelines so that their trainees have every chance of passing the final exam, which is organised jointly by the ministry and the federation.

The FFT's objective is to facilitate access to training throughout the country by offering more training opportunities to future candidates and, above all, by promoting work-linked training through the apprenticeship contract, which came into being in July 1992 (Aubry Law) and is better known today as the professionalisation contract, which took over in 2004.

This scheme gives young people under the age of 25 and/or jobseekers over the age of 26 easier access to training within a clearly defined framework (qualification contract introduced in 1992, then professionalisation contract from 2004). Training costs are absorbed by the OPCA (Organisme Paritaire Collecteur Agréé), to which employer clubs are expected to pay monthly contributions.

These OPCAs are responsible for collecting companies' (and therefore clubs') financial obligations in terms of professional training, and then redistributing them.

Before the arrival of approved BEES training organisations, candidates for the diploma had three options:

1. Training in their league and with the CTR (limited places, recruitment based on applications)

2. Take the exam as an independent candidate (low chance of success)

3. Training in the CREPS (only six in the whole of France offer training in 1981 -Paris/ Montry, Poitiers, Talence, Aix-en-Provence, Strasbourg and Montpellier/Port Camargue). This is a very demanding course, as it involves ongoing training spread over eight months (September to April).

So access to the course was not easy, but it did guarantee that everyone who enrolled would be motivated, which will not necessarily be the case later on...

Having taken the specific BE1 training course with ACTJ, the common core BE2 tennis option course at CREPS Châtenay-Malabry and finally the specific BE2 training course with Trans-Faire, I can say that these three organisations offered me solid preparation in all areas and I have excellent memories of all these training sessions where seriousness and good humour, work and relaxation reigned, whether on the court and/or in the room!

I would also like to pay special tribute to my various trainers, who were, in order: Jean Paul, Jean-Marie and Arnaud for ACTJ, Patrick, Philippe, Mélanie, David, Jacques V. and Jacques M. at the Chatenay-Malabry CREPS, Patrice, Gérard and Christian for Trans-faire.

Moreover, these organisations were as much concerned with developing our skills as they were with preparing us for the exam:

"If you give a man a fish, he feeds once. If you teach him to fish, he'll feed for life", a Chinese proverb dear to my colleague and friend Salam, with whom I took the BE2 training course for two years, and which perfectly sums up the two wonderful years we spent together with Trans-Faire Ile de France.

This vision subsequently led to changes in strategy in the structure of state diplomas, since from 2008, training will no longer focus on providing knowledge but rather on developing skills.

From now on, candidates will be assessed more on content than on form, and the job of tennis teacher will be seen in its entirety, with the teacher having to become an expert in areas as varied as teaching, technique, leadership, club management, management training, developing projects for the club, mastering IT tools, etc., as well as digitalisation.

But by opening up training to a wider audience and, above all, increasing the opportunities for training with the creation of new accredited centres, we are faced with a problem of uniformity from one league to another, from one centre to another.

What is even more unfair for candidates is the lack of harmonisation on the examination board: as the DE is a state diploma, future candidates should be treated in the same way from one territory to another, which in practice is not always the case...

In short, in the 21st century, the profession of tennis instructor or teacher has little in common with what it was at the time of the all-out development of the sport in the 1980s.

In-service teacher training: a major challenge

Like all professions, the teaching profession, particularly in sports, is constantly evolving, and teaching and/or learning methods - if indeed there are any - are constantly being called into question in line with changes, good or bad, in the society in which we live.

Curiously, the FFT initially focused its efforts on club instructors, who were asked - quite rightly, I might add - to attend refresher courses every 2/3 years in order to maintain their status, even though they remained 'voluntary' teachers under the responsibility of a professional teacher, usually a sports or technical director. These refresher courses, which began in the early 1990s, were organised by the leagues and/or departmental committees and were often decentralised to the clubs.

It was a very good initiative in that it enabled instructors from different clubs to get together and exchange ideas as freely as possible, with everyone contributing their skills.

And very often, the EC in charge of recycling also left with a more open mind, as sharing knowledge is always very rewarding.

A little later, in 1997, the FFT decided to create a Continuing Education Department for Professional Teachers, offering a wide range of training courses on different themes, and not just in Paris.

Having myself run a training course on school tennis for this department and for teachers from the Brittany League in 2009, I have some excellent memories of these exchanges.

And it was a great learning experience for me to spend time with Patrice Beust and ask him questions about his experience as a player, teacher and coach.

The creation of the Institut de Formation du Tennis (LIFT) in 2018 currently guarantees the ongoing training of teachers on behalf of the FFT, and this is a very good thing.

With a wealth of digitised content on its platform, it provides access to information for all its teachers who are the least bit curious.

But LIFT is not the only one, as social networks have also made it possible to disseminate information en masse: Facebook pages, blogs, etc.

Wouldn't a curious and passionate learner be able to train to become a professional tennis teacher and/or coach?

Haven't some self-taught artists gone on to become big names?

Towards closer ties between the federation and private centres?

In the daily L'Equipe of Tuesday 16 March 2021, Nicolas Escudé, recently appointed interim DTN by the new president of the FFT, Gille Moretton, had this to say:

"I don't think you can build yourself up as a tennis player and as a human being by staying in your own corner. It makes no sense to work against the academy of Thierry Ascione, Patrick Mouratoglou or Jean-René Lisnard.

Obviously, for us there is no business side. But there are countless bridges between them and us. The same goes for what's being done abroad. It's not good to keep to ourselves".

For a long time, the federation was very inward-looking, even hermetic towards its teachers. Individual initiatives have always been seen as "disturbing" for the federal world!

Personally, I think we have to learn to discuss and exchange ideas with people, coaches and teachers who haven't had the same training and/or who simply don't have the same vision as us.

When, in 1972, Pierre Barthes inaugurated his private tennis centre with no fewer than 44 courts in Cap d'Agde with great fanfare, it was viewed with suspicion.

The FFT was all the more suspicious of Barthes, who did not hesitate to enlist the services of a foreign coach, the South African Francis Rawstorne, who was technical director of the training centre for top sportsmen and women for fifteen years.

Francis Rawstorne was a lecturer at the University of Perpignan, where he was planning to study for a degree in literature. His teaching skills and command of both English - his mother tongue - and French made him the ideal candidate to head up the Barthes centre!

In 1965, at the age of 24, Pierre Barthes decided to set himself apart from traditional tennis by turning professional alongside the great players of the day: Rod Laver, Ken Rosewall, Lewis Hoad and many others. He travelled the world with them and, above all, observed the American and Australian training centres. In short, he was a trailblazer, and he put his experience at the service of the trainees:

"For 6 days, from sunrise to sunset, on or off the courts, sometimes with an imaginary racket in hand, the trainees react, talk and think, in a word, live with a single aim: to improve or even perfect their tennis".
reported journalist Gérard Albouy in *Le Monde on 27 October 1978.*

Pierre Barthes, who sees himself more as a player than a teacher, will take on the role of adviser to his instructors and trainees alike, and it won't be long before the mayonnaise takes hold!

A forerunner in the field, the Barthès/Rawstorne duo's 'tennis village' became the leading tennis training centre in Europe, welcoming no fewer than 2,500 trainees a year, just a few years before the creation of the Bollettieri Academy (1978) on the other side of the Atlantic.
!
The FFT saw this as a counter-power to its message and was never very comfortable with 'dissidents', even though they all had a common objective: to serve French tennis.

However, Rawstorne himself declared in *Le Monde o*n 27 October 1978:

"We're not denying the French method of teaching tennis. In fact, it's the basis on which we all work, as we have to pass the federal state certificate before we can teach. What makes us different is that we use very graphic language, because we know that pictures are worth more than words. And the originality of our method lies more in the fact that we favour tactics over technique".

All in all, a very appropriate statement, given that it is very difficult for the vast majority of players to change their technique in a week! What's more, in these tennis centres for all, the federation could find a valuable ally in spreading tennis throughout the country. Wasn't that one of the aims of the federal authorities at the end of the Second World War?

Of course, except that times have changed since 1945, the federation having become tentacular at the dawn of the eighties and it wants, it thinks it can control everything.

So when the promising young Catherine Tanvier, who had always chosen to live on the fringes of the federal structures, decided in 1980 at the age of fourteen to join Pierre Barthès' structure to benefit from Rawstorne's experience, the FFT frowned.

An article by Dominique Cazaux published in n°329 of *Tennis de France* magazine in September 1980 and entitled, *"Catherine Tanvier, comme une petite américaine"* explains the young girl's approach.

We learn that she already has a strong character and is determined to make her own way. So when the journalist asks her why, as well as dressing like Borg, she plays identically to the Swede, Tanvier replies:

"If you're going to imitate someone, imitate the best.

And when asked why not emulate Navratilova rather than Borg, Tanvier adds: *"Because I've admired Borg for a very long time [...] at the start I had a natural game that was similar to hers and then, you see, I think that the lift is the future of women's tennis".*

This very interesting article deals for the first time with the role of parents and the mistrust shown by the federal authorities towards parents who are considered to be detrimental to the careers of their offspring. The journalist states:

"One fine day, she and her mother decided to leave Cap d'Agde to run from tournaments to training sessions and vice versa in the company of an Australian, Steve Myers, one of the Mc Namara, Mc Namee etc. gang...

Myers is completely devoted to Catherine, watches all her matches and makes her programme. With this way of living and organising herself, Catherine Tanvier has become the first Frenchwoman to live almost completely in the American way. Always on the move with her mother to protect her and avoid emotional imbalance, and her coach to help her progress".

As early as 1980, the importance of the player/parent/coach trilogy was highlighted in this article about the young Catherine Tanvier, but the FFT chose not to consider this axiom. For a very long time, parents were sidelined by federal authorities, which led to a number of conflicts.

Yet many champions owe their success to a parent or mentor (Chris Evert, Jimmy Connors, Monica Seles, Martina Hingis, Jennifer Capriati, Maria Sharapova, not to mention the Williams sisters and Rafael Nadal).

And France is no exception to the rule: don't Marion Bartoli and Caroline Garcia owe their performances to their dads? There's no doubt about it, and we must take our hats off to Walter Bartoli and Louis Paul Garcia for the admirable results they have achieved for their daughter.

The antagonisms are crystallised even more by two private organisations that focus on top level football and which for a time overshadowed the FFT because most of the best players trained with them:

1. the unit set up by a certain Régis de Camaret in the early eightiesat the Marres tennis club in Saint Tropez

2. the one closer to home and the Roland Garros stadium, created in 2005 by industrialist Arnaud Lagardère, better known as Team Lagardère.

There was a time when the best French players (Nathalie Tauziat, Isabelle Demongeot, Karine Ricard...) trained outside the federal structures, which did not fail to disturb the federal authorities, who could see Régis de Camaret's structure as a counter-power?

Perhaps the latter, who did not fully hold the BE (he never obtained the common core syllabus), was not fully appreciated by the FFT?

The fact is that he had excellent results with several of the players he coached, even if these results were subsequently tarnished by a criminal conviction for practices unworthy of the profession.

However, Régis de Camaret is one of the few French coaches to have reached a Grand Slam singles final with a player they coach: in Régis's case, a female player, Nathalie Tauziat (Wimbledon finalist in 1998).

In the open era, there aren't many of them:

➤ Georges Deniau (Patrick Proisy Roland Garros 1972)
➤ Patrice Hagelauer (Yannick Noah, Roland Garros 1983)
➤ Henri Dumont (Cédric Pioline, US Open 1993)
➤ David Pierce (Mary Pierce, Roland Garros 1994)
➤ Pierre Cherret (Cédric Pioline, Wimbledon 1997)
➤ Philippe Rosant (Arnaud Clément, Australian Open 2001)
➤ Loïc Courteau (Amélie Mauresmo, Australian Open and Wimbledon 2006)
➤ Guillaume Peyre (Marcos Baghdatis, 2006 Australian Open)
➤ Walter Bartoli (Marion Bartoli, Wimbledon 2007 & 2013)
➤ Sam Sumyk (Victoria Azarenka, Australian Open and US Open 2012 & 2013 / Garbine Muguruza Roland Garros 2016, Wimbledon 2017)
➤ Patrick Mouratoglou (Serena Williams, 18 finals between Wimbledon 2012 and US Open 2019)
➤ Gilles Cervara (Daniil Medvedev, US Open 2021)

Only thirteen French coaches have managed to reach a grand slam final with their respective player since the Open era (1968), and four of them have achieved this feat with a foreign player (Guillaume Peyre, Sam Sumyk - with two different players -, Patrick Mouratoglou and Gilles Cervara).

The majority of these high-level coaches (75%) have never played on the tour themselves. It is worth noting that four of them have managed to take their player to the top of the world rankings (Loïc Courteau, Sam Sumyk - with two different players -, Patrick Mouratoglou and Gilles Cervara).

Having had the opportunity to discuss with Régis de Camaret in November 2021, I learned that he had started playing tennis late in life (at the age of seventeen) and completely by chance (he would have followed a friend).

He was soon ranked at 30 and was selected for a 'hopefuls' course at the Dauphiné-Savoie league in 1960, where he benefited from the skills of Henri Cochet.

Later he had the chance to take lessons from Joseph Stolpa (the same man who coached Françoise Durr), who was known to be a very pragmatic teacher, able to adapt to his pupils' abilities at a time when the relationship between teacher and pupil was still one of knowledge versus learning, with no possibility of compromise for the latter. De Camaret observed many of the champions of the time and was able to talk to some of them (Pietrangeli, Rosewall, Nastase), not hesitating to ask them for advice on how to train and master a particular shot. Gradually he moved away from the principles of the French method and focused on respect for biomechanical principles:

"A lot of foreign players came to the Côte d'Azur with their coaches during the tournament season, so I saw that they all had very different training methods, so I chose to focus on efficiency. I quickly realised that we shouldn't constrain our biomechanics, but rather try to be as thrifty as possible. And I became convinced very early on that every stroke is different for every individual. So I always let the players I coached choose the solution for themselves: I suggested it, they decided. For me, it's the player who chooses his or her coach, not the other way round. The coach gives the resources and the player does what he wants with them. And it's the player who makes the difference, not the coach. I set up my training centre to meet a need and it's worked rather well because I've had some very good results.

Régis de Camaret has won around 130 French youth championship titles (individual and team), and in some years 70% of the grants awarded to the Côte d'Azur league by the FFT were the result of his work.

Despite this, the DTN never sought to find out more about his training methods... Shame!

As far as Team Lagardère is concerned, for a time this highly organised structure with its huge resources eclipsed the CNE, attracting the best specialists in fields as diverse as physical preparation, physiology and nutrition/dietetics.

Team Lagardère began as a sponsorship initiative to support young hopefuls Richard Gasquet and Gaël Monfils - Arnaud Lagardère wanted to provide financial backing for the two young players to help them blossom - but it soon became a training centre of excellence just a stone's throw from the CNE.

The structure, which was set up on the premises of the Jean Bouin stadium at Porte d'Auteuil and had up to ten tennis players, did not hesitate to poach executives from the FFT, which may have felt weakened for a time.

However, it has to be said that Lagardère's investment has had the merit of getting things moving, and the FFT had to react to a new offer in terms of top-level training and, above all, 100% financed by the sponsor!

In all cases, high-level training requires constant commitment from both parties: players and coaches. There is no miracle formula, but what is certain is that success requires a great deal of effort and sacrifice, which not everyone involved in performance - players, coaches or parents - is prepared to make...

My friend Guillaume Peyre explains:

"To be a top performer, you have to sacrifice everything and impose an iron discipline. With time and experience, a coach ends up with convictions, but you always have to listen and be able to adapt to players and situations. Nothing can be taken for granted; everything can be done over and over again!

There's no substitute for experience. Diplomas and all kinds of training are all very well, but they won't make you a successful coach! Even though I got my BE2 in high-level training, I learned more on the circuit than during my initial training. Nothing teaches you more than travelling, being curious, exchanging ideas and observing. All the players on the circuit, including the French players, are very good technically, tactically and physically, but most of them lack faith in discipline and the quest for the grail.

And his colleague Sam Sumyk added:

"For the FFT, the immediate result is more important than the long term, which is not a criticism at all, just an observation. But training players capable of performing at the highest level is a very long-term process that requires patience and perseverance. Personally, I owe everything to Alain Cassaigne, who introduced me to top-level tennis. I received very good general training from the Brittany CTR at the time, but the fact that I took a year's unpaid leave to see what was happening elsewhere, particularly in the United States, and that, thanks to Alain, I was able to rub shoulders with coaches from different countries at the Palmer Academy in Florida, helped me a lot. I think that at the moment, the French federal system isn't open enough, the authorities don't go out enough to see what's being done elsewhere and the CNE is a real fortress, which is a shame!

Today, much more than in the past, it is possible to succeed outside the federal system, and many players take a variety of routes to reach the highest level at an advanced age: being very strong in junior is absolutely no guarantee of being one of the best on the big circuit.

On the other hand, you can be a very average player when you're twenty and then break into the top 20 a few years later!

The development of new technologies

France has always been an entrepreneurial nation, and the tennis sector is no exception.

René Lacoste is perhaps the French player who has done the most to make tennis easier to play, both in terms of clothing and improved equipment, as well as developing training techniques.

In fact, it was he himself who had the idea, in 1923, of putting a coating on the handle of the racket, which at first was bare, the hand being in direct contact with the wood.

Today, it's hard to imagine playing with a racket without an overgrip or even a grip, which was the case at the beginning of the last century!

It's easier to remember the eponymous polo shirt invented by the same René and emblazoned with an alligator, the famous Lacoste polo shirt that is still so popular at the time of writing. Once again, progress was made, as this clothing invention enabled the players of thetime to move around better, even in hostile environments, and therefore togive their very best both in very hot and very humid climates. But there were two inventions that revolutionised tennis more than any others: the ball-throwing machine created in 1927 in collaboration with Dunlop, and the first tubular steel tennis racket in 1963 in collaboration with France's number one tennis player at the time, a certain Pierre Darmon, who was in a way the luxury consultant chosen by René Lacoste himself for the tests and feedback.

First of all, let's take a look at this famous bullet-throwing machine: why was it invented?

? Quite simply and above all to allow René Lacoste to train on his own and at his own pace! Back then, even more than now, it wasn't easy to find a playing partner, especially when you were at a certain level, so having a machine capable of sending a certain number of balls in a row at a certain rate proved to be a particularly interesting teaching tool, and Monsieur Lacoste might never have earned the nickname crocodile without his machine!

Today's ball-throwing machines are extremely sophisticated, even though they are not so frequently used in clubs? Why not? The French training system has always banned the use of the ball basket and therefore the ball machine in favour of mixed situations (the teacher throws the first ball and then lets the game develop) and/or game situations.

And yet these machines are undeniably fun, as I've noticed every time I've used them at tennis school parties in the clubs I've visited: a bit like shooting with a rifle at a funfair, what could be more fun for youngsters than receiving a ball from a machine of any kind to try and hit a target and win a prize!

As we saw earlier, developments in equipment (rackets, balls, strings) have enabled players to hit the ball harder and harder without risking injury.

From 1976 onwards, the advent of rackets with enlarged heads, spearheaded by the Prince brand and its iconic Prince Pro model, gave more people the chance to try their hand at tennis, with the ball suddenly becoming easier to catch for novices!

Composite material rackets (Kevlar, graphite) appeared on the tennis market in the early 1980s, providing players with rackets that were both lighter and more rigid, making them easier to play for beginners, but also much more powerful for competitors, allowing for excess power without risk to the joints involved (shoulder/elbow/wrist).

But at the same time, the development of hard courts, which are much cheaper for local authorities to build and require less maintenance, has led to the appearance of new pathologies among tennis players, whatever their level: back, knee, calf, ankle, Achilles tendon, foot, etc. Despite the improved comfort of shoes (remember that in the sixties and seventies, players were practically wearing espadrilles), hard courts are still very traumatic and send far too many of our players to the infirmary. A study commissioned by the FFT a few years ago highlighted the fact that over a ten-year career, a French player spent around three years in the infirmary, which is of course highly regrettable. However, this phenomenon is not unique to French tennis; it affects all nations without exception.

Physical preparation has become central to the training of tennis players and can no longer be summed up by a few 'jogging' sessions here and there, as in the days of Connors/Borg/McEnroe... For several decades now, it has been a major issue with a dual objective: to make the player more effective on the court but also to enable him or her to reduce or avoid injuries.

So, despite the fact that tennis is a much more traumatic game than it was in its early days, players are playing for longer and longer, which leads me to believe that the 'senior' categories should start not at 30 or 35 but at 40 or even 45!

Changing the rules: a strategic and dangerous challenge

The rules of the game were codified in 1877 for the first Wimbledon tournament and have undergone only one technical change since then: the authorisation in 1958 to take both feet off the ground when serving.

This same service, which was originally intended as a courteous gesture to start the rally (the term 'tennis' comes from the Old French 'tenetz', referring to the start of the rally), gradually became a means of ending the point before it had begun!

"When lawn tennis first appeared in France in the 1880s, apart from the written rules, there were conventions and rules of etiquette that gave tennis a slower pace; serving too hard was incorrect, as it was considered to be a simple tee shot," explains Eugène Broquedis (1890-1973), a tennis teacher in Puteaux at the time when France went to war in 1914.

In fact, the Americans were the first to be "deceitful", trying to win the point before the exchange could get underway.

In 1913, Max Decugis, whom we have already mentioned, devoted a chapter to "American services" in his book _Tennis_.

Performed with a western forehand grip, these serves are similar to extremely slice serves, as the ball can be hit in reverse (from the inside to theoutside) so that it can be turned differently! Decugis distinguishes between the "ordinary" serve (with the racket moving from right to left) and what he calls the "reverse" serve (with the racket moving in the opposite direction). Closer to home, French-Iranian Mansour Bahrami, Australian Nick Kyrgios and Russian-Kazakh Alex Bublik have all been fans of the reverse serve!

As early as 1913, players from the other side of the Atlantic, who were baseball enthusiasts, were hitting the first cannonball serves, which a certain Maurice McLoughlin (1890-1957) specialised in well before his compatriot Roscoe Tanner...!

Before 1958, it was necessary to maintain contact with the ground throughout service, as the FFLT Technical Committee pointed out in an official bulletin in 1947 :

"At no time during the execution of the service, i.e. from the moment the serve is taken up to the moment the racket makes contact with the ball, may both feet leave the ground simultaneously" and to specify _"the server must not be considered to have changed his position by walking or running for the following movements :_

1. _slight movements of the feet that do not materially affect the position originally taken by the dog_

2. _any movement of one foot if the other foot maintains its original contact with the ground at all times_

But this rule, which had become very difficult to enforce in local tournaments, was relaxed in 1958: now the server can take both feet off the ground and jump, even over the baseline when serving.

This new rule led to an evolution in technique with the introduction of the rocking serve, which accentuated the thrust of the legs and thus increased the power of the strike.

Then, from 1970 onwards, the invention of the jump serve by the American Arthur Ashe (1943-1993) - the same man who discovered our champion Yannick Noah and whose name the Flushing Meadow centre court bears - coupled with the development of equipment (balls, rackets and strings) helped to make the serve increasingly important.

With the advent of composite rackets, which allowed players to hit the ball harder and harder without having to invent new techniques, and to protect themselves from injury, many players began to use their groundstrokes to hurt their opponents straight away, with the following players appearing on the circuit in order of appearance: Roscoe Tanner (USA), nicknamed 'The Rocket' and whose speed record set in 1978 (246 km/h) was not beaten until 2004 by his compatriot Andy Roddick (249.4 km/h).

And among those who have made, or are still making, the powder talk in the service, we can mention chronologically:

Roscoe Tanner (USA), Chip Hooper (USA), Yannick Noah (France), Kevin Curren (South Africa), Slobodan Zivojinovic (Yugoslavia), Boris Becker (Germany), Goran Ivanisevic (Croatia) and closer to home Mark Philippoussis (Australia), Andy Roddick (USA), Ivo Karlovic and Marin Cilic (Croatia), Kevin Anderson (South Africa), Albano Olivetti (France), Sam Groth (Australia), John Isner (USA), Reilly Opelka (USA), Maxime Cressy (Franco-American) and recently the young frenchy Giovanni Mpetshi Perricard.

The list of all those who liked or like to send toffees is of course not exhaustive, but it has led the international bodies to progressively ban certain playing surfaces (taraflex at Paris Bercy, parquet in the Davis Cup) and to slow down most of them (the grass at Wimbledon before 2002 is nothing like it is now!), particularly the hard surfaces whose speed index can be adjusted on demand...

At the moment, the authorities are even thinking of allowing only one service ball, which could completely change the game: the serve is the only shot in tennis that you can afford to miss - isn't that right, Miss Sabalenka, sic - even though it is the only shot with a closed skill (it only depends on you and absolutely not on your opponent).

So, by offering players just one service ball, we would be entering a new era... I'm not in favour of it!

New ways of playing tennis: more fun, more friendly and more accessible to all

Among the deviants that have appeared in mainland France, beach tennis, padel tennis and, more recently, pickleball, it's worth taking a closer look at padel tennis, whose sudden popularity in France and throughout Europe is comparable to that of tennis in the 1980s. Created in Acapulco, Mexico, in 1969 by a certain Enrique Corcuera, it was imported to Spain in 1974, near Marbella (Andalusia), and has taken almost twenty-five years to spread throughout the Iberian peninsula (a single padel club in 1974, five hundred in 2000, then one thousand in 2005 and finally 2,500 today).

Padel is currently the fastest-growing sport in the world, and France is no exception.

Padel became part of the FFT in 2014, with 680 members in 2014 and 9,208 members in 2019. According to Arnaud Di Pasquale, head of the FFT's padel mission, there are now around 300,000 regular padel players in France (compared to 4 million in Spain with 75,000 members)!

How do you explain this craze?

Having tried it with my children, who are young adults with no natural predisposition for racket sports, I have to say that we had fun straight away, which is not always the case for two beginners venturing onto a tennis court... Recently, as I was sitting quietly on my court, waiting for my students, my attention was drawn to the court next to me where three members of the LRC - the club where I've been teaching in Hong Kong since 2011 - who were clearly not very experienced, were trying to exchange a few balls from the back of the court to the back of the court.

I realised that these 3 good people spent more time chasing their bullets to pick them up than sending them back to themselves, and I think that if they had had this experience in more northerly latitudes, they would have put an end to the ordeal quickly and definitively... Although teaching methods have been adapted and developed considerably to make tennis more accessible to a wider audience, the fact remains that tennis is still a difficult sport for those with no particular physical ability.

As a result, membership of a gym where the premises are both heated and/or air-conditioned has become more attractive to this audience, particularly women. It's a way of doing sport as you like, when you like, without the constraint of a fixed session once a week, as is more often the case in tennis clubs.

And it's not easy to have fun in winter in halls that are often unheated and where the temperature can frequently approach zero degrees...

So yes, padel tennis could prove to be the solution to keeping these recreational players, whose membership is vital to the health of affiliated clubs.

A fun activity and a less demanding racket sport than its big brother, tennis, padel is a sport that can be enjoyed by everyone, and it is becoming firmly established in clubs.

The FFT has recently organised a training course leading to a federal diploma for padel instructors (DFMP).

This course is aimed solely at professional teachers with a Tennis State qualification (BE and/or DE).

A very big tournament was even organised very recently on the Roland Garros centre court, a tournament that is intended to be the equivalent of a Grand Slam for padel.

Personally, I don't see padel dethroning tennis in the long term because, like squash, it's not a very televised sport. Even today, everything is broadcast via the audiovisual media and this aspect could be an obstacle to the recognition of padel as a sport in its own right, in the same way as squash, which is widely practised throughout the world but is still not on the Olympic programme.

I'm much less enthusiastic about pickleball, which appeared on the other side of the Atlantic in 1965, the other trendy activity that's being talked about more and more these days.

Having tried it myself, I think the late Coluche's expression *"tennis is like ping pong except that you're standing on the table"* really comes into its own when describing this new game! A mix of tennis, ping pong and badminton, this activity invented by a certain Joel Pritchard to entertain his children is still a long way from tennis: hitting plastic balls, albeit with composite rackets, does not offer the same sensations of touch.

Plus, it's a very noisy sport and difficult to practice outdoors...

But with over four million people now practising it in the United States, it's still worth considering!

There's no doubt that padel and, to a lesser extent, pickleball will be able to reinvigorate tennis clubs and, who knows, perhaps act as a stepping stone to traditional tennis?

In any case, the FFT has clearly understood the stakes, the importance and the opportunity of being able to ride this wave, which can only have positive effects on its affiliated clubs.

And let's not forget that very soon after its creation in 1920, our federation was already reaching out to all racquet sports through its official magazine, _Revue du tennis, du badminton et du ping pong, the official organ of the FFLT_.

Unless private investors, who have no intention of affiliating their padel centres to the FFT, take over the activity and develop it on the fringes of the federation: that's a risk!

Beach tennis, which first appeared on Italian beaches in the late 1970s and early 1980s, primarily to entertain beach-going tourists, has been somewhat overshadowed in recent years. The main reason, in my opinion, is threefold:

1. It's an activity that's not for everyone, as you need a minimum of technical mastery and physical ability before you can enjoy it.

2. It's a seasonal business

3. It's complicated to create land outside coastal areas...!

A padel tennis court   *A pickleball court*

A beach tennis court somewhere in Vaucluse

<u>*What kind of tennis for tomorrow? Towards the uberisation of teaching?*</u>

I think it's very important for the FFT to open up to the outside world, because it's clear that every federation (there are almost two hundred of them at the moment) is facing the same problems.

Also, the solutions proposed by some are not always identical and so, in my opinion, there is an effort to be made in terms of analysis, because some interesting initiatives could be adapted to the French system?

We have a long and rich history of teaching and education, but it's not exclusive!

I've been lucky enough to practise in Hong Kong for nearly fourteen years now. It's a territory that counts for little or nothing on the international scene in terms of competitive tennis, but in

175

terms of teaching and teaching methods, it's an incredible melting pot and it's interesting and enriching to work alongside coaches who have been trained differently.

The ITF, PTR, PBI and the national federations all award diplomas whose content is somewhat different, but which deserve to be analysed and dissected in order to draw out the most relevant ideas and why not recreate a training reference framework for future generations of teachers?

Why not set up a council, attached to the FFT, representing French tennis teachers abroad (whether state-qualified or not) and organise seminars every two years online via zoom or other means of virtual communication?

All this, of course, in the interests of the FFT and French tennis in general.

As far as clubs are concerned, I think that France's system of associations is a very good thing for sport in general and tennis in particular, because it guarantees equal opportunities.

But I also think it could be improved by making the management more professional.

The teacher should also be the number one contact within the club, the referent, i.e. the one who can make proposals and even take decisions.

For that to happen, he would have to be interested in the club's development and not 'pauperised' as has been the case for too long already? But how?

Why not give him the responsibility of developing his club himself?

In this age of social networks, tennis teachers should be able to act like entrepreneurs, like company directors (the club) and be able to adapt their own teaching programmes to suit the problems of their club, their local area and the expectations of the population with regard to tennis?

Still the number one individual sport in France, and has been for several decades now, tennis has become a universal activity that is played on every continent and in every country, especially since it returned to the Olympic programme - thank you Mr Chatrier -.

Knowing also that the Roland Garros tournament is a sure and certain source of significant revenue for the FFT (90% of the federation's budget is fed each year by revenue from the organisation of the Paris Grand Slam) - revenue that has admittedly been weakened by the covid 19 health crisis - and visibility, it seems to me that the federation should be less concerned about attracting new members than trying to keep the ones it already has?

Although the renovation of the Roland Garros stadium has cost almost 400 million euros, partly financed by the federation itself, it will give the FFT greater visibility, as the stadium will now be used all year round and not just during the three weeks of the French internationals.

So Roland Garros, which is already a fully-fledged brand with an international reputation, is no longer just a sanctuary for French tennis, but also a magnet for events.

So perhaps the FFT should refocus its actions on the three areas of development that I feel are currently lacking:

1. training, monitoring and support for elite athletes
2. the assurance of having teachers who are passionate and 'committed' to making clubs more dynamic
3. better support for "leisure" members

As far as training is concerned, I wouldn't go so far as to say that it's not good at the federation, I think it's quite the opposite and the statistics show it. Every year we have new youngsters arriving on the circuit who are all very competitive.

But I'm sure there's room to do even better, in particular by planning training in more extreme conditions, outside the federal cocoon and above all closer to real tournament conditions. Training in very hot and humid conditions would be one way of better preparing our players to face their opponents in competition.

I also think it's vital to make training more transparent and therefore to protect the status of Professional Teacher by guaranteeing a quality label: training has become a business, and not just in sport, so I sincerely believe that we should put safeguards in place to ensure that all trainee instructors really want to make a long-term commitment to their future teaching career.

Why not impose a minimum of one or two full seasons as a club initiator (CQP/AMT) before any entry to DE training?

Couldn't the first training session, the one that gives you your foot in the door and allows you to discover yourself as a teacher, be done in your training club, the same one where you discovered the activity, where the future teacher would feel confident and where he or she could very easily see whether or not he or she is cut out for the job?

In any case, I think it's very important to look at these problems if we want to maintain the pyramid that is typical of the French system: federation/leagues/committees/clubs.

If this is not the case, is there not a risk that professional teachers will evaporate into private organisations such as major sports brands or tennis academies, or even move to more attractive countries in terms of consideration and remuneration? Or perhaps, in the age of digitalization, some might be tempted to become more independent, leading to the uberisation of teaching and coaching!

Finally, and I think this is the most significant and the most penalising for clubs and teachers, we don't take leisure members seriously enough, even though they are the ones on whom the health of our clubs depends.

We mustn't forget that out of the total number of licence holders, only a third are competitors, and yet the federal policy, and by cascade that of the clubs, is centred on, and almost blindly oriented towards, competitive tennis!

Very little is done to meet the expectations of ordinary members, who see tennis more as a way of keeping fit than as a competitive sporting activity.

We're fortunate to have a product (tennis) that's great fun and accessible to almost everyone, and we should be able to cultivate this specificity that most of our competitors' sports activities don't have: running, fitness, bodybuilding....

And if we take into account competitors alone (a third of all licence holders), we should be able to draw up the following typology:

1. Sunday" competitors: those who experience competition solely through interclub events and/or their club's own tournament (whether open or internal).

2. Ranked" competitors: those who are prepared to travel dozens of kilometres to play numerous individual tournaments throughout the year in order to improve their ranking, whatever their level of play.

Don't take it personally when I use the term "Sunday racer" - quite the contrary.

This category of member is often the one that invests the most in the life of the club, but in most cases receives nothing in return, and is even completely neglected by the teachers and managers who are always more interested in those who achieve results.

In contrast, those whom I have chosen to call ranking competitors, who represent around a tenth of licence holders, attract all the attention despite being very much in the minority?

Isn't there a dichotomy here, a source of division, conflict and therefore the evaporation of our licensees towards more peaceful horizons?

Unless our recreational members decide to practice only on public courts or in non-affiliated private clubs, using their smartphones to reserve a court and hire the services of a private coach without using the Ten Up federal application!

The risk is high and could prove dangerous for the federation in the long term...

CONCLUSION

The history of teaching our sport is therefore very rich and has its origins in Great Britain, where the first players, and therefore quite naturally the first teachers, arrived.

But it wasn't long before the French distinguished themselves with their teaching approach, usingtheir experience of the palm to train tennis players.

It is interesting to note that the first French teachers to be recognised for their skills came from the Basque country, a region where paume and pelote, two ball sports traditionally widely practised in this southern part of France, were very widespread. So it's obvious that there have been transfers of learning between these different sports.

The sport of tennis and the teaching of tennis were confidential at the beginning of the 20th century, but thanks to the success of Suzanne Lenglen and the Musketeers in major tournaments, the sport gradually became more popular between the wars and benefited from the expertise of its two champions: Lenglen and Cochet.

Lenglen for thinking about a teaching approach that would enable more young people to be introduced to the game at the same time.

Cochet, using his powers of observation to help the best young players, trying to adapt his approach to the specific nature of each player, with the aim of respecting each player's personal style.

The sudden death of Suzanne Lenglen and then the Second World War of course put the brakes on this movement, even though the federation benefited from the largesse of Borotra and Lacoste during the German occupation to enable French tennis to continue to exist and even strengthen its position in relation to other sports.

The Trente Glorieuses period (1946-1974) saw the development and/or implementation of new teaching methods introduced by the French federation, the aim of which was to spread the practice throughout the country and above all to get as many people as possible to join its affiliated clubs.

Firstly, the Lenglen method, which became widespread after the Second World War and enabled the schools of the same name to operate. Then there was the French teaching method, the aim of which was to unify the way in which tennis was taught and to introduce a greater number of people - young and old alike - to the game, shortly after tennis became 'Open'. Initially a confidential sport reserved for the elite, tennis in France enjoyed its heyday in the 1980s with improved television coverage of the French Open at Roland Garros, making duels on the Paris clay courts particularly attractive for both sexes, even for the uninitiated.

At a time when the range of leisure and entertainment activities was not as diverse as it is today, tennis, which is a mixed sport, attracted large numbers of men and women in search of physical exercise. Clubs have sprung up all over the country, making the sport accessible to as many people as possible and, above all, controlled by an increasingly sprawling federation. And the figures speak for themselves: in 1986, the FFT had 1,400,000 members in its 9,500 clubs and 2,500 state-qualified professional teachers (*Source: Roland Garros Magazine number 1, official programme of the 1987 French internationals*).

A time when the demand for teaching was greater than the supply. Today, even though teachers are better trained than they used to be, in the sense that their training covers all areas of the profession and not just technical education, the situation is reversed:

2,500 clubs have disappeared in 30 years and, at the same time, the federation has lost 400,000 members.

There are many reasons for this: thereis now a plethora of leisure activities on offer, society is much more individualistic and the younger generations are much less inclined to "hurt themselves" on any kind of sports field - hence the success of eSport, an activity for which I personally have no passion!

Today, even though tennis remains a major sport in France, it is facing competition from sporting activities that are easier and more accessible to everyone, even if they are less fun: fitness centres are in full swing, offering varied and different programmes and, above all, à la carte offers that allow greater flexibility and are accessible all year round, whereas tennis lessons remain fixed to a schedule and a day of the week from September to June, with no possibility of change.

It therefore seems obvious that we need to react to this problem by launching a major campaign to renovate and modernise our facilities in affiliated clubs. Having successfully modernised the Roland Garros stadium, the showcase for French tennis on the international stage, it seems to me that it is high time we looked after our tennis clubs, which are in a state of disrepair.are suffering from a general dilapidation of their facilities, a state of affairs that perhaps no longer encourages the French to join our clubs.

And what about the teachers (whether state-qualified or not) who enter training in ever-increasing numbers every year, and who end up pauperising themselves, many of them choosing to change careers after only a few years in the profession when they realise that it is now very difficult to make a decent living from their passion.

Perhaps they should react by organising themselves into a guild, because it's up to them to do everything they can to safeguard their profession, a noble profession moreover, but one that unfortunately isn't recognised for its true worth!

It also seems to me that it would be a good idea to emphasise the 'health' side of our business, especially after the covid crisis, in an attempt to bounce back and put or put the professional tennis teacher back at the centre of the game.

Performance and competition are all very well, as long as we don't abandon the heart of our profession, which is above all to educate the public in the practice of sport, a major social issue. And that's why tennis remains a magnificent, all-round sport that can be played by everyone, at any age!

NOTES

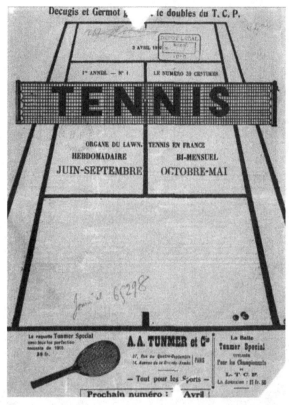

Opposite, the title page of the 1ˢᵗ issue of the first specialist magazine, very simply entitled "Tennis".

Article published in the July 1910 issue of Tennis magazine recounting the match between the 2 teachers, Thomas Burke and Eugène Broquedis.

quelques champions de l'escrime et du tennis avaient remporté la victoire par leur adresse plutôt que par une réelle valeur athlétique, on déclara que ces sports n'étaient pas athlétiques.

La vérité, on s'en rend compte aujourd'hui, c'est que dans tous sports, quelle que soit la part de l'adresse, le champion n'en est pas moins en fin de compte celui que la nature a le mieux construit, physiquement et moralement, pour ce sport. Avec la concurrence, avec la sélection sur des masses de plus en plus nombreuses, on en arrive fatalement à trouver un certain nombre d'athlètes, aussi habiles l'un que l'autre. Ce jour là c'est la seule valeur athlétique qui triomphe.

Regardez ce qui s'est passé en lutte: on vit tout d'abord triompher les scientifiques purs, les Bordelais, puis arrivèrent les colosses russes, aussi scientifiques que leurs rivaux, et devant lesquels ceux-ci n'existèrent point.

Regardez la nouvelle génération d'escrimeurs, c'est une génération d'athlètes qui pratique la culture physique à outrance.

Regardez encore le tennis. Il y a cinq ans, les Français étaient sans rivaux, à part les Anglais. Eux seuls savaient jouer. L'année dernière marqua la déception cruelle. Nos joueurs, habiles, d'un mécanisme adroit et divers, se heurtèrent aux rudes joueurs allemands, beaucoup moins scientifiques, mais qui s'étaient fait des muscles et du souffle. Ils furent écrasés. Cette année, instruits par la défaite, nos hommes se firent des muscles, travaillèrent moins encore leur sport spécial que leur culture physique générale. Ils triomphèrent à leur tour de leurs vainqueurs de 1912.

Comme quoi, s'il y a la manière, la manière n'est pas tout. Dans un bon habit, la coupe est quelque chose, mais encore faut-il qu'il y ait du drap.

WHIPPER.

Comment améliorer son jeu

Conseils d'entraînement
par une célèbre joueuse anglaise.

Le lawn-tennis est un jeu qui possède maint avantage. Il combine l'exercice et le grand air, et par là, se conforme aux premiers principes, bases de la santé. Il n'exige pas une somme de temps exagérée — (comme le golf) — grand avantage pour les deux sexes...

Certains joueurs éprouvent une grande difficulté à améliorer leur jeu. Ils atteignent un certain niveau, et semblent s'y arrêter, malgré tous leurs efforts. C'est, selon moi, qu'ils n'emploient pas les bons moyens. Une pratique « intelligente » voilà ce qu'il leur faudrait. Ne jouez pas un jeu d'entraînement comme une partie de match, où vous évitez vos coups faibles, votre unique but étant de gagner. Dans un jeu d'entraînement, ne vous préoccupez point d'être battu; travaillez vos coups faibles, jouez-les le plus possible, jusqu'à ce qu'ils deviennent vos coups forts. Un bon système est de ne pas marquer, mais d'obtenir d'un ami dévoué de vous envoyer encore et encore la balle où vous la voulez; votre patience sera récompensée par vos progrès continus.

Autre système: travailler contre le mur, qui a l'avantage d'être toujours là, et vous dispense de déranger personne... Ne travaillez qu'avec un objet précis, avec un point faible en vue. Jouez contre meilleur que vous. Surveillez les meilleurs joueurs et tâchez de pénétrer leurs méthodes. Il y a dans le tennis beaucoup de science; beaucoup à apprendre, toujours; c'est ce qui en fait et renouvelle l'intérêt. Jeu difficile, soit, mais amusant, même pour le débutant.

Tout autre le jeu de match; là, il faut éviter ses coups faibles, l'unique objet étant ici de gagner. Un des secrets du succès, c'est le don d'anticipation. Il y a un génie naturel à prévoir les coups, mais il se cultive. Observez vos adversaires d'abord, et vous découvrirez souvent qu'à certaines balles, ils font toujours la même riposte... Cela vous permettra d'anticiper leur coup, et vous donnera plus de temps pour aller prendre la meilleure position, d'où renvoyer. Obligez toujours l'adversaire à bouger pour répondre. Variez votre jeu, pour qu'il ne sache sur quoi compter, et déguisez le plus possible vos intentions.

Dans le simple, vous avez à protéger un terrain beaucoup plus grand, le jeu est plus dur que le double; il exige que le joueur soit en bonne condition. N'essayez pas de marquer sur chaque balle, mais préparez votre ouverture, et, alors, exécutez votre coup gagnant. Variez vos méthodes d'attaque et de défense. Ne laissez pas l'adversaire s'habituer à votre jeu, ne voir que vous êtes las ou inquiet, car son énergie en serait doublée. Tel joueur tombe dans un coup stéréotypé, et l'adversaire qui sait à quoi s'attendre, en profite.

Jamais de découragement ou d'abandon; des matches ont été gagnés par des joueurs moins forts, mais qui s'acharnaient jusqu'au bout. Si vous êtes trop lâchés, oubliez la marque, et luttez, et vous aurez le plaisir, parfois, de remonter le courant, de gagner une partie, semblait-il, perdue. Que si, par contre, vous menez et paraissez tenir le succès en main, n'en continuez pas moins à jouer de votre mieux; sinon, gare la défaillance dont on se remet trop tard.

Tâchez de rester calme devant la difficulté, l'accident. Ne vous laissez distraire par nul incident extérieur. Il arrive, quand vous perdez, que toute la chance, il y en a, semble aller à l'adversaire. Tâchez de n'en être pas démonté, et votre tour viendra sans doute. A la guigne, il faut opposer un front philosophique.

Les erreurs de l'arbitre, autre source d'ennui, d'irritation; il est dur sur un coup bien dirigé qui doit gagner, d'entendre l'arbitre crier : out, quand on est sûr qu'il se trompe. Et cela arrive toujours au moment critique.

« Accidents », erreurs, sont des quasi-fatalités, qu'il faut prendre comme telles, avec indifférence; s'en fâcher, c'est, en jouant plus mal, courir au devant de nouveaux malheurs.

En double, ne pas oublier qu'on a un partenaire. Il est bon de jouer avec le même partenaire le plus possible, et de le comprendre. Rappelez-vous, comme au bridge, que votre partenaire a peut-être un as ou deux; donnez-lui toutes les chances de les faire (je parle de doubles mixtes); aidez-le en lui préparant des ouvertures, dont, s'il n'est une parfaite mazette, il saura bien tirer parti. Le revers est presque toujours le point faible. Souvenez-vous en et vous comportez en conséquence. Il existe encore un autre point faible dans le double. C'est le centre, surtout si les deux joueurs sont au filet. Et ne vous fâchez pas contre votre partenaire s'il joue mal, ça ne servira à rien, au contraire.

Mieux vaut au contraire pardonner les fautes qu'il peut commettre, sans quoi, dans votre rage vous risqueriez à votre tour de mal jouer. Aux erreurs d'autrui, il convient de répondre par un jeu d'autant plus soigné, afin d'éviter le handicap qui pourrait en résulter et amener la perte de la partie, au moment où elle aurait pu être gagnée.

L'entraînement pour jeu de match réclame du bon sens avant tout. Le sommeil, voilà le premier besoin. Se coucher de bonne heure et dormir la fenêtre ouverte. De la promenade au grand air; repas léger avant la partie. Ne jouez pas dans trop de tournois, l'effort imposé au système nerveux est très grand, l'esprit et le corps réclament de temps à autre un repos complet, après la concentration intense que demande le tournoi. Ne jouez pas un match ou un tournoi avant d'avoir maîtrisé les divers éléments du jeu. C'est une erreur fréquente de commencer trop tôt, le style s'en ressent. Car si vous n'avez pas acquis d'avance la science des différents coups, vous n'aurez pas le temps de l'apprendre en match, et vous contracterez de mauvaises habitudes tenaces.

Mais, sous cette réserve et à condition de garder la mesure, le jeu de tournoi est la meilleure école, qui vous oppose à toutes sortes de joueurs et d'ordinaire meilleurs que vous... Ne regardez pas un match immédiatement avant de jouer le vôtre, cela peut troubler votre vue; de même n'occupez pas la chaise de l'arbitre, poste très fatiguant aussi pour l'œil.

Il n'est pas bon non plus de faire un long voyage en chemin de fer avant la partie; rendez-vous au lieu du tournoi, s'il est éloigné, la veille, de préférence; et accordez-vous une bonne nuit de repos d'abord.

Ne portez rien de lourd juste avant de jouer tel qu'un sac de tennis, etc, cela risquerait d'enlever à notre main sa sûreté, sans laquelle il n'est pas de bon jeu.

Et souvenez-vous toujours que le tennis est moins un jeu qu'un sport, un grand sport qui réclame de réelles qualités athlétiques. Si vous ne les possédez pas, jouez dans votre jardin tout ce que vous désirez, mais ne commettez jamais la sottise de vous engager dans une compétition quelconque. Vous y seriez simplement ridicules.

MRS. LAMBERT CHAMBERS.

Extract from the magazine La Vie au grand air, *21 June 1913, article by Miss Lambert Chambers: Comment améliorer son jeu.*

Opposite, an article written by tennis player Marguerite Broquedis and published in the special tennis issue of the magazine <u>La Vie au grand air</u> on 30 May 1914.

Marguerite Broquedis explains the tennis style in an article published on 15 November 1913 in the magazine <u>La Vie au grand air</u>

L'ENFANT

SES SPORTS : LE TENNIS

Ce que nous dit Suzanne Lenglen

Suzanne LENGLEN
Professeur de Tennis

Tout ce qui touche à l'éducation sportive de la jeunesse est de la plus brûlante actualité. Sur le rôle qu'on doit réserver au tennis, nous avons sollicité l'avis de Suzanne Lenglen. La grande championne, complétant sa réponse à une récente enquête de notre journal, nous a fait, pour nos lectrices et lecteurs, les déclarations suivantes :

Le tennis, son importance

« Le tennis est extrêmement important dans l'éducation physique de l'enfant, car il développe la plus essentielle des qualités athlétiques : la coordination des mouvements de l'ensemble du corps. En effet, l'exécution des différents coups du tennis nécessite la mise en jeu de tout le corps, depuis les pieds, dont la position est capitale, jusqu'à la tête. Cette coordination de tous les muscles du corps s'exerce non pas par rapport à un objet fixe, comme dans le golf par exemple, et d'autres sports, mais par rapport à une balle se mouvant avec une extrême rapidité et qui ne peut être frappée efficacement que pendant un temps excessivement court. A une coordination parfaite de mouvements, le joueur de tennis doit donc joindre une grande rapidité de réflexes, et doit être capable de se déplacer rapidement tout en conservant son équilibre.

Le tennis, sport des enfants

Contrairement à ce que croit l'immense majorité des gens, le tennis ne se joue que très peu avec le bras, et les muscles qu'il fait le plus travailler sont ceux des jambes, les dorsaux et les abdominaux.

Comme à aucun moment il ne demande de force brutale, qu'il tend à développer les qualités de vitesse, de détente et d'équilibre indispensables à tout épanouissement physique normal, ces caractéristiques le rendent particulièrement indiqué pour l'enfant, chez qui les exercices de force pure peuvent avoir des conséquences regrettables.

Enfin, pratiqué par un bon joueur de force moyenne, il suscite continuellement des problèmes tactiques demandant à être résolus dans l'espace d'un instant, ce qui détermine la décision et la rapidité de jugement.

Les débuts

Aux environs de la dixième année, on devra commencer par des mouvements exécutés sans la balle, de façon à faire jouer les muscles de l'enfant dans la bonne direction, à lui faire comprendre et exécuter des gestes aussi parfaits que possible. Lui apprendre ensuite à exécuter ces mêmes gestes en jeu, sur une balle de plus en plus difficile à atteindre. Dès que l'élève a acquis ce qu'on peut appeler la maîtrise de la balle, et que le geste de la frapper correctement est devenu chez lui instinctif et habituel, on lui apprendra à la diriger. Enfin, et comme dernier stade, on lui inculquera tous les principes de la tactique du jeu.

Premières leçons et entraînement

Les leçons ne doivent pas dépasser une heure, et pendant cette heure le travail effectif fourni par chaque élève ne doit pas excéder une quinzaine de minutes.

Il est absolument impossible à un enfant de conserver la concentration intellectuelle et la tension physique nécessaires à l'exécution de gestes nouveaux plus longtemps.

Le reste de la leçon doit se passer à absorber instinctivement les enseignements donnés par le professeur aux autres élèves du groupe. J'ai constaté que la plupart des élèves corrigent plus facilement leurs défauts en voyant le professeur rectifier les erreurs de leurs camarades.

Leçons collectives

L'enfant, et même l'homme, se rend rarement compte de l'imperfection de ses propres gestes. S'il n'en était pas ainsi, tous les êtres humains seraient parfaitement gracieux. Ce n'est que par la comparaison et l'imitation instinctive que l'enfant parvient à corriger ses défauts. C'est pourquoi j'insiste sur la leçon collective. D'autant plus qu'elle détermine entre les élèves une émulation extrêmement salutaire. »

Pour conclure, nous avons posé à notre grande championne les deux questions suivantes :

Que doit-on éviter dans les débuts ?

« D'une façon générale, il faut éviter que l'élève contracte de mauvaises habitudes qui semblent au premier abord rendre son exécution plus facile, mais qui, enracinées à la longue, deviendront un obstacle insurmontable à ses progrès.

En cas de mauvais débuts, comment y remédier ?

Impossible de vous répondre sans de trop longues considérations techniques. Pourtant, à moins de cas désespérés pour lesquels je conseille purement et simplement d'abandonner le tennis pour un autre sport mieux adapté à l'individu, un peu de patience et de fermeté donnent toujours des résultats. Dans le cas de mauvaises habitudes prises depuis trop longtemps, il faut tout simplement se résoudre à recommencer par le commencement. »

Above, an interview with Suzanne Lenglen, published in Le Figaro on 20 August 1936.

René Lacoste, his game-changing inventions

Opposite, presentation of the baling machine patented by René Lacoste in 1929.

On the right, an advertisement for the metal racket invented by René Lacoste in 1963 and published in <u>Tennis de France</u> magazine in June 1974.

Patrick Proisy was a finalist at the French Open at Roland Garros with this racket in 1972.

Centres Scolaire d'Initiation au Tennis (1938)

TENNIS

PLUS DE 80 ÉLÈVES
suivent le cours d'initiation au tennis

Les cours de l'Ecole des Juniors de tennis se poursuivent régulièrement chaque jeudi dans les trois centres désignés par la F.F.L.T. qui sont, rappelons-le : les courts couverts du R.C. de France, 154, rue Saussure, du T.C. de Paris, à la Porte de Saint-Cloud et du T.C. de France, 34, rue du Chemin-Vert.

Afin de permettre aux jeunes de 9 à 15 ans d'apprendre à jouer au tennis, la Fédération du Tennis a créé à leur intention, un cours d'initiation au tennis. C'est sur les courts couverts du Tennis Mozart, 100 bis, avenue Mozart, où fonctionna de longues années, l'école Suzanne Lenglen, que les dirigeants de la rue Volney ont fixé leur choix, et où sous la direction des professeurs Canavèse, Roux et Bagnaud, 80 élèves : filles et garçons, répartis en plusieurs groupes, apprennent l'A.B.C. du tennis.

C'est une rude et lourde tâche qu'ont accepté les trois professeurs; mais ils l'accomplissent avec joie, satisfaits des résultats qu'ils ont déjà obtenus.

Gageons qu'avant la fin du cours, ils auront « sorti » quelques espoirs. — H. G.

Cochet et Gentien joueront à Nice

Henri Cochet et Antoine Gentien participeront, à partir du 2 janvier, au tournoi organisé par le L.T.C. de Nice, sur les courts en terre battue.

Afin de permettre à ces deux joueurs engagés dans le tournoi de Noël, d'être à Nice en temps voulu, les organisateurs parisiens ont décidé d'avancer les finales des doubles, dans lesquels ils sont tous deux inscrits et de les faire jouer le 1er janvier.

Rappelons que le tournoi de Noël, organisé par le R.C. de France sur les courts couverts du 154, rue Saussure, commencera demain, à 11 h. 45, avec les parties du simple messieurs. — H. G.

Article published on 19 December 1941 in the daily newspaper Aujourd'hui about the tennis initiation centres set up by the federation in 1938.

Un professeur dans chaque lycée et collège de France

Opposite is an article that appeared in the regional daily L'express de Mulhouse on 9 June 1938, explaining the recruitment and training of future tennis teachers at the Écoles normales d'Éducation Physiques.

D'autre part, cette école de professeurs demandera des frais. C'est le gouvernement qui y pourvoira. Les cours auront lieu au Stade de Coubertin, sous la direction technique de Suzanne Lenglen, assistée de plusieurs professionnels.

Les raquettes et les balles seront fournies. Les élèves de l'Ecole Normale d'Education Physique, comme ceux de l'Institut régional, pourront donc, durant les deux ans de leur stage, apprendre gratuitement à jouer au tennis.

Bien sûr, ils ne seront pas obligés de le faire, cette nouvelle branche offerte à leur activité sera toute facultative, mais on peut estimer à 70% le nombre de ceux qui suivront ces cours.

A preuve, lors d'une conférence sur le tennis, que Suzanne Lenglen et Jean Tillier firent à l'Ecole, sur 50 élèves, 41 s'inscrivirent aussitôt avec enthousiasme.

A la sortie de l'Ecole, les élèves passeront un examen devant une commission composée de deux membres de la Fédération amateurs et de deux professionnels. S'ils sont reçus, ils partiront nantis d'un diplôme correspondant à leurs capacités; trois catégories sont prévues, comme pour tous les autres professeurs : MONITEUR (force d'un joueur de 3e série), PROFESSEUR (joueur de tête de seconde série), ET ENTRAINEUR (1re série).

Ce que l'on demandera surtout, ce sont des connaissances théoriques complètes. Il y aura probablement des « recalés », mais, sans doute, en nombre infime. Ajoutons d'ailleurs que cette école ne sera pas uniquement pour les futurs moniteurs d'éducation physique. Les premières places... Il y en aura en tout une quarantaine leur seront réservées, s'il en reste, tous ceux qui désireront devenir professeurs pourront suivre les cours et passer le même examen. Rappelons que tous les professionnels ont intérêt à avoir un diplôme, car, ainsi que nous l'avons dit récemment, la fédération conseillera à ses clubs de choisir les professeurs diplômés.

Précisons que Suzanne Lenglen sera la grande directrice technique de l'affaire, c'était tout indiqué, que Roger Dumont sera chargé des rapports entre la Fédération et les établissements scolaires, et que Baquet surveillera le côté culture physique afin que le programme comporte des mouvements appropriés au tennis.

Dans l'ensemble, c'est toute une éducation sportive tendant vers le tennis que l'on va inculquer à la jeunesse. On ne pouvait mieux faire que de la diriger vers ce sport qui a l'avantage de pouvoir être aussi bien pratiqué par les hommes que par les femmes et qui est un complément utile et agréable à l'indispensable culture physique.

Félicitons tous ceux qui sont à la base de cette nouvelle organisation. Dans quelques années, chaque collège et lycée de France aura son «prof» de tennis. Gageons que nos «potaches» ne seront pas les derniers à s'en réjouir.

The Cochet courses (1938) and propaganda tours (1943)

HENRI COCHET
part à la recherche de futurs champions pour leur enseigner l'art et les obligations de ce rôle

Henri Cochet a réuni, hier matin, les chroniqueurs sportifs parisiens spécialisés dans le tennis pour leur exposer un projet qu'il a conçu et dont il compte entreprendre la réalisation dès la semaine prochaine, secondé, pour les détails d'organisation, par Jean Foucault.

Laissons la parole à Cochet :

J'abandonne presque complètement les tournois ou exhibitions professionnels pour m'adonner au

Henri Cochet.

professorat : j'estime qu'on ne peut mener à bien les deux choses à la fois.

Mais je vais essayer d'appliquer dans mes cours une méthode autre que celle qui consiste à indiquer d'abord les positions réglementaires pour l'exécution des divers coups et ensuite à renvoyer inlassablement des balles à l'élève.

Mon intention est surtout de tenir compte du style personnel des joueurs et de donner ainsi à chacun d'eux son meilleur rendement. C'est, selon moi, une erreur de prôner une technique uniforme : voyez les « mousquetaires » Jean Borotra, René Lacoste, Jacques Brugnon et moi-même : aucun de nous n'avait la même façon de jouer.

N'êtes-vous pas surpris de voir que maintenant il y a en France plus de bons joueurs que voici une

dureront une heure ; pour le second, une heure trente ; pour le troisième, deux heures. Les prix de ces cours ne sont pas encore définitivement arrêtés ; néanmoins, je puis dire qu'ils seront établis de manière à ne pas constituer un gros obstacle pour ceux qui auraient le désir de les suivre.

Je vais commencer mes tournées à Paris. Puis, j'aborderai la province, qui est à mon sens un « réservoir à champions ». Peut-être y découvrirai-je de futurs, mais je n'ai pas l'intention de les entraîner. Je veux seulement leur indiquer la manière de progresser et leur exposer précisément les obligations du rôle de champion.

Il faut que les joueurs de tennis pratiquent un autre sport

Henri Cochet continue à parler du tennis, qui le passionne toujours :

Il est certain que la majorité des bons joueurs n'ont pas une condition physique suffisante. Il est mauvais de leur conseiller la pratique régulière de la culture physique, qui est sans aucun doute excellente, mais aussi terriblement monotone.

Il faudrait leur faire comprendre la nécessité de s'adonner à un autre sport conjointement au tennis, et plutôt à un sport d'équipe, car celui-ci comporte des obligations qui développent le goût d'une discipline et d'un courage absolument indispensables pour les luttes des courts.

Il y a quelques années, on avait créé des équipes de hockey composées justement de joueurs de tennis et qui disputaient une compétition organisée à leur intention. Pourquoi ne le referait-on pas ?

Cochet a passé son examen de professeur et d'entraîneur

Cochet nous quitte, car il lui faut, à 14 heures, « subir les foudres » des examinateurs de l'Association française des professionnels de tennis.

... Il est au stade Pierre de Coubertin à l'heure fixée, devant MM. Gallay, Darsonval et Tissot. Il fait quelques balles, donne quelques conseils à un joueur et... reçoit licence officielle de professeur et d'entraîneur, ce qui est, en l'espèce, le fin du fin.

Maurice Capelle.

Perspectives d'avenir.

Cette mission scolaire de Cochet pourrait s'étendre indéfiniment, mais il ne s'agit nullement pour lui d'amener à son sport favori tous les élèves de France. Ces séances ne s'adressent qu'à des volontaires, à des jeunes gens qui savent déjà ce qu'est le tennis, mais à qui il faut ouvrir des horizons qu'ils ignorent encore. Ce sont ces jeunes gens déjà convaincus qui feront ensuite la meilleure propagande auprès de leurs camarades profanes.

S'il était besoin d'une preuve de la réussite de ces manifestations, il suffirait d'avoir vu, après la réunion de Limoges, tous ces gosses enthousiastes, entourant les deux champions dans la cour de leur lycée, leur demandant des autographes, leur posant mille questions dont la plus fréquente était celle-ci : « Que faut-il faire pour arriver à jouer comme vous, comment apprendre ? » La réponse était aisée, à Limoges précisément, où une école Suzanne-Lenglen fonctionne d'une façon parfaite et ne demande qu'à recevoir des inscriptions.

Mais, répétons-le, ce travail en profondeur n'est pas le seul but que poursuivent la Fédération française et ses propagandistes ; ils en ont un autre qui est de trouver des champions. Pour cela, il faut que les clubs s'organisent pour grouper les jeunes qui font preuve de dispositions particulières et les suivre de façon efficace. Qu'ils suivent l'initiative prise il y a deux ans à Roland-Garros, sous la direction de Cochet et de Gentien, et qui n'a pas donné de si mauvais résultats puisqu'il est sorti de ces contacts entre les jeunes et les anciens, des joueurs d'avenir comme Lucot, Colin et Lévêque.

Aujourd'hui, Cochet et Gentien élargissent leur champ de prospection. Au cours de leurs tournées, ils ont l'intention de toujours jouer avec les gosses les plus doués. On peut être sûr que, s'ils en rencontrent un avec l'étoffe d'un champion, ils ne le laisseront pas échapper. Cochet l'a promis du reste. N'a-t-il pas dit : « Je trouverai des champions, dussé-je avoir autant de mal dans cette lutte que dans une finale de championnat du monde. »

On the left is an article published in the newspaper <u>Le Figaro</u> *on 6 December 1938, in which we learn that Henri Cochet had decided to devote himself to teaching tennis, having just obtained his teaching diploma.*

On the right is an article relating the propaganda tours carried out by Cochet from 1943 on behalf of the federation.

**Official magazines of the French Lawn Tennis Federation
(the word "Lawn" disappeared for good in 1976)**

*The first issue of Tennis Info (bottom right) is dated 1 December 1978 and was at the time the only federal
newspaper to reach all affiliated clubs free of charge.
More than 42 years after its creation, the magazine is still distributed every month in all clubhouses
affiliated to the FFT.*

Specialist tennis magazines

In order of appearance, Tennis Sports (1929), Tennis de France (1953), Tennis Magazine (1976), Le Monde du Tennis (1980) and Court Central (2003).

1st issue 1929   1st issue 1953   1st issue 1976

1st issue 1980   1st issue 2003

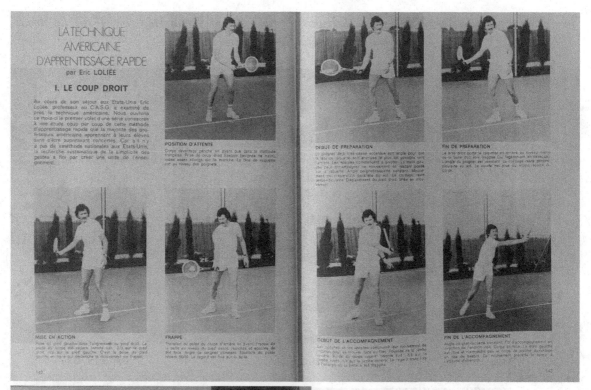

Extracted from the June and October 1974 magazines, a few years after the release of the French teaching method, the only specialist magazine of the time did not hesitate to mention other teaching approaches. Here the American technique explained and reported by French teacher Eric Loliée, who didn't hesitate to go and see how it was done across the Atlantic.

Letter from the Federal Club of Professional Teachers

This is an excellent initiative launched by the DTN at the end of 1999, with the aim of sharing knowledge with teachers in affiliated clubs.

Interview with Patrice Beust, 5 April 2020

1. What were the lessons like at the Suzanne Lenglen de Coubertin School, individual or group lessons, and who gave them?

The French Tennis Federation at the time had set up this school to detect 10/11 year olds and select those most suited to tennis so that they could be offered to clubs after a year. The two people in charge at the time were Mr CAVALINI and Mr PASQUIER. Lessons were given at the "petit Coubertin", near Porte de Saint-Cloud, on Thursdays (school holidays at the time) and took place on one half of the court for 15 minutes. Every fourth Thursday was reserved for service, with eight players on each side. I'd like to take this opportunity to point out that, having never played before, I got my first taste of the game at that school, particularly the volley, as it was the first shot I learnt, and it has steered my entire career towards the volley. Later, after reading a lot of tennis books, I came to the conclusion that it was more effective to teach tennis by starting with the simplest things. It's easier to add preparations for groundstrokeslater on than to do away with preparations when you come to the net. The same is true of chess, where you start with the endgame with few pieces, which is strategic, whereas the beginning of the game is the result of a library that you just have to learn by heart. The same goes for golf, where you start with putting, small touch and feel shots, then intermediate clubs and finally the big shots.

2. Did you make rapid progress, or did you find it difficult to learn?

From the moment I started playing, I had a dream: to become the best player in the world. That's obviously very presumptuous and utopian, but it was my driving force for all the years that followed. From that moment on, my motivation was total and it made it much easier for me to find the information I needed to progress. This meant that I never found training of any kind boring. My progress was rapid, even though at the time, under 14 were not allowed to play as adults because of the triple upgrade, and only had access to clubs on Thursdays and weekends. As a result, by the under 16 category, the best players were already playing in the second series, which explains this progression. In conclusion, when you're motivated, nothing is difficult, because it's your own choice.

3. At what age did you start at TCP (I understand that you had to go to the club accompanied by your parents)? Who was your teacher and how often did you play?

I joined the TCP when I was 11, a year after the Suzanne Lenglen school. In fact, to be a member of the club, you had to be 12 if your parents weren't members. As fate would have it, before refusing me entry, the Master Teacher, Mr Bagnaud, who was at the TCP, wanted to see how I was getting on; he had me play for half an hour, and at the end of this training, seeing that I must have some qualities, he decided to falsify my date of birth by one year so that he could enrol me at the TCP, even if it meant rectifying the error the following year, which he did. (A first sign of destiny). From thenon, I played every Thursday and every weekend. A second sign of destiny appeared to me in the person of Mr SIMÉON, the club's Director, who, seeing my motivation for tennis, arranged to reserve courts for me throughout the day so that I could play. So I was able to improve my skills between 6 and 8 hours every Thursday. Of course, I played a little less at the weekends because it was too busy, but I did slip in with a few adults from time to time.

4. When did you play your first competitions? How have you progressed?

As far as I can remember, I played my first competitions in Brittany when I was about 12 during the summer holidays; there was a series of tournaments at the time. My first ranking at 15 was 15/2, then 2/6, -4/6 and n°16... at 18. It was a fairly rapid progression, but I was able to win a few titles that opened up new prospects for me (French junior champion in singles and twice in doubles). If you want to know more, there's a summary on Wikipedia. These titles enabled me (a third sign of fate) to win my first Davis Cup cap at the age of 19. That selection was very important for me, because it enabled me to play in all the major international tournaments, including the four Grand Slams. In those amateur days, tournaments only invited the No. 1 players from each country or the Davis Cup players who made up a prestigious line-up for the organisers.

5. How did you become a teacher/coach yourself? Did you follow a training course or did joining the French Davis Cup team automatically make you a Teacher?

Gil De Kermadec, the National Technical Director at the time, advised me in 1967 to take my teaching qualification (the future BE2), knowing that it was the last year that it was possible to obtain it directly, as the creation of a monitorat (the future BE1) was planned for the following year and it would take two years to obtain the teaching qualification. Although I was in the middle of the Davis Cup period, I decided to listen to Gil's advice, knowing that at that time you could barely make a living from tennis because of your amateur status, and that I might have to consider giving lessons or coaching. It was a good thing I did, because I came of age, and it made me want to take the 3rd degree a few years later, the equivalent of the Master Teacher at the time, which is now called the BE3 (unless there's a new name for it), which I did by presenting to the jury the book I'd written on tennis technique.

At the time, teacher training consisted of a 15-day course at INSEP, which immediately preceded the exam, which lasted 3 days. It was at the end of my sixth year of Davis Cup (at the age of 26) that Philippe CHATRIER, with whom I had close ties, told me of his aim to create a training centre in Nice (to play all year round on clay and better prepare our French players for Roland Garros). He wanted to turn the Côte d'Azur into a kind of French California. (It's *strange that 50 years later, the current FFT is planning to repeat the same experiment...*).

To carry out his project, he asked me if I would be interested in taking over the management. I think Philippe had complete confidence in me, and intended to give me carte blanche to run the centre. The fact that I was married and had two young children to look after and provide for made me decide to accept Philippe's offer (which was very tempting for me, with a new experience at stake), forgetting (with some regret) about the Davis Cup. So I transferred my life to the south of France. At the time, I had a sports shop that wasn't doing very well, where I strung rackets every morning for 4 hours at a time.afternoon training sessions with my doubles partner Daniel CONTET, and twice a week group training sessions that I ran in a sports hall from 8pm to 11pm.

The challenge offered to me by President Philippe CHATRIER (who was only Vice-President at the time, as he had been keen to pay tribute to Marcel BERNARD by appointing him President for a term) was therefore very tempting, both financially and professionally. Admittedly, the salary was very low at the time, especially as it was fashionable to do big training courses in private centres which brought in alot of money. Without being laughed at by my friends, who found it hard to understand my choice, I put first and foremost my desire to share the values that had enabled me to achieve (almost) all my goals with those I was going to coach; I wanted to pass on the energy that had enabled me to overcome all the obstacles and above all to try to pass on messages, such as the dream, the main driving force behind overcoming mountains.

6. Did you work at a club before looking after the top players?

I never worked in a club except for the one my parents owned in Brittany, which allowed me to earn a little money during the summer between two or three 'beach' tournaments.

7. With regard to Tennis Études de Nice, how was training organised? Did you have a physical trainer? How were the players selected? Was the Tennis Études coeducational?

The first year was relatively complicated, because I had to deal with several difficulties. My group was made up of twelve boys aged between 11 and 19, ranging in level from NC (Christophe CASA went up to 2/6 during the year) to -15 with Denis NAEGELEN. You can imagine how many problems this can cause, from coordinating and harmonising training sessions to travelling to tournaments. Especially as there were no special timetables, and I was on my own to manage tennis, physical training and travel. Not to mention the fact that the teachers never missed an opportunity to nail the 'tennismen playing a rich man's sport' (at the time) by giving them tests first thing on Monday morning. I really felt that competitive sport was not part of traditional teaching. Fortunately, the club that warmly welcomed us (the Nice Lawn Tennis Club) made my task much easier, thanks in particular to the members of the club who acted as mentors for the younger players. All the players slept at the boarding school, which was run by someone who, unlike the teachers, was very understanding and always ready to help those who needed it. I was lucky enough to benefit from a time when, for the first time, young people could benefit from training and daily sports supervision. They were highly motivated and had complete confidence in me. The same applied to their parents, who never interfered with the way I applied my instructions. (We can see the evolution with our times where parents, claiming to know everything, take the liberty of advising the educator on what is good for their son). Subsequently, I did what was necessary to secure the services of a physical trainer who was sufficiently available to be able to accompany me to tournaments, and who adhered to my philosophy of preparing for the top level.

Players were selected at the end of rallies during the French championships, but I had suggested to Philippe CHATRIER the possibility of including from time to time a player that I would have noticed during the tournaments, who might not have the level, but from whom the following stood out great potential. As this proposal was approved by the Chairman, I was able to bring a '*wild-card*' into the team on several occasions. Once again, I was lucky enough to have Philippe's complete confidence, which is very rewarding, but also means that I have to be extremely rigorous if I am to live up to the responsibilities entrusted to me. The big advantage of having held the position of National Coach (compared to private individuals) is that I've always been free to recruit whoever I wanted (provided I had good arguments), and to let go of anyone who didn't meet my criteria (provided that it was justified). On the other hand, I've always believed that in a group it's never the strongest who push the group up, it's the weakest who pull the best down. That's why I made an agreement with the League whereby I would bring in one or two of the League's best juniors once or twice a week to give my best cadets a workout (which wasn't always the case). This proposal satisfied the League, which was able to benefit from part of the national training for these juniors and an additional opportunity for my team to progress.

This Tennis-Études has never been mixed.

8. Based on your experience, what qualities do you think are essential for becoming a professional tennis player and a good teacher/coach?

There are two questions in this question.

Pro tennis player

Above all, it's about a good pro tennis player, the pro being first and foremost a status. For my part, having played on the circuit for several years, I've always considered myself a pro in spirit (at least since my junior days) despite having amateur status. I later realised that some pros, by virtue of their status, behave like amateurs. The first quality is motivation, ambition, the will to succeed and to make the necessary investments. They say that faith makes mountains rise, and there's nothing more true than that. If a player had come to me and said that he preferred to train his own way to achieve his goals, I would have told him: "If you believe deeply in what you are saying, don't hesitate for a second and you have my blessing". This rarely happened, especially when one or other wanted to try the American camps that were all the rage. They often came back the following year, but after having had a different experience, which I think was constructive. The most important thing, and this has been my main line of conduct, is to have an approach to oneself that consists of playing (or training) as well as possible according to the form of the day; the result is only the consequence. This is the kind of 'key' message that needs to be conveyed from an early age, but which may take several years for the player to assimilate.

<u>Good teacher/coach</u>

Not having any certainties, but strong convictions, I would tend to say first of all that you need to have open ideas. I was once asked, at a time when teaching was characterised by a certain rigidity, what a reliable shot was (probably thinking that I was going to move towards two-handed grips or backhands, according to a certain fashion of the time). My answer was that a reliable shot is one that the player can reproduce perfectly. as much as the choice he has of being able to send the ball anywhere on the court with the spin, precision and speed he wants. It doesn't matter what grip he uses. Of course, as part of the early teaching process, the coach needs to be aware of the advantages and disadvantages of different grips and of holding the ball with one or two hands, particularly for backhands, as well as the importance of support and footwork. At a time when the instructions were still for one-handed backhands, I was coaching two players who had two-handed backhands (and forehands), including Fabrice Santoro. Fabrice used to centre all his balls perfectly and play tactically in the right way. Would you change something that was working perfectly if you didn't think you could do any better? I was talking earlier about the reliability of his shots, and he's a perfect example of that. I only worked with him to improve his ability to pick up the ball early, knowing that he had a great sense of observation and an excellent reading of his opponent's game. I also think that if I'd forced him to stick to a traditional technique, he would have stopped playing tennis; it's part of his personality. It's part of his personality. It's also the quality of a top-level coach to detect certain qualities in a player that are unique to him and that he needs to work on to make even better. Working on his weak shots, yes, but above all not forgetting his strong shots. All players are different, but champions have one thing in common: their desire to get the best out of themselves. Knowing how to play the right shot to the detriment of the shot you want to play to please yourself is part of the panoply of a champion. A good coach is one who gives his players the best weapons. Coaches who try to impose their 'trademark' by breaking down their pupils' personalities will achieve nothing.

9. Did you have a lot of freedom in the way you taught/coached or were you obliged to follow the Federal recommendations?

As it happens, being the perfectionist/self-taught type, I've always had a few problems complying with certain requirements imposed on me by coaches, unless they were part of my philosophy or were the result of an inescapable logic. As I said in the previous chapter, I've sometimes had a way of playing imposed on me that didn't suit me, but it didn't usually last very long. I think (I hope) that some of these people didn't hold it against me too much, knowing my strong motivation. In the previous chapter, I explained my behaviour towards the federal authorities, which I did not criticise insofar as my experience as a player allowed me to cross the yellow line slightly. The fact is that I never received the slightest remark about the way I coached. My teaching always respectedanatomy, logic, morphology and the search for the language I had to use with each player, which was different depending on their personality. I also realised that sometimes you have more to learn from the player than the other way round. Of course, subjects like motivation and getting the best out of yourself can be part of a joint meeting. Whatever the case, I think it's necessary to respect the segments, the joints, as much as possible in natural positions. Roger FEDERER is the model in every respect. To conclude this chapter, a champion is first and foremost an individuality that we must try to understand so that we can work positively with him.

10. Do you think you've exploited your full potential as a player? Do you think you would have been a stronger player if you'd started out in the evolutionary pedagogy era?

I have no regrets about my career. I feel I've made the most of it. Of course, there have been times when I've taken a path I thought was the right one, but mistakes are made in order to progress, which is why, in tennis, you can only win, either the match or the apprenticeship. I was convinced I could do it, with or without a coach. I used to (at around 16/18 years old) go and get the information myself. Why would I do that? Because it was my life and my will. So, when a few good former players attended my matches from time to time, I would systematically go and see them afterwards to pick up a few tips. In this way, I gradually learned as I went along. I'd like to take this opportunity to point out that for the coach/player pairing to work, each must play their part, the player must be the driving force and the coach the conductor. One doesn't work without the other. The best coach in the world can't produce a champion; his only power is to buy him time.

One final thought concerns the Tennis-Études programme, which worked perfectly in my day and which, little by little over the years, has become a little less productive in favour of personal projects (at least some of them). I think that my main asset as far as my playing career is concerned is the fact that my greatest motivation came when I was around 16/18 years old because I was lacking in my game, I had a hunger to play that I don't find in the youngsters of today. The weakness of French tennis lies first and foremost in the comforts of life in France, which don't help to motivate players, and the excessive assistance they are given, which leads to a kind of carelessness. It's good to live in France. Obviously, to reach the top level, you have to start young with a slightly crazy programme. It's a necessary condition, but it doesn't guarantee success, and that's what parents find hard to understand. That said, the difficulty for a coach is to get the player to 17/18 as well prepared as possible without undermining his motivation (watch out for *burn-out* and injuries caused by growing up).

11. How do you explain the widespread use of the 2-handed backhand over the last 20 years, despite the introduction of evolutionary tennis, which in my opinion should/could have had the opposite effect?

Often, over the decades, new ideas appear claiming to hold the truth, but generally motivated by an objective of renovating learning methods. The proof of this is the position taken by my friend Patrice Dominguez, then National Technical Director, in advocating the elimination of the cut backhand. It was an announcement that was intended to make an impression, but which subsequently proved to be a mistake. (Of which I'm sure he was aware, given his very high level of tennis).

In my many years as a coach, I've seen a number of different technical and physical approaches come and go, before finally coming back to the basics; that's how life goes. We think we hold the truth, but in fact there are many truths, just as there are many forms of intelligence. This is where the quality of a teacher comes into its own. Through his knowledge and experience, he will be able to pass on the only part that concerns the player he is coaching. It would be too easy to have a blanket method that enables everyone to become a champion. Progressive tennis certainly has its positive aspects, but as soon as a young hopeful stands out from the crowd, he or she needs to be removed from the group and given a different approach.particular programme. If you look at the history of the game, at one point the two-handed backhand was banned, then the cut backhand, and now all the strokes are used. NADAL plays well with two hands, but when he has to cut, he only uses one. So I still say that a player who wants to reach the top level has to be able to do all the shots without restriction.

Talking about the physical side of things, there was a time when working the right/left with a basket of balls was all the rage. It was all over the place. And yet it was a technique in which the player put more balls out than in. I really don't see what it could do. I've very rarely seen a coach teach players to touch the ball, to work with their hands, to learn to play with the racket and occasionally with the other arm; that's how, not so long ago, we observed that matches consisted of a duel at the back of the court, and that players were very clumsy on drop shots or touch shots. In recent years, tennis has become a little more varied. My philosophy is that there's no work without a goal (even in the warm-up).

As for two-handed backhands (I'm talking about those that use two forehand grips), they have their advantages and disadvantages. At present, however, there is a balance between the two techniques. One-handed backhands are magnificent and equally effective. On the other hand, learning the two-handed backhand requires the addition of a one-handed backhand for chopping shots and especially for volleys.

Here are some of my thoughts, delivered in a bit of a jumble, each of which would merit an entire chapter on its own. I hope I've answered some of your questions. I remain at your disposal and wish you every success with your project.

Best regards

BIBLIOGRAPHY

a- General works

E. de Nanteuil, G. de Saint Clair & C. Delahaye, *La paume et le lawn tennis,* Bibliothèque du Sport, Paris, Librairie Hachette, 1898

Henry Claremont, *Le livre des sports athlétiques et des jeux de plein air*, Pierre Roger & Cie, Paris, 1910

Max Decugis, *Tennis*, Editions Slatkine, 1913

Suzanne Lenglen, *Lawn tennis for girls, covered techniques and advices on tactic for beginner players*, American Sports Publishing Co, New York, 1920

Etienne Micard, *La Légende des sets. Réflexions sur le tennis,* Paris, Editions Fast, 1923

Suzanne Lenglen, *Lawn Tennis: The game of nations*, Harrap, 1925, London

Claude Anet, *Suzanne Lenglen*, Paris, Simon Kra, 1927

René Lacoste, *Tennis*, Grasset, 1928

Martin Plaa, *Seize leçons de tennis,* Société Parisienne d'éditions, 1932

Henri Cochet, *Tennis. Sa technique et sa psychologie*, Éditions Guy le Prat 1933

Suzanne Lenglen & Margaret Morris, *Initiation au Tennis, principes essentiels et préparation physique*, Albin Michel, Paris, 1937

Henri Cochet & E.L Broquedis, *Le tennis, Henri Cochet parle aux jeunes,* Paris, 1938

Alfred Estrabeau & Jacques Feuillet, *Apprendre le Tennis,* Éditions La Table Ronde, 1952

René Pelletier, *For a French tennis school - The school of champions - The school of style - L'ecole de la volée,* Édition Susse, 1952

Antoine Gentien, *Aventures d'un joueur de tennis*, La Palatine, Paris-Geneva, 1953

Bernard Destremau, *Tout le tennis*, Édition Amiot Dumont, 1955

René P. Pelletier, *Précis de tennis moderne*, Editions Grasset Paris, 1955

Aimé Gremillet, *Tennis-digest, toute la formation du joueur*, Lyon, 1962

Henri Cochet & Jacques Feuillet, *Le tennis de A à Z, une nouvelle méthode d'enseignement accélérée*, La Table Ronde, 1966

Georges Deniau, *Tennis total*, JC Lattès, 1970

Pierre de Coubertin, *Pédagogie Sportive*, 1972 (reprint)

Timothy Gallwey, *The inner game of tennis*, 1972, translated into French by Alain Cassaigne in 1977 under the title *Tennis et psychisme*, then a second time under the title *Tennis et concentration* in 1985.

Asher J. Birnbaum, *Tennis strokes & strategies*, the classic instruction series from Tennis Magazine USA, New York City, 1975

Christian Quidet, *La Fabuleuse Histoire du Tennis*, Editions Odile Jacob, 1976

Gianni Clerici, *Cinq Cents ans de Tennis*, Édition Hatier, 1976

Jacques Brugnon, *L'épopée des Mousquetaires*, Les cahiers de Tennis de France, special issue, 1977

Georges Deniau, *Tennis la technique, la tactique, l'entraînement*, Marabout, 1979

Henri Cochet & Jacques Feuillet, *Tennis, du jeu mondain au sport athlétique*, éditions Stock 1980

Dr. Michel Rota *Gagner au tennis, psychologie du jeu et des joueurs*, éditions Pierre Belfond, Paris, 1982

Odile de Roubin & Catherine Gerbaud, *Guide du Tennis Naturel*, Editions Calmann-Lévy 1983.

Didier Masson, *Le Rôle du bras libre*, Editions Chiron, 1984

Christophe Roger Vasselin & Charles de Raissac, *Mc Enroe est-il génial*, Editions Ramsay, 1985

Jean Claude Marchon & Christian Rieu, *Mini Tennis Maxi Tennis*, Vigot, 1986

Alain Mourey, *Tennis et pédagogie*, Vigot, 1986

François Lacaze, *Tennis : 15 ans de recherches pour une vérité*, Les presses de l'INAM, Editions Louis Musin, 1987

Association des Enseignants d'Éducation Physique et Sportive, _Tennis, la formation du joueur_, 1987

Roland Glaszmann, _Tennis, quand tu nous tiens_, 1989

Didier Masson, _Quel Tennis pour le XXIème siècle_, 1995

Francoise Rollan & Martine Reneaud, _Les étapes de la diffusion du tennis en France 1913-1992_, Maison des Sciences de l'Homme d'Aquitaine, 1995

Anne-Marie Waser, _Sociologie du tennis, genèse d'une crise (1960-1990)_, l'Harmattan, Paris 1995

Daniel Amson, _Borotra, de Wimbledon à Vichy_, éditions Tallandier, May 1999
Vincent Cognet, Romain Lefebvre and Philippe Maria, _Le tennis feminin français_, éditions du stade, May 1999

Olivier Letort & Jean Claude Marchon, _Tennis évolutif_, Tennis Cooleurs, August 1999

Olivier Letort, _Tennis évolutif, Tennis cooleurs_, Editions Arts & Littérature, 2002

Jean Claude Marchon & Christian RIEU, _Tennis : corriger ses défauts_, Amphora, 2006

Jean Christophe Piffaut, _L'invention du tennis_, Les quatre chemins, May 2007

Jean Pierre Chevalier, _Tennis in France, 1875-1955_, Nouvelles Editions Sutton, Mémoire du sport collection, June 2007

Lionel Crognier, _Tennis in tomorrow's society_, Dijon 2008 conference

Fabrice Abgrall & François Thomazeau, _La saga des Mousquetaires, la Belle Époque du tennis français_, Calmann-Lévy, May 2008

Éric Belouet and Michel Dreyfus, _Robert Abdesselam, une vie criblée de balles_, Editions les Quatre Chemin, April 2009

Patrick Clastres and Paul Dietschy, _Paume et tennis en France, XVe-XXe siècle_, Editions Nouveau Monde, May 2009

Jean-Michel Peter, _Tennis, leisure class and new representations of the body in the Belle Epoque_, Staps, 2010

Jean Lovera, _Tennis : art du jeu, art de vivre_, Glénat, May 2010

Paul Jalabert, *L'album de souvenirs filmés du tennis français*, Groupe Horizon, Gémenos, November 2010

Georges Deniau, *Des Mousquetaires à Federer*, Edilac éditions, November 2011

Elizabeth Wilson, *Love game: A history of tennis*, October 2014

Florys Castan-Vicente, *Suzanne Lenglen et la définition du professionnalisme dans le tennis de l'entre-deux-guerres*, Éditions La Découverte, 2016

Valerio Emanuele, *Dictionnaire du tennis*, Honoré Champion éditeur, Paris 2019

Chris Davies, *Balles neuves*, Davies Christop, July 2019

Petter B. Kettle, *The Suzanne Lenglen Phenomenon: Myths & Reality*, PK Associated, June 2020

John Barrett, Wimbledon, *The Official History of the Championship*, Vision Sports Publishing, June 2020 (latest edition)

Didier Masson & Pr Fabrice Duparc, *Un tennis fin dans un corps sain*, Presses d'Escourbiac, July 2020

Gilles Simon, *Ce sport qui rend fou : réflexions et amour du jeu*, Flammarion, October 2020

Lionel Crognier & Francois Ousset, *Le tennis dans la société de demain, proceedings of the 2nd international symposium*, Dijon 2021

Jacques Thamin, *Mes belles rencontres, from Borotra to Federer*, January 2022

Jean Claude Marty, *Roland Garros, un stade, un tournoi, des vainqueurs, des raquettes*, éditions Book Envol, July 2022

b- Federal works

French Lawn Tennis Federation, *Yearbook 1928*

Jean Tillier & René Lacoste, *La méthode d'initiation au tennis de Suzanne Lenglen*, Fédération Française de Lawn Tennis, Gallimard, Paris, 1942

Pierre Boyard, *Fiches Techniques et pédagogiques*, Ligue Poitou-Charents de Lawn Tennis, 1971
Gil de Kermadec, *La Méthode Française d'enseignement*, published by FFLT, 1972

FFT, *Guide annuel de la fédération française de tennis, année 1981*, published by Tennis-info, 1981

FFT, *Guide annuel de la fédération française de tennis, année 1983*, published by Tennis-info, 1983

Pierre Boyard, *Le cahier de l'Éducateur Fédéral*, 1987

DTN, document number 5: *La pédagogie Fédérale*, 1990

DTN, *Classeur Noir*, éditions FFT, 1992

DTN, document number 1: Les *différentes étapes de la détection et de l'entraînement des jeunes*, September 1993

DTN, document number 2*: Tennis School tests*, March 1993

DTN, document number 6: *Initiation Adults, teaching programme*, March 1998

DTN, document number 7: *Le cahier de l'Enseignant, initiation & perfectionnement*, 1999

DTN, document number 2: *Les Tests du Club Junior et de l'école de tennis*, December 2001

DTN, *Animations sportives, Tennis évolutif*, July 2006

DTN, document number 1: *Le Club Junior: Organisation & Pedagogy*, September 2006

DTN, document number 2: *Le cahier de l'enseignant, programming, tests et chronologie de l'apprentissage*, November 2012

DTN, document number 3: *Le cahier de l'enseignant: l'organisation et les principes d'enseignement pour les jeunes*, October 2014

c- Research work

Anne Marie Waser, *La genèse d'une politique sportive : l'exemple du tennis*, 1992, Actes de la recherche en sciences sociales pages 38-48

Christophe Cazuc, *La construction d'une carrière internationale de joueur de tennis professionnel : approche sociologique d'une profession au sein de neuf pays*, sociology thesis under the supervision of Charles Suaud, University of Nantes, September 2001.

Nicolas Stanajic, *En quoi et comment le tennis en milieu scolaire peut-il dynamiser les écoles de tennis*, BE2 core curriculum dissertation, CREPS Ile de France Chatenay-Malabry, May 2005

Patrick Vitel, *Une histoire de l'entraînement en tennis en France au XXème siècle (A history of tennis coaching in France in the 20th century)*, BEES 3ème degré research dissertation under the supervision of Jean Michel Delaplace, Université de la Réunion, September 2005.

Aurélien Zieleskiewicz, *La transmission du tennis en France : sociographie d'une relation de service,* sociology thesis under the supervision of Jean-Marc Leveratto and Roland Huesca, University of Lorraine, March 2015

Pierre-Marie Bartoli, *Les dieux du kiosque,* Ecole des Chartes thesis, under the supervision of Christophe Gauthier and Bertrand Tillier, May 2020

François Lacaze, *Le coup droit*, St-Honoré éditions-Paris, July 2020

d- Official Federation magazines

Revue Tennis et Golf, official organ of the French and Belgian golf federations, number 347 of 16 December 1937, presentation of the tennis school by Suzanne Lenglen.

Revue du tennis et du badminton, Organe officiel de la FFLT, number 173, November 1938, reply from Mr Jehan Kuntz, member of the FFLT technical committee, to Mr Gremillet about his son.

Bulletin Officiel de la Fédération Française de Lawn-Tennis, number 113, March 1947

Bulletin Officiel de la Fédération Française de Lawn-Tennis, number 114, May 1947

Smash : la revue française de Lawn Tennis, de badminton, de ping pong et de tennis de table, Organe officiel de la FFLT, numéro 31 de juin 1953, liste complète des membres de l'Association Française des Professeurs de Tennis pour l'année 1953

Tennis, official magazine of French tennis, number 65, March 1967

e- Physical Education and Sport Journals

Revue EPS number 66, July 1963, *Can tennis become a school sport?* by Louis Dutertre, PE teacher in Tananarive

Revue EPS number 104, July-August 1970, *Tennis, aspects d'une technique de base* by Gil de Kermadec & Jean Paul Loth

Revue EPS number 110, July-August 1971 *Le tennis, sport d'équipe* by Gil de Kermadec Revue EPS number 121, May-June 1973 *Tennis la conception novatrice de Gilbert Omnes* by Gil de Kermadec

Revue EPS number 131, January-February 1975 and number 132, March-April 1975 *Enseigner*

ou permettre d'apprendre. Reflections on tennis pedagogy by Bernard Pinon

Revue EPS number 136, November-December 1975 *Tennis, le jeu de volée* by Pierre Boyard

Revue EPS number 152, July-August 1978, *Mini-tennis by Pierre Larcade,* EPS educational adviser, Poissy Yvelines.

Revue EPS number 240, March-April 1993 *Tennis, les coups à deux mains,* by Anne Marie Rouchon

f- Daily press

Le Monde, 12 July 1946, *Le tennis à deux mains,* article by Olivier Merlin

Le Monde, 14 October 1947, *Le tennis de compétition se transforme-t-il (Is competitive tennis changing?)*, article by Olivier Merlin

Le Monde, 13 December 1962, *La préparation hivernale des joueurs français,* article by Jean Marival

Le Monde, 20 October 1965, *La fédération refuse chaque année des centaines de jeunes candidats*, article by Gérard de Ferrier

Le Monde, 24 July 1971, *La méthode française d'enseignement sera prête à l'automne*, article by Jean Marquet

Le Monde, 21 October 1971, *Il faut dix ans pour former un champion déclare M. Chatrier, responsable de l'équipe de France*, article by Michel Castaing.

Le Monde, 27 October 1978, *Analyser le tennis,* article by Gérard Albouy

Le Monde, 21 March 1981, *Frappe la balle et tais-toi*, article by Gérard Albouy

Libération of 30 May 2020, *Retrosport: Marguerite Broquedis, the great forgotten tennis player*, article by Gilles Dher

FILMOGRAPHY

F. Watts, *How I play tennis - by Mlle Suzanne Lenglen*, filmed in June 1925 by K. Gordon & F. Bassill for British Pathé

C. Eades, *Sports Shots No 18: Suzanne Lenglen*, British Pathé, 1933

British Movietone News, *Suzanne Lenglen's school*, February 1936

Marcel Martin, *Tennis*, Production des films JK Raymond-Millet, 1947

ORTF, Les coulisses de l'exploit, *Australian Tennis*, June 1962

ORTF, Les coulisses de l'exploit, *Tennis professionnel*, September 1965

François Reichenbach, *Les Internationaux de France 1975*, Les films du prisme, 1976

Les dossiers de l'écran *Once upon a time, Roland Garros, 1928-1978*, Procitel, Antenne 2, May 1979

William Klein, *The French*, 1981

J. Leclerc, *Professeur de tennis*, programme antenne 2 "Je veux être toi", broadcast in 1981

(INA) Gil de Kermadec & Torben Ulrich, *La balle au mur*, 1988

Gil de Kermadec, *Naissance d'un Tennis au Burkina Faso*, INSEP, 1989

Gil de Kermadec, *Les Maîtres du Jeu*, DTN, 1990

Paul Jalabert, *Tennis d'antan, Porte d'Auteuil, 1930-1952 des 4 Mousquetaires à Patty et Drobny*, mémoires filmées du tennis, 2009

Paul Jalabert, *Tennis d'antan, Porte d'Auteuil, 1953-1968 from Rosewall to Rosewall*, filmed memories of tennis, 2009

Paul Jalabert, *Tennis d'antan, Porte d'Auteuil, 1969-1980 from Laver to Borg...and Noah*, filmed memories of tennis, 2009

Paul Jalabert, *En souvenir des quatre Mousquetaires*, filmed memories of tennis, 2009

Paul Jalabert, _Tennis sur la Riviera d'antan_, filmed memories of tennis, 2010

Paul Jalabert, _Racing club de France d'antan_, filmed memories of tennis, 2010 Paul

Jalabert, _Le tennis professionnel d'antan_, filmed memories of tennis, 2010

British Pathe, _A Day that shook the world: Suzanne Lenglen breaks Wimbledon record 1925_, BBC 2011

Julien Faraut, _The empire of perfection_, UFO Production, Paris, 2018

SEHENOLAND
LIMITED

Company Registered n. 63726057, Scenecliff, 33 Conduit
Road, Tower 1, F12/C Mid-Levels, Hong Kong

ABOUT THE AUTHOR

Nicolas Stanajic Petrovic is a 53-year-old French professional tennis coach with a passion for history. He began teaching tennis in 1991 while studying history at La Sorbonne University Paris IV (bachelor in 1993).

Nicolas very quickly developed a passion for teaching tennis and followed the entire French Tennis Federation training program: level 1 assistant coach in 1991, then level 2 in 1993. He obtained the common core of the National coaching license in 1996 while preparing for the exam to become a history teacher. After 1 year training in a national center near Paris, Nicolas graduated top of the national exam in June 2001 (200 candidates) to become a fully French Professional tennis coach level 1.

After becoming tennis director in a club near Paris, he obtained level 2 certification (equivalent to a master's degree) after 2 years training in 2 different centers in the Paris area. After that Nicolas was appointed by a consultancy cabinet to become coach's trainer for Paris center.

Nicolas left France in May 2011 to go teach tennis in Hong Kong. He was appointed by TennisAsia, a tennis coaching service provider company in the Chinese city-state. He has been teaching for 13 years now at the Ladies Recreation Club (LRC), a very prestigious centenary country club created in 1883 by the British.

Nicolas is now assistant tennis director and oversees the adult program at the LRC. He manages more than 200 players every week and no less than 10 coaches from 5 different continents.

Until this day, he has given more than 15,000 hours of tennis lessons to members of over 60 different nationalities. Nicolas recognizes the excellence of the French training system and wishes to explain its origins and developments through this book.

Printed in the United States
by Baker & Taylor Publisher Services